WILLIAM

THE
COMING
EPIPHANY

**Your Guide To Understanding
End Times Bible Prophecy**

©Copyright 2004, 2007, 2010, 2013, 2014 William Frederick. All rights reserved. No part of this book may be reproduced, stored in a retrieval system, or transmitted by any means, electronic, mechanical, photocopying, recording, or otherwise, without written permission from the author. All comments herein are without malice or prejudice.

Book cover design: William Frederick

Book cover photos:
© leaf. Image from BigStockPhoto.com.
© Suebluey. Image from BigStockPhoto.com
© Karimala. Image from BigStockPhoto.com

Scripture quotations are taken from the King James Version of the Bible.

Take note that the name satan and related names are not capitalized. I believe that he does not deserve that honor, even to the point of violating grammatical rules.

ISBN: 978-1-4303-1383-0

Dedication

This book is dedicated to the great God, Lord, and Savior Jesus Christ, who gave His life and shed His blood for the remission of our sins. May this book be used for His glory and honor. I also dedicate this book to all of God's children, especially my family and friends, who love the Lord but are still asleep in regards to what will shortly come to pass on the earth. I pray that all of God's children will be awakened.

Acknowledgments

All praise, glory, and thanksgiving belong to the Lord Jesus Christ, who saved me from a terrible hell and who has indwelt me since salvation and shall never leave me nor forsake me. Through His wisdom, strength, and power, this book was written, and to Him and Him alone is due the credit. I look forward to the day when I can bow before Him and worship.

Special thanks are given to Roy Reinhold, whom the Lord has greatly used to awaken me to the prophetic events that will transpire in the near future.

I would also like to acknowledge H. L. Nigro, whom God has used in pruning and shaping this book and helping it to more effectively say what I meant it to say.

Preface

Thomas angrily pounded his fist on the table saying, "You are crazy, the world is flat! If you sail too far, you will fall off!"

Christopher responded, "No, you are wrong. The world is round, and I will not fall off!"

I can easily imagine this type of argument between Christopher Columbus and one of his peers. We all know who was eventually proved right; but at the time, because of the limited knowledge many possessed, the topic of whether the world was round or flat was a heated topic of debate. Today, there is another heated and complicated topic of debate: biblical prophecy and especially the timing of the rapture. The information presented in this book deals with this complicated topic. The information presented in this book deals with this complicated topic and will prove by scripture which one of the many rapture theories is the correct one.

There are many books on the market that deal with biblical prophecy. Why is this book different? Why listen to me? Who am I to say what is right or wrong? Should you listen to me because I have been involved in preaching and teaching God's Word on a daily basis for the last 20 years, or because I have memorized and meditated on scripture every day for the last 23 years, or because I have a Master of Divinity degree from a conservative fundamental Christian university, or because I have fasted and prayed over this book? No, even though credentials have their place, you should not listen to anyone because they have "credentials." You should only listen to me or any Bible teacher or preacher because what they say agrees with the Word of God. We all have the responsibility before God to go to the scriptures ourselves and see if what we are being taught agrees with all of scripture just like the Bereans did. "These [Bereans] were more noble than those in Thessalonica, in that they received the word with all readiness of mind, and searched the scriptures daily, whether those things were so" (Acts 17:11).

Scripture and scripture alone is the standard by which everything must be judged. Unfortunately, many approach end-times scriptures with a predetermined theological mindset and then try to make scripture fit into their theology. What sets this book apart from all the rest is that it attempts to approach the topic with all of scripture, and scripture alone, as its basis. A theological belief is then formed on the basis of what all of the scriptures dictate.

In this book scripture will be interpreted according to the following principle: "When the plain sense of scripture makes common sense, seek no other sense; therefore, take every word at its primary, ordinary, usual, literal meaning unless the facts of the immediate context, studied in the light of related passages and axiomatic and fundamental truths, indicate clearly otherwise."[1] In other words, scripture will be interpreted literally unless it is evident that a symbolic interpretation is warranted by the text. Theological systems will then be evaluated in light of what the Bible says and not the other way around, as many books on this topic do.

Many end-times books also are based solely or partly on various extra-biblical ancient and modern-day prophecies. It is apparent that many of these prophecies are man-made or even demonic in origin, and even though they may contain some truth, they do not contain *all* truth and thus cannot be trusted. The only sure foundation that we have for faith and doctrine is the Word of God. When this book uses extra-biblical sources, it is only to support a point that has already been made from the scriptures.

The understanding of prophecy and formulating correct prophetic beliefs is much like putting together the pieces of a complicated jigsaw puzzle. In putting together a puzzle, one first examines all the pieces, then selects the border pieces and starts to assemble the border. After the border of the puzzle is completed, one works on filling in the center. As we know, to complete the puzzle, we must fit every piece perfectly with its surrounding pieces. When every piece is fitted in, the picture is complete.

The pieces of the "prophecy puzzle" are the numerous prophetic verses found throughout the Bible. The border pieces are the prophetic principles set forth in scripture, such as the principle that God will not allow His children to be subject to His wrath (1 Thess. 5:9), that no one knows the day or hour of the return of Christ Jesus, etc. In attempting to formulate a correct prophetic view of future events, one must put all the pieces within this framework so that all the pieces fit together perfectly. In other words, one must establish a prophetic belief system that is in agreement with all of the prophetic principles and all of the prophetic scriptures so there are no contradictions. We can check any

---

[1] The Golden Rule of Interpretation, by David L. Cooper.

theological position for its correctness by comparing it to *all* of the scriptural principles and truths found in the Bible. If it contradicts any of them, that theological position is in error. The theological position presented in this book has undergone the scrutiny of such an analysis. Do not take my word for it. Go to the Lord and the scriptures, and prove to yourself that what is being presented is in agreement with all scripture.

In this book, I will endeavor to present what the whole of scripture says with regard to prophetic events and not necessarily what any theological system dictates. I ask that you would prayerfully compare what I present with scripture. If I have been accurate in presenting the truth of God's Word—and these pages represent the truth of what is to come—then all of scripture will agree with what I am stating. And in all of your prophetic study, whether through this book or any other, let me remind you of one of God's wonderful promises: "If any of you lack wisdom, let him ask of God, that giveth to all men liberally, and upbraideth not; and it shall be given him. But let him ask in faith, nothing wavering" (James 1:5–6). I pray that this book will be a blessing to you

A proper understanding of biblical prophecy is extremely important and is essential to the life of the believer (or unbeliever, for that matter). Without it, regardless of your spiritual background, you could be caught off guard and be unprepared for what is going to take place on the earth in the near future. Should this occur, you would most likely place yourself in spiritual and or physical jeopardy. If the rapture occurs and you are left behind, you will most likely suffer a terrible fate. Thus, I beseech you to take very seriously the information presented in this book, for it will be of such profound importance that I liken it to the importance of Christopher Columbus saying that the world is round.

Table of Contents

Introduction	11
Chapter 1: The Essence of the Day of the Lord	13
Chapter 2: The Signs of the Day of the Lord	23
Chapter 3: The Beginning of the Day of the Lord	31
Chapter 4: Who's Right?	55
Chapter 5: Why Does it Matter?	71
Chapter 6: The Great Day of His Wrath is Come	81
Chapter 7: The Millennium and Beyond	97
Chapter 8: O America	113
Chapter 9: The Fourth Beast	129
Chapter 10: The Son of Perdition	165
Chapter 11: A Chronology of the End	183
Chapter 12: When?	199
Chapter 13: Be Prepared	215
Chapter 14: Jehovah Jireh	237
Conclusion	245
Reference	249

Introduction

The student exclaimed, "Oh! I get it!" I have taught mathematics for many years, and sometimes, after explaining a new concept, a few just don't quite get it. When that happens I usually try explaining the concept another way, and many times I have heard them say, "Oh! I get it!" When somebody finally gets it, that is what is known as an epiphany. Here is the formal dictionary definition of an epiphany.[2]

> A sudden manifestation or perception of the essential nature or meaning of something.
>
> An intuitive grasp of reality through something (as an event), usually simple and striking.

One of the central themes of this book concerns the explanation of the epiphany that is coming to all mankind. It will happen on a day when men cry out with the sudden perception of the essential nature or meaning of Christ. It will happen on a day when they will gain a grasp of reality through a very special prophetic event. The reality that they will be awakened to will cause their hearts to melt in terror. This event is known in the Bible as the Day of the Lord, and it will follow several signs that will be given to let all the world know that the day is approaching.

The epiphany that will come upon mankind at the Day of the Lord will be part of a larger series of events that will occur during the seven-year end-times period known as the 70th Week of Daniel or, as some call it, the "tribulation." This period constitutes the last seven years on earth before Jesus Christ returns and establishes His millennial reign. The most incredible series of events yet experienced on the earth will take place during the 70th Week. These events will span seven years of 360 days (based on the ancient Jewish "prophetic" year), for a total of 2,520 days. Some of these events will be so cataclysmic that men will try to hide themselves in crevices of the earth, their hearts will fail, and they will cry out for fear.

---

[2]*Webster's Ninth New Collegiate Dictionary* (Springfield, Mass.: Merriam-Webster, Inc., 1985).

The reason that the Day of the Lord is so cataclysmic is that it is a period of time in which God pours out His wrath upon the world. This event culminates with the Lord Jesus Christ's return to earth to rule and reign over the whole world. In the first few chapters this book will focus in on the event known as the Day of the Lord. As you will see the Day of the Lord, as outlined by scripture, has profound theological implications. Specifically we will examine what will occur before, during, and after that Day. We will also examine several related aspects associated with the Day of the Lord such as America in Bible prophecy, the coming world kingdom—the New World Order, the antichrist, the prophetic implications of the feasts of the Lord, a chronology of the sixty nine and seventy weeks, and give practical spiritual applications to these essential prophetic truths.

We will begin our discussion of prophetic truths by first establishing a framework of prophetic principles. The first piece in the framework is to define or examine the essential nature of the Day of the Lord.

Chapter 1
The Essence of The Day of the Lord

The sun is suddenly darkened, the moon glows the color of blood, the ground shakes violently, the sky splits and rolls away like a scroll, and the stars fall. Grown men run frantically to and fro, screaming like babies, trying to find somewhere to hide, while others just faint from terror.

It is at this time that all the people of the world will have an epiphany. The epiphany will occur at the yet future event known as the Day of the Lord, which is mentioned many times in scripture. It is even the subject matter of the entire book of Joel. Many parts of scripture have whole chapters and paragraphs devoted to the topic. Understanding the Day of the Lord is foundational to a proper understanding of all biblical end-times prophecy. In this chapter, we will examine the essence, reason for, and duration of this Day.

First, we need to come to an understanding of the essential nature of what this future event entails. Renald Showers describes its essence beautifully.

> The Day of the Lord refers to God's special interventions into the course of world events to judge His enemies, accomplish His purpose for history, and thereby demonstrate who He is— the sovereign God of the universe.[3]

This time of God's special intervention known primarily as The Day of the Lord has been referred to by other terms in scripture, such as the Time of Jacob's Trouble (Jer. 30:7); His Strange Work/Act (Isa. 28:21); the Day of Israel's Calamity (Deut. 32:35); the Indignation (Isa. 26:20; Dan. 11:36); the Overflowing Scourge (Isa. 28:15, 18); the Day of Vengeance (Isa. 34:8; 35:4; 61:2); the Day of Wrath/Distress/Wasteness/Desolation (Zeph. 1:15); the Day of Darkness/Thick Darkness/Gloominess (Zeph. 1:15, Joel 2:2); the Day of Trumpet and Alarm (Zeph. 1:16); the hour of trial (Rev. 3:10); the Wrath to Come (1 Thess. 1:10); the Wrath (1 Thess. 5:9), and the Hour

---

[3] Renald E. Showers, *Maranatha, Our Lord Come* (Bellmawr, NJ: The Friends of Israel Gospel Ministry, 1995), 38.

of His Judgment (Rev. 14:7). In some instances, the Day of the Lord, due to its unique nature and importance, has been referred to as simply "that day" (Isa. 2:11, 17; 2:20; 4:2; Joel 3:18; Mark 13:32; Luke 21:34; 2 Tim. 1:12, 18; 4:8).

In relation to the events of the last seven years on earth, the yet future Day of the Lord can be characterized as a time of wrath and vengeance poured out upon mankind for their wickedness. As it says in Isaiah 2:10–22:

> Enter into the rock, and hide thee in the dust, for fear of the Lord, and for the glory of his majesty. The lofty looks of man shall be humbled, and the haughtiness of men shall be bowed down, and the Lord alone shall be exalted in that day. For the day of the Lord of hosts shall be upon every one that is proud and lofty, and upon every one that is lifted up; and he shall be brought low…and the loftiness of man shall be bowed down, and the haughtiness of men shall be made low: and the Lord alone shall be exalted in that day. And the idols he shall utterly abolish. And they shall go into the holes of the rocks, and into the caves of the earth, for fear of the Lord, and for the glory of his majesty, when he ariseth to shake terribly the earth…To go into the clefts of the rocks, and into the tops of the ragged rocks, for fear of the Lord, and for the glory of his majesty, when he ariseth to shake terribly the earth.

The pouring out of God's wrath during the end times is only part of the Day of the Lord. The Day of the Lord will also include the pouring out of His blessings during the millennium.

> The future Day of the Lord will have at least a twofold nature. First, it will be characterized by darkness and a tremendous outpouring of divine wrath upon the world (Joel 2:1–2; Amos 5:18–20; Zeph. 1:14–15; 1 Th. 5:1–11). Amos 5:18–20 emphasizes that this will be the total nature of the Day of the Lord for God's enemies. It will bring no divine light or blessing to them. This will be the nature of the Day of the Lord during the 70th week of Daniel. Second, the Day of the Lord will also be characterized by light, an outpouring of divine blessing, and the administration of God's rule. The Prophet Joel, after talking about the darkening of the sun, moon, and stars and God's Day of the Lord judgment of the armies of the nations gathered in

Israel (Joel 3:9-16), foretold great divine blessing "in that day" (Joel 3:17–21).[4]

So even though the portion of the Day of the Lord that occurs before the millennium will consist of the wrath of God being poured out on a sinful world, after that aspect of the Day of the Lord is finished, then blessings will be poured out during the Millennium.

There have also been past fulfillments of the Day of the Lord:

> The Bible indicates that there have been several Days of the Lord in the past in which God demonstrated His sovereign rule by raising up several nations to execute His judgement on other nations. He raised up Assyria to judge the northern kingdom of Israel during the 700s B.C. (Amos 5:18, 20), Babylon to judge the southern kingdom of Judah during the 600s and 500s B.C. (Lam. 1:12; 2:1, 21–22; Eze. 7:19; 13:5; Zep. 2:2–3), Babylon to judge Egypt and its allies during the 500s B.C. (Jer. 46:10; Eze. 30:3), and Medo-Persia to judge Babylon during the 500s B.C. (Isa. 13:6, 9).[5]

Many passages concerning the Day of the Lord speak not only of some of these past fulfillments but also a future fulfillment of a yet to come great Day of the Lord. These double reference passages[6] can be difficult to interpret. However, upon reading them, it is clearly evident that their remains a yet future great Day of the Lord. For example in Amos 5:18 it says "Woe unto you that desire the day of the Lord! to what end is it for you? the day of the Lord is darkness, and not light." This passage in Amos, as referenced above, refers to the judgment brought upon the Northern tribes during the 700's B.C. but yet it is clear to see that the passage also makes reference to the yet future Day of the Lord in which there will be darkness over the whole earth as described in Acts 2:20.

---

[4] Showers, *Maranatha, Our Lord Come*, 32–33,39.
[5] Ibid., 30.
[6] "This law observes the fact that often a passage or a block of Scripture is speaking of two different persons or two different events which are separated by a long period of time. In the passage itself they are blended into one picture, and the time gap between the two persons or two events is not presented by the text itself. The fact that a gap of time exists is known because of other Scriptures." Arnold G. Fruchtenbaum, *The Footsteps of Messiah*, rev. ed. (Tustin, CA: Ariel Ministries, 2003), 4.

Scripture also makes it clear that there is only one Day of the Lord that is yet to come. "For thus saith the Lord of hosts; Yet once, it is a little while, and I will shake the heavens, and the earth, and the sea, and the dry land" (Hag. 2:6). "Whose voice then shook the earth: but now he hath promised, saying, Yet once more I shake not the earth only, but also heaven" (Heb. 12:26). The passage from Hebrews tells us, in reference to the Mount Sinai occurrence, that it was the voice of the Lord that shook the earth and that the shaking of the earth from the Lord's voice will happen only once more. The Isaiah 2 passage above tells us that this will occur during the Day of the Lord, "when he ariseth to shake terribly the earth." This yet future one remaining great Day of the Lord—when God will shake the heavens and the earth—is the time in which God's wrath will be poured out upon men and they will be so afraid, as we read in the Isaiah passage, that they will try to hide themselves in the clefts of the rocks because of their fear of the Lord and the glory of His majesty. At that time, all men will be humbled and God will be exalted. Isaiah again describes it as a day of destruction, fierce anger, and wrath; and again echoes that men will be terrified during this time. They will experience extreme anguish like they have never experienced before:

> Howl ye; for the day of the Lord is at hand; it shall come as a destruction from the Almighty. Therefore shall all hands be faint, and every man's heart shall melt: And they shall be afraid: pangs and sorrows shall take hold of them; they shall be in pain as a woman that travaileth: they shall be amazed one at another; their faces shall be as flames. Behold, the day of the Lord cometh, cruel both with wrath and fierce anger, to lay the land desolate: and he shall destroy the sinners thereof out of it. For the stars of heaven and the constellations thereof shall not give their light: the sun shall be darkened in his going forth, and the moon shall not cause her light to shine. And I will punish the world for their evil, and the wicked for their iniquity; and I will cause the arrogancy of the proud to cease, and will lay low the haughtiness of the terrible. I will make a man more precious than fine gold; even a man than the golden wedge of Ophir. Therefore I will shake the heavens, and the earth shall remove out of her place, in the wrath of the Lord of hosts, and in the day of his fierce anger. (Isa. 13:6–13)

This last passage not only reiterates the fact that the Day of the Lord is a time when God's wrath is poured out upon the world, but it also tells us the reason for it. Namely, it is a punishment for the sins and wickedness of the world. As it says in verse 11, "And I will punish the world for their evil, and the wicked for their iniquity." Thus scripture tells us that the purpose for the Day of the Lord is to punish the world for its sin.

Isaiah 34:8–10 also brings this out, describing the Day of the Lord as a day of vengeance.

> For it is the day of the Lord's vengeance, and the year of recompenses for the controversy of Zion. And the streams thereof shall be turned into pitch, and the dust thereof into brimstone, and the land thereof shall become burning pitch. It shall not be quenched night nor day; the smoke thereof shall go up for ever: from generation to generation it shall lie waste; none shall pass through it for ever and ever.

God is the one responsible for pouring out judgment upon mankind for their sins at this time. It is the righteous punishment for sinning against a holy God. God has a limit to the sin that He allows. Once a society or a people group reaches a certain level of sin, they are in danger of His wrath being poured out on them. This was the case in the days of Noah when the world was hit with a devastating worldwide flood. This was the case with Sodom and Gomorrah when they were obliterated with fire and brimstone. This was the case with the Egyptians who received God's wrath through the hand of Moses. This will also be the case with our world when the Day of the Lord arrives. It will be the day when wicked unrepentant men reap the just retribution for their evil deeds.

This is again echoed in Jeremiah 46:10: "For this is the day of the Lord God of hosts, a day of vengeance, that he may avenge him of his adversaries."

Consider what Zephaniah and Malachi say about this day:

> The great day of the Lord is near, it is near, and hasteth greatly, even the voice of the day of the Lord: the mighty man shall cry there bitterly. That day is a day of wrath, a day of trouble and distress, a day of wasteness and desolation, a day of darkness and gloominess, a day of clouds and thick darkness, a day of the trumpet and alarm against the fenced cities, and against the high towers. And I will bring distress upon men, that they shall walk like blind men, because they have sinned against the Lord: and their blood shall be poured out as dust, and their

> flesh as the dung. Neither their silver nor their gold shall be able to deliver them in the day of the Lord's wrath; but the whole land shall be devoured by the fire of his jealousy: for he shall make even a speedy riddance of all them that dwell in the land. (Zeph. 1:14–18)

> For, behold, the day cometh, that shall burn as an oven; and all the proud, yea, and all that do wickedly, shall be stubble: and the day that cometh shall burn them up, saith the Lord of hosts, that it shall leave them neither root nor branch. (Mal. 4:1)

Again, we see that the Day of the Lord brings great destruction upon the world because they have sinned against Him and remained unrepentant. Zephaniah sums it up, describing it as a day of wrath.

The book of Joel is an expose that exclusively refers to the Day of the Lord and contains a wealth of information about that time. Among other things, it reveals to us another purpose for the Day of the Lord: that people would be brought to repentance. This is clearly seen in Joel 2:11–14:

> For the day of the Lord is great and very terrible; and who can abide it? Therefore also now, saith the Lord, turn ye even to me with all your heart, and with fasting, and with weeping, and with mourning: And rend your heart, and not your garments, and turn unto the Lord your God: for he is gracious and merciful, slow to anger, and of great kindness, and repenteth him of the evil. Who knoweth if he will return and repent, and leave a blessing behind him; even a meat offering and a drink offering unto the Lord your God?

God does not take pleasure in judging people. It breaks His heart, and He earnestly desires that sinners might turn to Him and not be judged.[7] He pours out His judgment only as a last resort.

There are many reasons judgment falls. One is that He is a just judge and will righteously recompense those who have broken His holy law. He also brings judgment because He does not want cancerous sin to spread to others—such was the case with Sodom and Gomorrah. And He brings judgment or the threat of judgment because

---

[7] O Jerusalem, Jerusalem, thou that killest the prophets, and stonest them which are sent unto thee, how often would I have gathered thy children together, even as a hen gathereth her chickens under her wings, and ye would not! (Mt 23:27)

He wants people to repent and experience a wonderful relationship with Him. God is very merciful and always wants people to repent; and judgment or the threat of judgment is always the last resort.

God never springs judgment upon people unawares. He will always warn them before the final judgment comes. Sometimes, this warning comes through lesser judgments. Many times these warnings come by way of His prophets in His holy Word, who through the ages have proclaimed His warnings, even for us today. A classic example of this was with what happened to the city of Nineveh. God sent the prophet Jonah to proclaim the message that their city was to be destroyed in 40 days because of their wickedness. After this warning was issued, the people repented, and the judgment was stayed.

The Day of the Lord will be a time of severe judgment that God has been warning us about for thousands of years. Those who choose to repent before that day will escape His wrath.

> Before the decree bring forth, before the day pass as the chaff, before the fierce anger of the Lord come upon you, before the day of the Lord's anger come upon you. Seek ye the Lord, all ye meek of the earth, which have wrought his judgment; seek righteousness, seek meekness: it may be ye shall be hid in the day of the Lord's anger. (Zeph. 2:2–3)

Even during the time that His wrath is being poured out people can still repent. In fact, Joel goes on to tell us that as a result of the Day of the Lord, many in the nation of Israel will be brought to repentance. In Joel 2:15–21, it says,

> Blow the trumpet in Zion, sanctify a fast, call a solemn assembly: Gather the people, sanctify the congregation, assemble the elders, gather the children, and those that suck the breasts: let the bridegroom go forth of his chamber, and the bride out of her closet. Let the priests, the ministers of the Lord, weep between the porch and the altar, and let them say, Spare thy people, O Lord, and give not thine heritage to reproach, that the heathen should rule over them: wherefore should they say among the people, Where is their God? Then will the Lord be jealous for his land, and pity his people. Yea, the Lord will answer and say unto his people, Behold, I will send you corn, and wine, and oil, and ye shall be satisfied therewith: and I will no more make you a reproach among the heathen: But I will remove far off from you the northern army,

and will drive him into a land barren and desolate, with his face toward the east sea, and his hinder part toward the utmost sea, and his stink shall come up, and his ill savour shall come up, because he hath done great things. Fear not, O land; be glad and rejoice: for the Lord will do great things.

In this passage, we see that as a result of some of the events of the Day of the Lord, Israel will repent. This is evidenced by their blowing a trumpet, sanctifying a fast, and calling for a solemn assembly. Their turning to the Lord will result in the blessings of God being bestowed upon them.

Blessings in the Day of the Lord

We have established that the Day of the Lord is a day of wrath and destruction upon mankind. God brings judgment because He wants to cleanse the world of sin and because He sincerely desires for people to repent. Some will choose to repent and they will experience blessings during the Day of the Lord in the millennium:

> So shall ye know that I am the Lord your God dwelling in Zion, my holy mountain: then shall Jerusalem be holy, and there shall no strangers pass through her any more. And it shall come to pass in that day, that the mountains shall drop down new wine, and the hills shall flow with milk, and all the rivers of Judah shall flow with waters, and a fountain shall come forth of the house of the Lord, and shall water the valley of Shittim. (Joel 3:17–18)

> And it shall come to pass in that day, that the light shall not be clear, nor dark: But it shall be one day which shall be known to the Lord, not day, nor night: but it shall come to pass, that at evening time it shall be light. And it shall be in that day, that living waters shall go out from Jerusalem; half of them toward the former sea, and half of them toward the hinder sea: in summer and in winter shall it be. And the Lord shall be king over all the earth: in that day shall there be one Lord, and his name one. (Zech. 14:6–9)

So even though the Day of the Lord will primarily be a day of wrath, it will cause some to repent and will culminate in blessing. Next, we will consider the length of time that the Day of the Lord will encompass.

How Long Will the Day of the Lord Last?

How long will the Day of the Lord last? Will it be a literal 24-hour day or will it be longer? In the Bible, the word "day" can refer to part of a day, a whole day (24 hours), or a longer period of time. In Matthew 20:2, it refers to part of a day: "And when he had agreed with the labourers for a penny a day, he sent them into his vineyard." Clearly, this refers to only the working part of a day. In Genesis 7:17, the word "day" refers to a 24-hour period: "And the flood was forty days upon the earth; and the waters increased, and bare up the ark, and it was lift up above the earth." But the word "day" can also refer to an undetermined period of time as in John 9:4, "day" refers to an undetermined period of time: "I must work the works of him that sent me, while it is day: the night cometh, when no man can work." Clearly, "day" in this context refers to a longer period of time, namely the time that God has given to each of us for service to Him.

So when we talk about the Day of the Lord, what are we referring to? A part of a day, a whole day, or a longer period of time? I contend that the Day of the Lord is a period of time and not a single day. In Chapter 7, I will detail many of the events that will transpire in the Day of the Lord. One of those events will be demon locusts torturing people for five months (Rev. 9:1–6). Thus, it stands to reason that if it is one of the events of the Day of the Lord, then the Day of the Lord refers to a period of time longer than a day.

The pouring out of God's wrath during the Day of the Lord—the Day of wrath—will be one of the most horrific times the earth will ever go through. It is a time in which God's wrath is poured out upon men as just retribution for their wickedness. Hopefully, many will heed the clear call to repent and be spared from this time of great wrath. This is the essence of the Day of the Lord.

Now that we have an understanding of the essence of the Day of the Lord we will turn our attention to the signs that precede it—letting all who recognize the signs know of the imminence of that great day.

Chapter 2
The Signs of The Day of the Lord

Before the Lord does a mighty work He gives the world signs. He gave Egypt and the Israelites many signs when He delivered Israel out of bondage. "And the Lord brought us forth out of Egypt with a mighty hand, and with an outstretched arm, and with great terribleness, and with signs, and with wonders" (Deut 26:8) The Lord also gave many sign gifts to his servants to validate and show the world that Jesus was the true Messiah. "And fear came upon every soul: and many wonders and signs were done by the apostles." (Acts 2:43) God will also use signs in the future to let us know that the Day of the Lord is approaching. In His Word, God has revealed to us several signs that must occur before the Day of the Lord. In this chapter, we will examine the signs that signal that the Day of the Lord is almost upon us.

The Sign of the Sun and Moon
One of the most prominent signs of the Day of the Lord is listed in Joel 2:31. It states:

> The sun shall be turned into darkness, and the moon into blood, before that great and notable day of the Lord come.

This scripture is also quoted in Acts 2:20:

> The sun shall be turned into darkness, and the moon into blood, before that great and notable day of the Lord come.

These scriptures give us crucial information regarding the Day of the Lord. It tells us in no uncertain terms that two celestial events must occur before the Day of the Lord arrives: the moon's light will be turned to the color of blood and the sun will become darkened. What type of event would cause such occurrences? Many have speculated as to the cause. Some have asserted such things as a pole shift[8], the

---

[8] The 'pole shift theory' is the hypothesis that the axis of rotation of a planet has not always been at its present-day locations or that the axis will not persist there; in other words, that its physical poles had been or will be *shifted*. From Wikipedia

passing of planet x[9], or even a super volcano. Amos 8:9 makes a strong case for the Day of the Lord entailing a pole shift, "And it shall come to pass in that day, saith the Lord God, that I will cause the sun to go down at noon, and I will darken the earth in the clear day." The phrase "that day" is in reference to the Day of the Lord and it says that the sun will go down at noon. The only way for that to happen would be for a pole shift to occur.[10] Though we can only speculate as to the exact cause, we know for certain that it will occur and will most certainly be noticed by all who dwell on the earth. Those who heed it will realize that the Day of the Lord is very near.

Great and Mighty Signs

The parallel passages in Joel and Acts also bring out other signs that will occur. Namely, God will pour out His Spirit in a great and mighty way, and great signs will be done by God's people. "That I will pour out my spirit upon all flesh; and your sons and your daughters shall prophesy, your old men shall dream dreams, your young men shall see visions" (Acts 2:17). Thus, another sign before the Day of the Lord is that God will pour out his Spirit in a great and miraculous way, and many of the gifts that were so prolific in the first century will flourish once again.

The Falling Away

Two other events in scripture that must occur before the great Day of the Lord are found in 2 Thessalonians 2:3. God, through the apostle Paul, in referring to the Day of the Lord, says, "Let no man deceive you by any means: for that day shall not come, except there come a falling away first, and that man of sin be revealed, the son of perdition." The Thessalonians had been deceived into thinking that they missed the rapture and were in the Day of the Lord period. Paul tells them that the falling away must occur before the Day of the Lord.

The word used in the Greek for falling away is *apostasia*, from which we get our word "apostasy," which basically means "backsliding." Clarke's commentary describes it like this: "a dereliction of the essential principles of religious truth—either a total

---

[9] Planet x is claimed to be an undiscovered brown dwarf star that orbits our sun and every five to ten thousand years comes close to the earth and causes cataclysmic events.
[10] This passage will most likely have a double fulfillment, the first when Jesus was crucified and the second at the Day of the Lord.

abandonment of Christianity itself, or such a corruption of its doctrines as renders the whole system completely inefficient to salvation."[11] The great falling away will be a time when professing Christians, in large numbers, will turn away from the faith. "The article makes it even more significant; this is not *a falling away*, but *the falling away*, the great and final rebellion."[12] J. Hampton Keathley, III , Th.M. describes the coming apostasy like this: "The *apostasy* or *rebellion* clearly refers to a special departure and rebellion against the true God. This will become a worldwide movement and will provide the seed bed for the great system of revolt which will be headed up in the person of the Beast who will be the very personification of satan himself."[13] In order for a great falling away to take place, I believe that an alternative belief system to the true gospel will be promoted with such believability that nominal Christians (not true Christians) will reject the God of the Bible. We can only speculate as to the exact reasons for the "falling away," but there are many plausible theories.

One such theory involves aliens. Specifically, I am talking about the theory that aliens are real space beings and are the originators of life on earth. While many believers may initially bristle at this outrageous suggestion, there is much support for this theory that "another gospel" will come at the hand of what many mistakenly believe to be alien beings. It might sound crazy at first, but it is highly likely that much of what we hear about regarding "aliens" is really demonic activity.[14] If you have ever researched the UFO phenomena, what is compelling is that, consistently, alien theology, as recounted in many "close encounters," parallels the plans and purposes of satan as presented in scripture. These manifestations present themselves as angels of "light and intellectual illumination," claim to provide leadership and hope to a suffering world, provide a source of awe, wonder, and worship that is an alternative to the God of the Bible, and even claim to be the originators of life on earth. Here is an interesting quote from a website promoting this alien theory containing an actual message from on of these aliens.

---

[11] *Clarke's Commentary*, http://www.godrules.net/library/clarke/clarke2the2.htm
[12] David Guzik, *Study Guide for II Thessalonians,*
http://blueletterbible.org/Comm/david_guzik/sg/2Th_2.html
[13] http://www.bible.org/page.asp?page_id=1696
[14] http://www.ufodigest.com/news/0307/tremble.html

In other words, they look like us, and we look like them. In fact, we were created "in their image" as explained in the Bible. He told Rael that: *"We were the ones who designed all life on earth. You mistook us for gods. We were at the origin of your main religions. Now that you are mature enough to understand this, we would like to enter official contact through an embassy."*

The messages dictated to Rael explain that life on Earth is not the result of random evolution, nor the work of a supernatural 'God'. It is a deliberate creation, using DNA, by a scientifically advanced people who made human beings literally "in their image" -- what one can call "scientific creationism." ...For example, in Genesis, the Biblical account of Creation, the word "Elohim" has been mistranslated as the singular word "God", but it is actually a plural word which means "those who came from the sky", and the singular is "Eloha" (also known as "Allah")...

Leaving our humanity to progress by itself, the Elohim nevertheless maintained contact with us via prophets including Buddha, Moses, Mohammed, etc., all specially chosen and educated by them. The role of the prophets was to progressively educate humanity through the Messages they taught, each adapted to the culture and level of understanding at the time. They were also to leave traces of the Elohim so that we would be able to recognize them as our Creators and fellow human beings when we had advanced enough scientifically to understand them. Jesus, whose father was an Eloha, was given the task of spreading these messages throughout the world in preparation for this crucial time in which we are now privileged to live: the predicted Age Of Revelation.[15]

If satan's demonic hoard can mask as alien beings presenting a false gospel, and if this will cause many in the world to follow satan at just the right point in history to accomplish his goals, he will do it. For more information on this topic, visit thecomingepiphany.com[16] By the way, NASA has recently released video clips of several "alien encounters" lending more credence to the alien theory[17] Many people

---

[15] http://rael.org/rael_content/rael_summary.php

[16]. Other excellent resources include *UFOs: Friend, Foe, or Fantasy*, by William R. Goetz (Camp Hill, Pennsylvania); *UFOs and the Alien Agenda*, by Bob Larson (Nashville: Thomas Nelson Publishers); and *Facts on UFOs and Other Supernatural Phenomena*, by John Ankerberg and John Weldon (Eugene, Oregon: Harvest House).

[17] http://www.youtube.com/watch?v=3p9vrhLJfEU

in the world have already been deceived to some degree and believe that aliens are really outer space beings, and unfortunately many Christians believe the same.

Another theory as to why the great falling away may occur regards the rise of pagan religions and their elements of heresy that attack Christian doctrines. In fact there is a film entitled Zeitgeist, meaning spirit of the time, which is promoting pagan heresies and is destroying the faith of many nominal Christians.

> An online movie documenting the close ties between ancient pagan religions and today's Christianity is "antichrist" in nature, destroying the faith of believers by combining some astonishing truth with plenty of error...."Millions of believers have watched 'Zeitgeist' and many are throwing away their long held faith in Jesus as a result. I am receiving calls from people concerned about family members who are doing just that."[18]

As you can see this evil movie is being used by Satan to pull people away from God. I am sure heresies like this will unfortunately cause many to fall into error.

Revealing of "the Man of Sin"

Another sign that will occur before the Day of the Lord as listed in 2 Thess. 2:3 is that the "man of sin be revealed, the son of perdition." We all know that the man of sin is the antichrist. What does this revealing entail? 2 Thessalonians 2:4 gives us the answer:

> Let no man deceive you by any means: for that day shall not come, except there come a falling away first, and that man of sin be revealed, the son of perdition; Who opposeth and exalteth himself above all that is called God, or that is worshipped; so that he as God sitteth in the temple of God, shewing himself that he is God.

The scripture speaks clearly that the antichrist must be revealed and set himself up as God in the Temple before the coming of the Day of the Lord. The Greek word *naos* is used for temple. Thayer's lexicon defines *naos* as: "Used of the temple at Jerusalem, but only of the sacred edifice (or sanctuary) itself, consisting of the Holy place and the

---

[18] http://www.worldnetdaily.com/index.php?fa=PAGE.view&pageId=92903

Holy of Holies." Thus scripture indicates that the antichrist will enter the Holy place and possibly the Holy of Holies.

In other parts of scripture, this event has been termed "the Abomination of Desolation":

> When ye therefore shall see the Abomination of Desolation, spoken of by Daniel the prophet, stand in the holy place, (whoso readeth, let him understand:) (Matt. 24:15)

> And they shall pollute the sanctuary of strength, and shall take away the daily sacrifice, and they shall place the abomination that maketh desolate." (Dan. 11:31)

The most likely scenario is that the antichrist will enter the Temple—even into the Holy sanctuary—proclaim himself as god/messiah, desecrate the temple by some means, stop daily sacrifices, and possibly set up some image of himself. This is another sign that must be fulfilled before the Day of the Lord begins.

Will the Temple Be Rebuilt?

This brings us to another consideration. At present, the temple does not exist. In order for the antichrist to perform the Abomination of Desolation, there must be a temple where sacrifice rituals are performed. It is reported that the Jews are ready to build this temple. They are just waiting for the go-ahead. To perform sacrifice rituals there must also be certain items such as the table of shew bread, the golden lamp stand, and the Ark of the Covenant. The late archeologist Ron Wyatt has claimed to have found and seen all of these items and has told leading Jews where they are.[19]

Even if they do not find the originals, many dedicated Jews have already made copies to use in the new temple, which can be viewed at the Temple Institute Web site.[20]

The Mysterious Sign

There is a fifth, kind of mysterious, sign that will happen before the Day of the Lord comes. This sign was given to us in Malachi 4:5–6:

---

[19] For more information on this find, see the article entitled "The Ark of the Covenant Discovered?" at *The Coming Epiphany* Web site.
[20] http://www.templeinstitute.org/main.htm

> Behold, I will send you Elijah the prophet before the coming of the great and dreadful Day of the Lord: And he shall turn the heart of the fathers to the children, and the heart of the children to their fathers, lest I come and smite the earth with a curse.

We see here that the prophet Elijah will return to earth before the Day of the Lord occurs. It is considered by some to be mysterious because it is not clear exactly how this will transpire. Will he just appear? Or will he be born as a baby? Will he be in a physical body or a spiritual one? These are questions that the scriptures do not detail, making his appearance a bit of a mystery. We *do* know that one of the main things that he will accomplish is to turn the hearts of the Jewish people to the true Messiah, Jesus Christ. Many Jews are looking for Elijah's return and believe that, because he did not die and was taken up into heaven, he will come back to earth and will signal to all that the Messianic era is about to begin. Even the Jewish Passover Seder speaks of this anticipation, for the fifth cup is left for Elijah who, according to Jewish tradition, will return on Passover.

Some Christians believe he will most likely be one of the two witnesses listed in Rev. 11:3–14:

> And I will give power unto my two witnesses, and they shall prophesy a thousand two hundred and threescore days, clothed in sackcloth. These are the two olive trees, and the two candlesticks standing before the God of the earth. And if any man will hurt them, fire proceedeth out of their mouth, and devoureth their enemies: and if any man will hurt them, he must in this manner be killed. These have power to shut heaven, that it rain not in the days of their prophecy: and have power over waters to turn them to blood, and to smite the earth with all plagues, as often as they will.

It is debated as to when the witnesses will perform their miraculous works. It is also debated as to whether or not the exact identity of these two witnesses can be known. What we do know for sure is that Elijah, whether he is one of the witnesses or not, will return before the Day of the Lord.

In Summary

In summary, at least five events/signs must happen before the Day of the Lord comes:

1. The moon is turned to blood.
2. The sun will be darkened.
3. The great falling away will occur.
4. The antichrist will be revealed and the Abomination of Desolation will occur.
5. The prophet Elijah returns.

Just as God has shown signs in the past before He does a great and mighty work so will He give signs to let the entire world know that the Day of the Lord is close at hand.

Chapter 3
The Beginning of the Day of the Lord

"Gentlemen start your engines" is a sign that the Indy 500 is about to begin. Then with the waving of the green flag the race begins. Just as in many things in everyday life there is an event that starts a certain period of time so there is an event that starts the time period of the Day of the Lord. What will be the event that starts this great period of time? That is a question of utmost importance that we will address in this chapter.

Not only is it a question of great importance but it is also a very easy question to answer, especially if you keep in mind what signs must occur before this Day takes place. As we have discussed, two of the signs that will occur—which will be easily recognized—are that the moon must be turned to blood and the sun will be darkened.

When is the moon turned to blood and the sun darkened? Look at what Revelation 6:12–14 says:

> And I beheld when he had opened the sixth seal, and, lo, there was a great earthquake; and the sun became black as sackcloth of hair, and the moon became as blood; And the stars of heaven fell unto the earth, even as a fig tree casteth her untimely figs, when she is shaken of a mighty wind. And the heaven departed as a scroll when it is rolled together; and every mountain and island were moved out of their places.

The passage from Revelation above tells us that the moon is turned to blood and the sun is darkened after the sixth seal is opened. Thus scripture plainly tells us that the Day of the Lord occurs after the sixth seal is opened. Notice also at this time that the stars fall as figs after being shaken of a mighty wind; and every island and mountain is moved as a result of the whole earth being shaken.

So if the sixth seal must be opened before the Day of the Lord, that means that the first five seals must also be opened before the Day of the Lord. Before we get back to our discussion of what event starts the Day of the Lord we will consider these events, which precede the Day of the Lord.

The Events Preceding the Day of the Lord

"The four horsemen of the apocalypse," as detailed in Revelation 6, symbolically represent the first four seals. It is hard to know for certain what exactly these seals entail because their descriptions are partially in symbolic language. However, a careful examination of Revelation 6 leads to the probable scenarios listed below. I would also like to add that the scriptures indicate that the start of each seal occurs in chronological order. They may overlap in duration or effect, but they occur chronologically.

The First seal

> And I saw when the Lamb opened one of the seals, and I heard, as it were the noise of thunder, one of the four beasts saying, Come and see. And I saw, and behold a white horse: and he that sat on him had a bow; and a crown was given unto him: and he went forth conquering, and to conquer. (Rev. 6:1–2)

The first seal is represented by a conquering warrior riding a white horse. Notice that the warrior has a bow, but the text does not mention that he has any arrows. This leads me to believe that possibly this conquering force will accomplish the takeover without war and will be of a political and or religious nature, and most likely involve deception. I also believe that this takeover is global, rather than regional as some have suggested, because the symbolism does not specify a place. Thus, by implication, we can assume this involves the entire world. Several commentaries agree with this analysis.

> Overall, the white horse and its rider are vivid representations of a powerful, aggressive, victorious force running unrestrained over mankind. Like a knight in armor or a soldier in full dress uniform, the first horseman appears to the eye as glorious and noble, but its intent is to kill, destroy, and subdue its enemies. Its white façade is deceptive, concealing a deadly, unholy purpose.[21]

---

[21] http://bibletools.org//index.cfm/fuseaction/Library.show/CT/PW/k/909

Thus, the white horse and his rider symbolize the spirit of conquest and militarism. . . . Economic power, propaganda, the use of religion, diplomacy and political shrewdness are also part of successful conquest.[22]

Scripture makes it clear that, during the end times, there will be a world religion and government. I believe this conquering warrior most likely represents the takeover of the world by these entities, undoubtedly involving deception. Look at what one "New Age" pastor said about the coming religious deceptive takeover of the world:

> The twenty-first century is the final stretch of the history of mankind. Not much time remains before the Second Coming. During this short period of time, God will bring into fulfillment all of the promises that have yet to come to pass. One of the most important of these is the New World Order under the banner of righteousness.[23]

Some think the rider of the white horse is the antichrist. I disagree with this assessment, for the antichrist is only allotted 3.5 years to reign at the end of the 70th Week, not at the beginning. The antichrist will, however, eventually rule the world through the New World Order system. We will discuss this in detail later in the book. The takeover of the world religiously and or politically by the New World Order, represented by the white horse and rider of the first seal, are the antithesis of the true and righteous world religion and government that will be started after the Lord Jesus Christ rides the white horse out of heaven when He establishes the millennial kingdom.

The Second seal

> And when he had opened the second seal, I heard the second beast say, Come and see. And there went out another horse that was red: and power was given to him that sat thereon to take peace from the earth, and that they should kill one another: and there was given unto him a great sword. (Rev. 6:3–4)

A fiery red horse represents the second seal. The rider of the red horse is given power to remove peace from the entire earth. The result

---

[22] http://www.wcg.org/lit/bible/Rev/sixseals.htm
[23] http://www.ngteam.org/TextEn.htm

is that people will kill one another on a scale never previously seen. This seal undoubtedly involves war and could be the infamous WWIII, and or it could involve total anarchy within countries where gangs, thieves and hoodlums would rule the streets. The great sword probably represents the fact that many will be killed during this time. The red color of the horse most likely represents the blood that will be spilled as a result. While it is true that we are experiencing wars and riots in various places throughout the world now, the distinguishing factor in this event is that peace will be taken from the *entire* world, and thus death will spread to the entire planet. In fact (as we will see in the fourth seal), up to one-quarter of the earth's inhabitants will be killed as a result of famine, war, and disease. This has never happened before in the history of the world.

The Third seal

> And when he had opened the third seal, I heard the third beast say, Come and see. And I beheld, and lo a black horse; and he that sat on him had a pair of balances in his hand. And I heard a voice in the midst of the four beasts say, a measure of wheat for a penny, and three measures of barley for a penny; and see thou hurt not the oil and the wine. (Rev. 6:5–6)

The black horse represents the third seal. The rider of this horse has a pair of balances in his hand. One of the ancient (and even modern) uses of balances is to measure out food. The phrase, "a measure of wheat for a penny, and three measures of barley for a penny," indicates that grains and possibly other foods will become very expensive. This could be caused by food shortages due to crop failures and/or a worldwide economic crisis. The average worker in the apostle John's day made about a penny a day. Thus, these verses indicate that one measure of wheat will cost a whole day's wages. Normally a penny would buy from sixteen to twenty measures of wheat. By today's standards, figuring the average worker in the United States earns $8 per hour, a half-loaf of bread would cost $64. The second part of the phrase, "see thou hurt not the oil and the wine," indicates that this affliction will not affect beverages made from grapes and oil, probably olive oil. Thus, if this affliction only affects some food items and not others, this would indicate that the most probable cause would be crop failures from drought, floods, and/or disease. The word used for the color black is *mevla*: "Of clothing used in mourning…as the color of evil."[24] Here the color black speaks of death from this worldwide famine.

The Fourth seal

> And when he had opened the fourth seal, I heard the voice of the fourth beast say, Come and see. And I looked, and behold a pale horse: and his name that sat on him was Death, and Hell followed with him. And power was given unto them over the fourth part of the earth, to kill with sword, and with hunger, and with death, and with the beasts of the earth. (Rev. 6:7–8)

A pale horse represents the fourth seal. The word translated "pale" has an explicit meaning in Greek and can be best described by the color gangrenous green—like a corpse in an advanced state of decay. This is a fitting color for the horse that depicts death. One fourth of the world's population will suffer death by the sword, hunger, plagues, and even attacks by wild animals or diseases spread by them. This extraordinary death count may be the culmination or result of all the first four seals put together, or it may represent the number who die from this seal alone.

The Fifth seal

> And when he had opened the fifth seal, I saw under the altar the souls of them that were slain for the word of God, and for the testimony which they held: And they cried with a loud voice, saying, How long, O Lord, holy and true, dost thou not judge and avenge our blood on them that dwell on the earth? And white robes were given unto every one of them; and it was said unto them, that they should rest yet for a little season, until their fellow servants also and their brethren, that should be killed as they were, should be fulfilled. (Rev. 6:9–11)

The fifth seal gives a clear picture of what it entails. Those holding the testimony of Jesus during this time will be persecuted and martyred for the cause of Christ.

---

[24] Danker, *A Greek-English Lexicon of the New Testament and Other Early Christian Literature*, 499.

In summary, to the best of my knowledge, based on the language employed in the passages above, the first six seals will most likely entail the following:

> **First seal (white horse):** Establishment of a world religion and or government through deception.
>
> **Second seal (red horse):** War and/or anarchy on the earth.
>
> **Third seal (black horse):** Famine due to crop failures and/or a worldwide economic collapse.
>
> **Fourth seal (pale horse):** Death of one-quarter of the world's population by various means, possibly culminating from the first four seals.
>
> **Fifth seal:** Persecution and martyrdom of saints.
>
> **Sixth seal:** Great earthquake, sun darkened, moon turned to blood, stars fall, heaven departs as a scroll, and every island and mountain moved.

As already stated, since the moon is turned to blood before the Day of the Lord, and the moon is turned to blood during the sixth seal event, then the events associated with the first six seals as listed above will also occur before the Day of the Lord.

Now that we have established that the Day of the Lord will occur after the sixth seal is opened, and we have examined the events and signs that will occur before the Day of the Lord, we will come back to our original question posed in the beginning of this chapter—What will be the event that starts this great period of time? It is a very important event, but I am not going to tell you what it is outright. First, I am going to see if you can discover it for yourself.

The Answer

The Day of the Lord and its alternative term, the Day of Christ, are both listed in Thessalonians and reveal to us what will occur in connection with the beginning of the Day of the Lord. Read carefully the next two passages and answer the question: What event is associated with the Day of the Lord or the Day of Christ?

> For this we say unto you by the word of the Lord, that we which are alive and remain unto the coming of the Lord shall not prevent them which are asleep. For the Lord himself shall descend from heaven with a shout, with the voice of the archangel, and with the trump of God: and the dead in Christ shall rise first: Then we which are alive and remain shall be caught up together with them in the clouds, to meet the Lord in the air: and so shall we ever be with the Lord. Wherefore comfort one another with these words. But of the times and the seasons, brethren, ye have no need that I write unto you. For yourselves know perfectly that the day of the Lord so cometh as a thief in the night. (1 Thess. 4:15–5:2)

> Now we beseech you, brethren, by the coming of our Lord Jesus Christ, and by our gathering together unto him, That ye be not soon shaken in mind, or be troubled, neither by spirit, nor by word, nor by letter as from us, as that the day of Christ is at hand. (2 Thess. 2:1–2)

What event is Paul referring to in these verses that he says will happen at the Day of the Lord—the Day of Christ? What event comes as a thief in the night? "And this know, that if the goodman of the house had known what hour the thief would come, he would have watched, and not have suffered his house to be broken through. Be ye therefore ready also: for the Son of man cometh at an hour when ye think not" (Lk. 12:39–40). What event were the Thessalonians afraid that they had missed because they thought they were now living in the Day of the Lord period? In both passages Paul is referring to the rapture; and it is clear from these passages that the event that is associated with the Day of the Lord is the rapture! 1 Thessalonians 4:15–5:2 describes the rapture and then goes on to make the association of the rapture with the Day of the Lord.

Let me put the two parts of 1 Thess. 4:15–5:2 together so you can see this more clearly:

> Then we which are alive and remain shall be caught up together with them in the clouds, to meet the Lord in the air. . . . For yourselves know perfectly that the day of the Lord so cometh as a thief in the night.

This passage indicates that the rapture occurs at the Day of the Lord event. In 2 Thessalonians, the rapture is again described, but here it is called the Day of Christ: "By the coming of our Lord Jesus Christ, and by our gathering together unto him . . . the day of Christ." Here, clearly the rapture is called the Day of Christ. The phrase "the Day of Christ" is synonymous with the phrase "the Day of the Lord." Many church fathers agree.

> It should be said that the formula, "The day of Christ," occurs in our translation in 2 Thess. 2:2, but that all the church fathers who quote the text have, "day of the Lord." The same is all but universally true of all the manuscripts. Thus the evidence is overwhelmingly in favor of the latter reading, and we may add, the internal evidence apparently requires this reading.[25]

Both of these passages in Thessalonians tell us that the rapture will occur in the time period known as the Day of the Lord. Thus, it stands to reason that since the Day of the Lord, or the Day of Christ, occurs after the opening of the sixth seal, and the rapture occurs as part of the Day of the Lord, then the rapture must also occur after the opening of the sixth seal!

Let me now present a formal proof of this fact. For purposes of our proof, we will use the following symbols and meanings.

R	Rapture
D	Day of the Lord
B	Moon turns to blood
S	Sixth seal
=	Means the first event happens during the second event
>	Means that the first event happens after the second

Using those symbols, we can then create the following logic statements and proof:

---

[25] J. B. Smith, *A Revelation of Jesus Christ* (Scottdale, Penn.: Mennonite Publishing House, 1961), 321.

Statement	Reason
1. D>B	Acts 2:20
2. R=D	1 Thess. 4:15–5:2
3. B=S	Rev. 6:12
4. R>S	Substitution

This logically proves that the rapture occurs after the sixth seal is opened.

Unless you are familiar with logic proofs, you probably did not understand the statements and conclusion. So let me explain it more fully:

1. D>B	Day of the Lord occurs after moon turns to blood. (Acts 2:20)
2. R=D	Rapture occurs during Day of the Lord. (1 Thess. 4:15–5:2)
3. B=S	Moon is turned to blood during the sixth seal event. (Rev. 6:12)
4. R>S	Therefore, the rapture occurs after the sixth seal is opened.

Statements 1, 2, and 3 are scriptural facts. In Statement 1, if you replace the D with the R, and the B with the S, which you can do by the mathematical law of substitution— because D & R and B & S happen at the same time—then you arrive at Statement 4, which says that R > S—the rapture occurs after the sixth seal is opened. Thus, the three scriptural truths (the rapture occurs during the Day of the Lord, the moon is turned to blood after the sixth seal is opened, and the Day of the Lord occurs after the moon is turned to blood) logically lead us to conclude that the rapture occurs after the moon is turned to blood. Let me put the logic into symbols.

The above symbols illustrate the scriptural facts that after the sixth seal is opened, represented by the **6,** the moon is turned to blood, represented by the crescent moon, and after the moon is turned to blood the Day of the Lord occurs, represented by the **D**. Realizing that scripture tells us that the rapture occurs at the Day of the Lord, represented by the arrow below, we can then create the following illustration;

This simple illustration puts all the facts together and clearly shows that the rapture occurs after the sixth seal is opened.

Deductive reasoning has now formally proved this fact.

> Deductive reasoning is an argument to establish that a statement is absolutely certain. An argument is valid if the reasoning proceeds logically from the premises to the conclusion. An argument is sound if it is valid and the premises are true. [26]

We have used deductive reasoning to prove that the statement "the rapture occurs after the sixth seal is opened" is absolutely certain. This argument is valid because it proceeds logically, as shown above, from the premises to the conclusion. The argument is sound because it is valid, and the premises (that the rapture occurs during the Day of the Lord, the moon is turned to blood after the sixth seal is opened, and the Day of the Lord occurs after the moon is turned to blood) are true. There is no way around it. The rapture occurs after the sixth seal is opened. Thus, scripture clearly tells us that the rapture will not occur before the start of the last seven years—the 70th Week—or what is commonly called "the tribulation." The rapture will, however, occur *during* the 70th Week, after the sixth seal is opened and simultaneous with the beginning of Day of the Lord.[27] Let's state it one more time:

---

[26] Ron Tagliapietra and Kathy Pilger, *Geometry for Christian Schools*. (Greenville, S. C: BJU Press, 2000), 182–183.

[27] Many post-trib adherents agree with the logic and conclusion that the rapture occurs after the sixth seal is opened. However, they place the occurrence of the sixth seal at the end of the 70th Week by claiming that the seal, trumpet, and bowl judgments overlap. This notion is easily shown to be false by realizing that scripture presents the seal, bowl, and trumpet judgments as proceeding chronologically. Also,

The Day of the Lord occurs after the moon is turned to blood.
The rapture occurs during the Day of the Lord.
The moon is turned to blood after the sixth seal is opened.
Therefore the rapture occurs after the sixth seal is opened.

Some object to this reasoning, saying that the rapture does not occur after the moon is turned to blood because there are two Days of the Lord yet to come. One occurs at the rapture before the 70th Week, and one at Armageddon. They then conclude that Acts 2:20 and Joel 2:31 are in reference to the Day of the Lord that will occur at Armageddon. This reasoning is in error because, if you remember our discussion about the essence of the Day of the Lord, we established the fact that there is only one Day of the Lord yet to come: "Whose voice then shook the earth: but now he hath promised, saying, Yet once more I shake not the earth only, but also heaven" (Heb. 12:26). The Day of the Lord is when the earth will be shaken, "And they shall go into the holes of the rocks, and into the caves of the earth, for fear of the Lord, and for the glory of his majesty, when he ariseth to shake terribly the earth (Is 2:19)," and there is only one Day of the Lord yet to occur.

Still others object to this reasoning, saying that the rapture is not part of the Day of the Lord, but happens before the Day of the Lord and not during it. However that is not what scripture indicates in

---

Rev. 7:2–3: "And I saw another angel ascending from the east, having the seal of the living God: and he cried with a loud voice to the four angels, to whom it was given to hurt the earth and the sea, Saying, hurt not the earth, neither the sea, nor the trees, till we have sealed the servants of our God in their foreheads"—tells us that the earth and sea cannot be hurt (which happens in the trumpet and bowl judgments) until after the sealing of the 144,000. The sealing of the 144,000 happens after the rapture and the sixth seal. Therefore the trumpet and bowl judgments cannot occur until after the sixth seal is opened. Thus the seal, trumpet, and bowl judgments cannot overlap. There are some pre-trib adherents that also agree that the rapture occurs at the sixth seal but place the sixth seal at the start of the 70th Week. This notion is also shown to be false by realizing that one of the signs that must occur before the Day of the Lord—as previously discussed—is that the antichrist must set himself up as god, which occurs at the Abomination of Desolation, which happens near the midpoint of the 70th Week. Thus the opening of the sixth seal and the Day of the Lord must occur after the midpoint of the 70th Week. Joel 1:15,16 supports this fact and clearly shows that the Day of the Lord occurs after the sacrifices are stopped at the abomination of desolation. "Alas for the day! for the day of the Lord is at hand, and as a destruction from the Almighty shall it come. Is not the meat cut off before our eyes, yea, joy and gladness from the house of our God?"

Thessalonians and many stanch pre-trib commentators believe that the rapture is part of the Day of the Lord:[28]

> He must explain what he means by "the coming of our Lord Jesus Christ and our being gathered to him" or else the solution to the problem cannot be grasped. *Episynagoges* ("being gathered") defines what part of the *parousias* ("coming") Paul has in mind. This is the great event he has described more fully in 1 Thessalonians 4:14–17—i.e., the gathering of those in Christ to meet him in the air enroute to the Father in heaven. This begins the day of the Lord. . . . He had told them that the coming of the Lord to gather his saints into heaven would initiate both the tribulation and the day of the Lord. They were promised immediate "rest" (1:7) and glorification with Christ (1:10), not increased persecution. . . . Despite their "persecutions and trials" (1:4) these Thessalonian Christians were not living in the day of the Lord as they had been erroneously told. A right understanding of "being gathered to him" reveals that they could not be so enmeshed, because for them Christ's *parousia* will antedate the awful period to come. In fact, their "being gathered to him" will be the event that signals the day's beginning.[29]

Also, as discussed earlier, and expounded upon by Mr. Keathley—a pre-trib author—2 Thessalonians 2:2 clearly tells us that the rapture is part of the Day of the Lord and is the event that starts it, by the coming of our Lord Jesus Christ, and by our gathering together unto him, "the day of Christ." Therefore, in reference to the logic proof: If the premises are valid and the argument is sound, then the proof stands—the rapture occurs after the sixth seal is opened. In fact, many other scriptures confirm this.

But before we examine this fact, let me discuss an emotional aspect of this discussion. The realization that the rapture will not occur until after the sixth seal is opened will probably scare you; that is a natural reaction that is to be expected. Let me state, however, that it is neither God's nor my intention to scare you. God does not want you to be afraid, and neither do I. Remember, He loves you more than you

---

[28] Many pre-trib commentators agree that the rapture is part of the Day of the Lord: Coffman, Matthew Henry, La Haye, to name a few.
[29] J. Hampton Keathley, III, Th.M., *Correction Concerning the Day of the Lord, Part 1.http://www.bible.org/page.asp?page_id=1696#P336_80025*

can imagine. He will take care of you better than any loving father takes care of his children. Even though these things may be scary to you, you must know the truth, for "the truth will set you free" (John 14:6). Would you rather know a hurricane was coming your way so you could prepare, or would you rather have it come upon you unawares? In the same way, God wants you to know what will transpire so you can prepare and not be caught unawares. We will devote a couple of chapters to these issues later in the book. But for now let's continue our discussion and confirm the fact that the rapture will not occur until after the sixth seal is opened.

Confirmation

You can find confirmation of the fact that the rapture will not occur until after the sixth seal is opened in many places in scripture. Look, for example, at Rev. 6:12–17:

> And I beheld when he had opened the sixth seal, and, lo, there was a great earthquake; and the sun became black as sackcloth of hair, and the moon became as blood. And the stars of heaven fell unto the earth, even as a fig tree casteth her untimely figs, when she is shaken of a mighty wind. And the heaven departed as a scroll when it is rolled together; and every mountain and island were moved out of their places. And the kings of the earth, and the great men, and the rich men, and the chief captains, and the mighty men, and every bondman, and every free man, hid themselves in the dens and in the rocks of the mountains. And said to the mountains and rocks, Fall on us, and *hide us from the face of him that sitteth on the throne, and from the wrath of the Lamb.* For the great day of his wrath is come; and who shall be able to stand? [italics mine]

Take note of the italicized portion and ask yourself why the people cry, "Hide us from the face of Him that sitteth on the throne?" Simply, the text tells us that they want to hide because they have seen the face of God. They want to hide because Jesus has come to the clouds and is visible for all to see, and the rapture has occurred; and men are scared to death because the Day of the Lord—the great day of His wrath—has come upon them.

In other words, they had an *epiphany!* Yes, when Christ comes to the clouds for his bride, He will be visible for all to see just as He foretold "Jesus saith unto him, Thou hast said: nevertheless I say unto you, Hereafter shall ye see the Son of man sitting on the right hand of power, and coming in the clouds of heaven." (Mt 26:64). And upon seeing Christ, those who are not raptured will experience an epiphany. That is, they will have "a sudden manifestation or perception of the essential nature or meaning of something." They will realize that Jesus is God and they have been wrong in following the antichrist. As a result, they will cry out; "hide us from the face of him that sitteth on the throne, and from the wrath of the Lamb."

This passage confirms that Christ will come after the opening of the sixth seal and will rapture His church. Then the wrath of God will be poured out upon mankind. Remember our definition of the Day of the Lord? It is primarily a day of wrath. After the rapture, the wrath of God will begin. The use of the aorist tense in the phrase "For the great day of his wrath is come" confirms that the great Day of His wrath—the Day of the Lord—has started after the opening of this seal and the occurrence of the rapture, and also confirms that the Day of the Lord/Christ referred to by Paul was in reference to the rapture.[30]

This scenario is clearly seen in other parts of scripture, too. Another passage that clearly confirms this fact is Matthew 24:29–31:

> Immediately after the tribulation of those days shall the sun be darkened, and the moon shall not give her light, and the stars shall fall from heaven, and the powers of the heavens shall be shaken: And then shall appear the sign of the Son of man in heaven: and then shall all the tribes of the earth mourn, and they shall see the Son of man coming in the clouds of heaven with power and great glory. And he shall send his angels with a great sound of a trumpet, and they shall gather together his elect from the four winds, from one end of heaven to the other.

The first thing I would like to bring out about this passage is that it begins by saying "after the tribulation of those days." Thus, the events talked about in the passage all occur after the "tribulation period" during the 70th Week of Daniel. The "tribulation period" entails the first six seals, which includes the sorrows of the first four seals, plus the great tribulation, which begins at the fifth seal. It does not refer to the entire 70th Week; we will discuss this more in detail later in this book.

---

[30] http://spiritandtruth.org/teaching/Book_of_Revelation/commentary/htm/030617.htm

The passage also says that, after this time of tribulation, the sun will be darkened, the moon shall not give her light, the stars shall fall from heaven, and the powers of the heavens shall be shaken. From our previous discussions, we know that these signs in the sun, moon, and stars occur before the Day of the Lord. We have also determined that these signs will occur after the opening of the sixth seal.

The passage goes on to indicate that after these signs, "then shall appear the sign of the Son of man in heaven: and then shall all the tribes of the earth mourn, and they shall see the Son of man coming in the clouds of heaven with power and great glory. And he shall send his angels with a great sound of a trumpet, and they shall gather together his elect from the four winds, from one end of heaven to the other." This is a description of the rapture when Jesus comes through the clouds and all the Christians are gathered together and caught up with the Lord, and all the earth sees Him and mourns.

This passage again confirms and summarizes that the Day of the Lord and the rapture occur during the 70th Week of Daniel, after the tribulations of the first five seals, and after the occurrence of the signs in the sun, moon and stars, which Revelation 6 says will occur after the opening of the sixth seal.

Some erroneously believe that because this event occurs at the sound of the trumpet, this event occurs at the last of the seven trumpet judgments. That is not correct. The triple sign of sun, moon, and stars clearly places the event described in the passage—the Day of the Lord—at the sixth seal. By the way, the trumpet referred to above is most probably in reference to the trumpet blown during the feast of Rosh Hashanah, which we will discuss in more detail later.

These scripture passages clearly confirm that the beginning event of the Day of the Lord is the rapture of the church, which occurs after the opening of the sixth seal. Just in case you are not convinced, here are more scriptures that confirm this. Look at how beautifully this passage from Mark 13 mirrors the exact chronology of events that we have been talking about thus far:

> And Jesus answering them began to say, Take heed lest any man deceive you: For many shall come in my name, saying, I am Christ; and shall deceive many. And when ye shall hear of wars and rumours of wars, be ye not troubled: for such things must needs be; but the end shall not be yet. For nation shall rise against nation, and kingdom against kingdom: and there shall

be earthquakes in divers places, and there shall be famines and troubles: these are the beginnings of sorrows. But take heed to yourselves: for they shall deliver you up to councils; and in the synagogues ye shall be beaten: and ye shall be brought before rulers and kings for my sake, for a testimony against them. And the gospel must first be published among all nations . . . And ye shall be hated of all men for my name's sake: but he that shall endure unto the end, the same shall be saved. But when ye shall see the Abomination of Desolation, spoken of by Daniel the prophet, standing where it ought not, (let him that readeth understand,) then let them that be in Judaea flee to the mountains . . . for in those days shall be affliction, such as was not from the beginning of the creation which God created unto this time, neither shall be. And except that the Lord had shortened those days, no flesh should be saved: but for the elect's sake, whom he hath chosen, he hath shortened the days . . . But in those days, after that tribulation, the sun shall be darkened, and the moon shall not give her light, And the stars of heaven shall fall, and the powers that are in heaven shall be shaken. And then shall they see the Son of man coming in the clouds with great power and glory. (Mark 13:5–26)

Notice in the above passage, the sequence of events aligns exactly with the prophetic timeline that has been presented thus far. In the beginning of the passage, we see wars, rumors of wars, famines, earthquakes, and troubles that align with the first four seals. Then we see the persecution that will take place during the fifth seal. After the persecution we see a description of the Abomination of Desolation and associated events. Then, in the last part of the passage we see the sixth seal events and the rapture.

Take notice that, like Matthew 24, this passage places the rapture after the Abomination of Desolation. The abomination occurs near the middle of the 70th Week. Thus, this passage firmly places the rapture as occurring after the middle of the 70th Week and after the first six seals.

We also see this timing reflected in the Old Testament in a passage in Isa. 26:19–21, which talks about the rapture:[31]

---

[31] Technically, the rapture itself is not referenced in the Old Testament. Paul clearly tells us that the rapture was a mystery only revealed to him (1 Cor. 15:51). However, we know from other passages, such as 1 Thess. 4:16–17, 5:2 and Matt. 24:30–31, that the rapture occurs at the same time as the resurrection. Therefore, because the

Thy dead men shall live, together with my dead body shall they arise. Awake and sing, ye that dwell in dust: for thy dew is as the dew of herbs, and the earth shall cast out the dead. [The resurrection of the dead at the rapture] Come, my people, enter thou into thy chambers, and shut thy doors about thee: hide thyself as it were for a little moment, until the indignation be overpast. For, behold, the Lord cometh out of his place to punish the inhabitants of the earth for their iniquity [The Day of the Lord]: the earth also shall disclose her blood, and shall no more cover her slain.

This passage places the resurrection of the dead, which occurs at the rapture before the outpouring of God's wrath, at the Day of the Lord.

And yet another Old Testament passage brings out this timing:

And he [antichrist] shall plant the tabernacles of his palace between the seas in the glorious holy mountain [performs Abomination of Desolation and rules the world from Jerusalem]; yet he shall come to his end, and none shall help him. And at that time shall Michael stand up, the great prince which standeth for the children of thy people: and there shall be a time of trouble [the great tribulation], such as never was since there was a nation even to that same time: and at that time thy people shall be delivered, every one that shall be found written in the book. And many of them that sleep in the dust of the earth shall awake, some to everlasting life, and some to shame and everlasting contempt. [rapture and resurrection of the dead] (Dan. 11:45–12:2)

This passage clearly shows that the Abomination of Desolation will be followed by a period of great tribulation, then the resurrection and rapture. Taken together, these passages further substantiate that the persecution of saints by the antichrist during the great tribulation will be followed by the resurrection of the saints at the rapture when the Day of the Lord begins.

Here is another scripture passage that confirms this scenario:

---

resurrection *is* mentioned in the Old Testament, by inference, we can place the rapture there.

> And after these things I saw four angels standing on the four corners of the earth, holding the four winds of the earth, that the wind should not blow on the earth, nor on the sea, nor on any tree. And I saw another angel ascending from the east, having the seal of the living God: and he cried with a loud voice to the four angels, to whom it was given to hurt the earth and the sea. Saying, Hurt not the earth, neither the sea, nor the trees, till we have sealed the servants of our God in their foreheads. And I heard the number of them which were sealed: and there were sealed an hundred and forty and four thousand of all the tribes of the children of Israel. (Rev. 7:1–4)

In Revelation 7:1–4, notice the phrase "after these things." This indicates that this event chronologically follows the sixth seal events in Revelation 6. In this passage, we see two groups of people. One group is the 144,000 Israelites who are sealed to be God's ambassadors on earth after the saints have been raptured. The passage also says, "Hurt not the earth, neither the sea, nor the trees, till we have sealed the servants of our God in their foreheads." This indicates that the 144,000 will be sealed before the wrath of God is poured out during the trumpet and bowl judgments, which will severely "hurt" the earth and those who live on it.

In the second part of the chapter, we see a group of people in heaven with white robes.

> After this I beheld, and, lo, a great multitude, which no man could number, of all nations, and kindreds, and people, and tongues, stood before the throne, and before the Lamb, clothed with white robes, and palms in their hands . . . And one of the elders answered, saying unto me, What are these which are arrayed in white robes? and whence came they? And I said unto him, Sir, thou knowest. And he said to me, *These are they which came out of great tribulation,* and have washed their robes, and made them white in the blood of the Lamb. Therefore are they before the throne of God, and serve him day and night in his temple: and he that sitteth on the throne shall dwell among them. They shall hunger no more, neither thirst any more; neither shall the sun light on them, nor any heat. For the Lamb which is in the midst of the throne shall feed them, and shall lead them unto living fountains of waters: and God shall wipe away all tears from their eyes. [italics mine]

In verse 13, the elder asks John who these people are. John did not know, so the elder gives him the answer. They are those who came out of great tribulation. They are the raptured saints of God, raptured out of the great tribulation, which starts after the opening of the sixth seal.

70th Week, Three Time Periods

As already mentioned there are three distinct periods of difficulty during the 70th Week of Daniel: 1) sorrows or tribulations, 2) the great tribulation, and 3) the Day of the Lord.

The first four seals constitute sorrows:

> And Jesus answered and said unto them, Take heed that no man deceive you. For many shall come in my name, saying, I am Christ; and shall deceive many. And ye shall hear of wars and rumours of wars: see that ye be not troubled: for all these things must come to pass, but the end is not yet. For nation shall rise against nation, and kingdom against kingdom: and there shall be famines, and pestilences, and earthquakes, in divers places. *All these are the beginning of sorrows.* (Matt. 24:4–8) [italics mine]

The great tribulation starts when the antichrist comes to power. It will include the fifth seal and the beginning part of the sixth seal.

> When ye therefore shall see the Abomination of Desolation, spoken of by Daniel the prophet, stand in the holy place, (whoso readeth, let him understand:). Then let them which be in Judaea flee into the mountains. Let him which is on the housetop not come down to take any thing out of his house. Neither let him which is in the field return back to take his clothes. And woe unto them that are with child, and to them that give suck in those days! But pray ye that your flight be not in the winter, neither on the sabbath day. *For then shall be great tribulation,* such as was not since the beginning of the world to this time, no, nor ever shall be. And except those days should be shortened, there should no flesh be saved: but for the elect's sake those days shall be shortened. (Matt. 24:15–22) [italics mine]

As already discussed, the rapture occurs at the beginning of the Day of the Lord. So the fact that there are saints in heaven who came out of the great tribulation, as told to us by Rev 7:13, supports the fact that the rapture occurs after the opening of the sixth seal, at the end of the great tribulation. It is comforting to note that the passage above says that the Lord will shorten the days of the great tribulation for the elect's sake. God will cut the time of the great tribulation short for the sake of His people who are living during this terrible time. See the chart entitled "The Afflictions of the 70th Week" at the end of this book for a pictorial representation of these facts.

Luke 17 also brings out very clearly the timing of the rapture. It irrefutably places it after the Abomination of Desolation.

> *In that day,* he which shall be upon the housetop, and his stuff in the house, let him not come down to take it away: and he that is in the field, let him likewise not return back. Remember Lot's wife. Whosoever shall seek to save his life shall lose it; and whosoever shall lose his life shall preserve it. I tell you, *in that night* there shall be two men in one bed; the one shall be taken, and the other shall be left. Two women shall be grinding together; the one shall be taken, and the other left. Two men shall be in the field; the one shall be taken, and the other left. (Luke 17:31–36) [italics mine]

Here we notice the phrase "in that day" and "in that night." These phrases are referring to a period of time, namely the great tribulation. It starts with the Abomination of Desolation—at which time Israel is told to flee to the wilderness—and ends with the rapture. The Abomination of Desolation is referred to as happening in "the day," and then the rapture "at night." No matter how you look at it, the use of these chronological phrases, "in that day" and "in that night," irrefutably places the rapture after the Abomination of Desolation.

The Harmony of Scripture

Look at how beautifully scripture harmonizes to show and confirm the scriptural truths we have been talking about:

	Revelation 6,7	Matthew 24	Mark 13	Luke 21
Deception	2. And I saw, and behold a white horse: and he that	5. For many shall come in my name,	6. For many shall come in my name,	8. And he said, Take heed that ye be not

	sat on him had a bow; and a crown was given unto him: and he went forth conquering, and to conquer.	saying, I am Christ; and shall deceive many.	saying, I am Christ; and shall deceive many.	deceived
War	4. And there went out another horse that was red: and power was given to him that sat thereon to take peace from the earth	6. And ye shall hear of wars and rumours of wars:	7. And when ye shall hear of wars and rumours of wars	9. But when ye shall hear of wars and commotions
Famine, Pestilence, Earthquakes	5. And I beheld, and lo a black horse; and he that sat on him had a pair of balances in his hand. 6. A measure of wheat for a penny, and three measures of barley for a penny; and see thou hurt not the oil and the wine.	7. and there shall be famines, and pestilences, and earthquakes, in divers places.	8. there shall be earthquakes in divers places, and there shall be famines and troubles	11. And great earthquakes shall be in divers places, and famines, and pestilences
Sorrows		8. All these are the	8. these are the	

		beginning of sorrows.	beginnings of sorrows	
Persecution	9. And when he had opened the fifth seal, I saw under the altar the souls of them that were slain for the Word of God, and for the testimony which they held:	9. Then shall they deliver you up to be afflicted, and shall kill you:	9. for they shall deliver you up to councils; and in the synagogues ye shall be beaten:	
A of D		15. When ye therefore shall see the abomination of desolation	14. But when ye shall see the abomination of desolation	
Great Tribulation		21. For then shall be great tribulation	19. For in those days shall be affliction, such as was not from the beginning of the creation	23. for there shall be great distress in the land, and wrath upon this people
Signs in sun, moon, stars	12. And I beheld when he had opened the sixth seal, and, lo, there was a great	29. Immediately after the tribulation of those days shall the sun be	24. after that tribulation, the sun shall be darkened, and the	25. And there shall be signs in the sun, and in the moon, and in the stars

	earthquake; and the sun became black as sackcloth of hair, and the moon became as blood; 13. And the stars of heaven fell unto the earth	darkened, and the moon shall not give her light, and the stars shall fall from heaven	moon shall not give her light, 25. And the stars of heaven shall fall	
See the Lord	16. Fall on us, and hide us from the face of him that sitteth on the throne, and from the wrath of the Lamb:	30. And then shall appear the sign of the Son of man in heaven…and they shall see the Son of man coming in the clouds	26. And then shall they see the Son of man coming in the clouds	27. And then shall they see the Son of man coming in a cloud
Rapture	7:9,14. lo, a great multitude, which no man could number…These are they which came out of great tribulation,	31. And he shall send his angels with a great sound of a trumpet, and they shall gather together his elect	27. And then shall he send his angels, and shall gather together his elect from the four winds	

In Summary

In summary, scripture clearly and undeniably shows us that the Day of the Lord is a period of time in which God's wrath is poured out upon mankind. There are several signs that precede this event to let us know that the time is approaching. Those signs, which must occur before the Day of the Lord, combined with the teaching in 1 and 2

Thessalonians, which equates the rapture with the Day of the Lord, irrefutably place the rapture as occurring after the start of the sixth seal. As we have seen there are many scriptures that confirm this chronology. Thus, scripture clearly indicates that the rapture occurs simultaneously with the beginning of the Day of the Lord after the opening of the sixth seal.

Chapter 4
Who's Right?

"Hopefully we will be raptured before . . . " Have you ever heard anyone talk that way? Back in college, I remember we used to wish the rapture would come so we would not have to take our finals. Many people are looking for and believe that the Lord will return and that the rapture will occur before the tribulation, or 70th Week of Daniel. This is commonly known as the "pre-trib rapture" theory. This theory teaches that the rapture could occur at any moment—imminence—which will be followed by the revealing of the antichrist, signing of the peace treaty, and the other events of the seven-year, so-called "tribulation period." In the last chapter, we showed why the rapture will not occur until after the sixth seal is opened. In this chapter, we will show why the pre-trib rapture belief cannot be correct.

One of the main arguments cited in defense of the pre-trib view reasons that since God has promised to not allow the Christian to be subject to His wrath; and since His wrath starts at the first seal, thus Christians will be removed before the 70th Week begins. It is true that God will not allow the righteous to be subject to His wrath. Verses that clearly bring out this principle are 1 Thessalonians 1:10: "And to wait for his Son from heaven, whom he raised from the dead, even Jesus, which delivered us from the wrath to come"; and 1 Thessalonians 5:9: "For God hath not appointed us to wrath, but to obtain salvation by our Lord Jesus Christ." We also see it in Romans 5:9: "Much more then, being now justified by his blood, we shall be saved from wrath through him."

The reasoning that God will not allow a Christian or any righteous person to be subject to His wrath is correct. This principle is illustrated in God's actions with Noah, Lot, the Israelites in Egypt, and others, and applies to Christians alive today. However, this does not mean that Christians will not go through trials and sorrows like those that occur during the first part of the 70th Week. The wrath of God does not start until the Day of the Lord, which occurs after the opening of the sixth seal. We have already defined the Day of the Lord as a time of wrath (Amos 1:14–15, Rev. 6:16–17). Therefore, the period before the Day of the Lord precedes God's wrath. Jesus Himself only called the first part of the 70th Week "sorrows" (Matt. 24:8).

We have already listed what will most likely occur during the first five seals:

> **First seal (white horse):** Establishment of a world religion and or government through deception.
>
> **Second seal (red horse):** War and/or anarchy on the earth.
>
> **Third seal (black horse):** Famine due to crop failures and/or a worldwide economic collapse.
>
> **Fourth seal (pale horse):** Death of one-quarter of world's population by various means, possibly culminating from the first four seals.
>
> **Fifth seal:** Persecution and martyrdom of saints.

If you consider these events, you will realize that there have been localized instances of these things occurring throughout history. There have been conquering powers, famines, pestilence, persecution, financial collapse, and martyrdom. And yes, some Christians and saints of God have gone through all of them, and some are going through them now. Since these sorrows are not part of God's wrath and since God's people have gone through these types of sorrows before, why shouldn't they go through them during the 70th Week? Even the Israelites were subject to the first three plagues in Egypt. They were only protected from the last seven.

From the sixth seal on, after the Christians are raptured, only then is God's wrath poured out. The first five seals are not described as being God's Wrath, just as *sorrows*.

When Is God's Wrath?

Some disagree, believing that the first six seals *are* part of God's wrath. However, this is impossible because we know that God's wrath does not include persecution and martyrdom of Christians. Martyrdom and persecution is an action of satan and men. God allows it, but it is an action of satan, not God. The story of Job is a clear example. The persecution, sorrows, and tribulations that Job experienced were allowed by God, but were caused by satan. When Saul was persecuting the early church, God allowed it, but satan was behind it. It would make no sense for Jesus to appear to Saul and ask why Saul was persecuting Him if God was the one responsible for it. "Saul, Saul, why persecutest thou me? And he said, Who art thou, Lord? And the Lord said, I am Jesus whom thou persecutest: it is hard for thee to kick against the pricks" (Acts 9:4–5).

How does this principle that persecution and martyrdom of believers is an action of satan and not of God apply to the 70th Week? The fifth seal is the persecution and martyrdom of believers:

> And when he had opened the fifth seal, I saw under the altar the souls of them that were slain for the Word of God, and for the testimony which they held: And they cried with a loud voice, saying, How long, O Lord, holy and true, dost thou not judge and avenge our blood on them that dwell on the earth? And white robes were given unto every one of them; and it was said unto them, that they should rest yet for a little season, until their fellow servants also and their brethren, that should be killed as they were, should be fulfilled" (Rev. 6:9–11).

Jesus also spoke about this persecution, as recorded in the gospels of Matthew and Mark:

> Then shall they deliver you up to be afflicted, and shall kill you: and ye shall be hated of all nations for my name's sake. And then shall many be offended, and shall betray one another, and shall hate one another" (Matt. 24:9–10).

> But take heed to yourselves: for they shall deliver you up to councils; and in the synagogues ye shall be beaten: and ye shall be brought before rulers and kings for my sake, for a testimony against them. And the gospel must first be published among all nations. But when they shall lead you, and deliver you up, take no thought beforehand what ye shall speak, neither do ye premeditate: but whatsoever shall be given you in that hour, that speak ye: for it is not ye that speak, but the Holy Ghost" (Mark 13:9–11).

Since the fifth seal is the persecution and martyrdom of believers, it cannot be part of God's wrath. God's wrath starts during the Day of the Lord, which starts with the rapture after the sixth seal is opened.

That is why men cry out and say, "hide us from the face of Him that sitteth on the throne," because the rapture has just occurred and men have seen Christ and go into hiding. That is also why they say, "For the great day of his wrath is come; and who shall be able to stand?" It is at this time that God's wrath has begun.

This verse tells us precisely that God's wrath does not start until after the sixth seal is opened and the rapture occurs. To say that the wrath of God starts at the first seal would require God to be the one persecuting and martyring Christians, which is impossible. God would never pour out His wrath on His children. Therefore, we must conclude that God's wrath—at the very least—cannot start until after the fifth seal, and that is exactly what we see. It starts at the sixth seal after the rapture. Thus scripture confirms that the Christian will be subject to the sorrows and tribulations of the first five seals and be raptured out of the great tribulation before God's wrath is poured out.

The belief that Christians will not be subject to God's wrath in no way necessitates a "pre-trib" rapture, because the seals are not part of God's wrath. It does, however necessitate the rapture occurring before the wrath of God is poured out, which occurs after the start of the sixth seal.

What About Revelation 3:10?

Some pre-trib adherents make further claims, citing Revelation 3:10 as evidence that God will not only keep the Christian from His wrath, but will also keep them from the hour of temptation—that is, the entire 70th Week: "Because thou hast kept the word of my patience, I also will keep thee from the hour of temptation, which shall come upon all the world, to try them that dwell upon the earth." However, a careful examination of the Greek used in this passage actually shows that the passage supports the view that believes that the rapture will occur at the sixth seal.

Robert Van Kampen, in *The Rapture Question Answered Plain & Simple,* has made a thorough analysis of this verse. Let us examine a few excerpts from that section.

> When the underlying Greek text is studied carefully, comparing Scripture with Scripture, we will discover that the "hour of testing" refers specifically to that time associated with antichrist's persecution. . . . More importantly we will see that the Greek words underlying our English translations argue that

this terrible time of testing cannot be the wrath of God, but must be the wrath of satan. . . . If the Greek word *peirasmos*, as used in the Revelation 3:10 passage, is compared to its use in other New Testament passages, we will see that the "hour of testing" cannot refer to the wrath of God but, quite the opposite, to the wrath of satan. . . . They all say the same thing: satan is the source of all *peirazo*, not God. Like the logical argument, the biblical argument from scripture demonstrates that the "hour of testing" in Rev. 3:10 cannot refer to the wrath of God but, by definition, must be the wrath of satan.[32]

Another phrase in Revelation 3:10 that we need to consider is "will keep thee from." The Greek phrase used here is *tereo ek*. Van Kampen has this to say about that phrase:

Tereo ek, is used in conjunction, can only refer to guarding or protecting those who persevere while they are within the sphere of danger, and then bringing them safely out from the midst of that danger. Thus the meaning of the text is clear. *Tereo ek* should be translated, "a watchful protection within the sphere of danger, with a safe deliverance out from the midst of it.[33]

Combining the analysis of the Greek into a translation of Revelation 3:10 yields a rendering that shows that the Christian will not be spared from the great tribulation, but will be rescued out of it:

Because thou hast kept the word of my patience, I also will *rescue you out of the midst* of the hour of *satan's* temptation, *the great tribulation,* which shall come upon all the world, to try them that dwell upon the earth.

So the analysis of the Greek in Revelation 3:10 does not support a pre-trib view, but supports a pre-wrath view of the rapture.

Revealing of the antichrist

Another argument presented by pre-trib adherents against the rapture occurring during the 70th Week is that they assert that the rapture occurs at the same time or immediately following the revealing of the antichrist. They reason further that since the antichrist is

---

[32] Robert Van Kampen, *The Rapture Question Answered Plain & Simple,* (Grand Rapids, Mich.: Revell, 2002), 173–174.
[33] Ibid., 177.

revealed at the signing of the peace treaty (the event that many believe starts the 70th Week), the rapture must occur at the beginning of the 70th Week.

Proponents of the pre-trib rapture formulate this belief from two passages:

> Let no man deceive you by any means: for that day shall not come, except there come a falling away first, and that man of sin be revealed, the son of perdition. (2 Thess. 2:3)

> And he shall confirm the covenant with many for one week: and in the midst of the week he shall cause the sacrifice and the oblation to cease, and for the overspreading of abominations he shall make it desolate, even until the consummation, and that determined shall be poured upon the desolate. (Dan. 9:27)

2 Thessalonians 2:3 does, indeed, tell us that the antichrist is revealed before the rapture will take place, but Daniel 9:27 does not necessitate that the antichrist be involved in the initial signing of the peace treaty. When you examine the Hebrew, the true meaning becomes clearly evident. Roy Reinhold, author of *The Day of the Lord* and an expert in Hebrew, has this to say about the verse:

> The "he" is the same person throughout the verse. Higbir is a hifil 3ms perfect verb, and the Qal root verb is gavar meaning "to be strong, to conquer." A Hifil is "causative," and so in this case the usage is "and he caused to be made strong" a covenant for the many for one period of seven. In no way does this imply that the "he" the antichrist originates the peace treaty. What it clearly shows is that the antichrist comes along *after* the peace treaty is in effect and he agrees with it and enforces its provisions.[34]

So an analysis of the Hebrew brings out the fact that, when the antichrist is revealed and comes to power in the midst of the 70th Week, the peace treaty will already be in effect and "he," the antichrist, will merely confirm and or strengthen it. Thus, a more accurate translation of the verse would read: "And he will strengthen the covenant that was made with many for a week: and in the midst of the week he shall cause the sacrifice and the oblation to cease."

---

[34] Unpublished personal correspondence.

So if the antichrist will not be the one to make the peace treaty, who is? The Hebrew rendering of this verse tells us the peace treaty will be made with "the many." This suggests that the treaty will probably be the result of an effort by many nations—like we see now with the "Road Map"—to bring peace to the tumultuous Middle East situation.

We also cannot assume that the signing or beginning of the peace treaty aligns with the beginning of the 70th Week. The peace treaty may simply be a treaty with terms in effect for 7 years signed sometime during the 70th Week that the antichrist strengthens during "in the midst" of the 70th Week.

Scripture tells us that the antichrist does not come to power and reign until the last 3.5 years of the 70th Week of Daniel after the Abomination of Desolation has occurred. In reference to the antichrist, Revelation 13:5 says, "and there was given unto him a mouth speaking great blasphemies; and power was given unto him to continue forty and two months." Thus his reign starts shortly after the occurrence of the Abomination of Desolation in which he deceives the world into thinking that he is God and his reign continues until he is thrown in the lake of fire at the conclusion to the battle of Armageddon.

2 Thessalonians 2:4 confirms when the revealing takes place:

> Let no man deceive you by any means: for that day shall not come, except there come a falling away first, and that man of sin be revealed, the son of perdition; Who opposeth and exalteth himself above all that is called God, or that is worshipped; so that he as God sitteth in the temple of God, shewing himself that he is God.

That verse tells us that the man of sin will not be revealed until he sets himself up as God, and he does that at the Abomination of Desolation: "and that man of sin be revealed, the son of perdition . . . so that he as God sitteth in the temple of God, shewing himself that he is God." The verse further tells us "that day shall not come," in reference to the Day of the Lord and the rapture, until after the antichrist sets himself up as God. As we have just pointed out, that does not happen until after the Abomination of Desolation.

Daniel 7:24 further confirms that the antichrist does not arise until after the peace treaty is signed, showing us that the antichrist (little horn) comes after the New World Order (NWO)—the "ten horns"—is established. "And the ten horns out of this kingdom are ten kings that shall arise: and another shall rise after them; and he shall be diverse from the first, and he shall subdue three kings." The establishment of the NWO does not begin until after the first seal is opened, which we will discuss in detail in another chapter. Thus, Daniel 7:24 confirms that the antichrist arises after the establishment of the NWO, which comes after the peace treaty is signed.

Therefore, to say that the antichrist will be revealed before the rapture is correct, but to say that he will be revealed before the 70th Week, or that the rapture occurs before or at the same time that he is revealed, has no scriptural support. In fact, the scriptures make it clear that the Day of Christ will not come until after he is revealed at the Abomination of Desolation.

'No One Knows the Day or the Hour'

Another argument pre-trib adherents put forth to support their view is that they say if the rapture does not occur before the 70th Week of Daniel, then you will know the time of Christ's return, and as Jesus said, "no one knows the day or hour." Believing that the rapture occurs during the 70th Week after the opening of the sixth seal does not mean that one knows the "day and hour" of His return. Even though I know that the rapture will not take place until after the sixth seal is opened, I still do not know the "day or hour" because I do not know exactly when the sixth seal will be opened and I do not know how long after the opening of the sixth seal that the rapture will occur. We know the name of that day as the Day of the Lord, but no one can give you an exact date for when that will occur. We only know that it will begin sometime between the Abomination of Desolation and Armageddon, but that's a very broad period of time.

Only after the 70th Week starts and we see the signs will those who have not been deceived by the devil be able to recognize and believe that the day is iminent—but they will still not know the exact time. Christians are to watch for that day and should be able to sense that the day is near so that the day will not overtake them as a thief:

> For yourselves know perfectly that the day of the Lord so cometh as a thief in the night. For when they shall say, Peace and safety; then sudden destruction cometh upon them, as travail upon a woman with child; and they shall not escape. But

ye, brethren, are not in darkness, that that day should overtake
you as a thief. (1 Thess. 5:2–4)

Thus, the Day of the Lord will only overcome the unbelieving as a thief, not the saved. Christians who know their scriptures will be able to recognize the signs and realize that it is very near. So the argument that "if the rapture does not occur before the 70th Week of Daniel, you will know the time of the rapture" is invalid.

What About Imminence?

Yet another argument put forth by pre-trib adherents is their belief in the doctrine of the imminent return of Christ. They reason that since the apostles were awaiting the return of Christ with great expectancy—and that they may even have believed that Christ could return and the rapture could occur at any time—that nothing has to occur prophetically before the rapture can take place. This includes the peace treaty or any parts of the 70th Week of Daniel.

This is a doctrine that was shown to be false by the apostle Paul himself. In 2 Thessalonians 2:1–3, Paul had to address the Thessalonians concerning a doctrinal problem they had regarding the timing of the Second Coming:

> Now we beseech you, brethren, by the coming of our Lord Jesus Christ, and by our gathering together unto him, that ye be not soon shaken in mind, or be troubled, neither by spirit, nor by word, nor by letter as from us, as that the day of Christ is at hand. Let no man deceive you by any means: for that day shall not come, except there come a falling away first, and that man of sin be revealed, the son of perdition.

The Thessalonians falsely believed that the Day of the Lord and the rapture were ready to occur (or had already occurred) and that they missed it and were in the Day of the Lord period. Paul told them that they did not miss it. He also told them about two signs that must occur beforehand, namely the great falling away and the revealing of the antichrist.[35] We have also elaborated on three other signs that need to

---

[35] Some, in their attempts to bolster the pre-trib position, have claimed that the phrase "falling away" comes from the Greek word *rapturem* and is better translated "rapture." Thus, they argue that the verse says that the rapture must precede the coming of the antichrist. In my opinion, this is nothing more than an attempt to make the Word of God say something that it does not. The word used in the Greek New

occur before the Day of the Lord or the Day of Christ: the moon being turned to blood, the sun being darkened, and the prophet Elijah returning to earth. Therefore, since God has made it clear that certain things must occur before the rapture occurs at the Day of the Lord, and since those things have not happened yet, there can be no doctrine of imminence. Christ's return will not be imminent until the signs mentioned above have first occurred.

Van Kampen elaborates on this point:

> The return of Christ has never been truly imminent and will never be imminent until the great tribulation of antichrist begins and the surrounding Gentile nations come together against Jerusalem in the valley of Jehoshaphat. Only then are the elect of God told to look for the sign of Christ's coming which will be seen in the heavens, but only after the earth is first plunged into darkness by the sign of the end of the age.[36]

So while the first-century church, as recorded in the New Testament writings, showed a great expectation and anticipation of the return of Christ, the scriptures themselves tell us that the rapture cannot occur at any time, but only after the signs are fulfilled.

Identifying the Restrainer

Yet another argument put forth by pre-trib adherents is that they say that the Holy Spirit is removed before the antichrist is revealed; and since the Holy Spirit indwells Christians, they will be removed also. They draw this conclusion from 2 Thessalonians 2:6–7: "And now ye know what withholdeth that he might be revealed in his time. For the mystery of iniquity doth already work: only he who now letteth will let, until he be taken out of the way." They have made the assumption that it is the Holy Spirit who is the restrainer and that when He is removed—and Christians with Him—the antichrist will be revealed.

This is an incorrect assumption, for the Holy Spirit is recorded as still being on the earth indwelling believers during the last days of the 70th Week. This is clearly evident in Joel 2:

Testament is *apostasia*, or "falling away," from which the English term "apostasy" is derived. "Falling away" means to backslide. Backslide from what? From the truth.[35] Thus, the phrase "falling away" means just that—a falling away from the truth; and the verse tells us that this must take place before the rapture and the Day of the Lord.

[36] Robert Van Kampen, *The Sign* (Wheaton, Il.: Crossway Books, 1992), 315.

> And it shall come to pass afterward, that I will pour out my spirit upon all flesh; and your sons and your daughters shall prophesy, your old men shall dream dreams, your young men shall see visions: And also upon the servants and upon the handmaids in those days will I pour out my spirit. And I will shew wonders in the heavens and in the earth, blood, and fire, and pillars of smoke. The sun shall be turned into darkness, and the moon into blood, before the great and the terrible day of the Lord come. (Joel 2:28–31)

To those of you that think the restrainer is the Holy Spirit, I would like for you to ponder a couple of questions. How can the Holy Spirit still be on earth during the 70th Week if the verse says the restrainer (Holy Spirit) is removed? And if He is removed, will He leave and come back? One individual told me that the Holy Spirit is not really removed, but just His restraining power; and after His restraining power is removed, that is when the rapture occurs and the Holy Spirit reverts back to His Old Testament mode. In responding to this, I would like to call your attention to Acts 2:16–21:

> But this is that which was spoken by the prophet Joel; And it shall come to pass in the last days, saith God, I will pour out of my Spirit upon all flesh: and your sons and your daughters shall prophesy, and your young men shall see visions, and your old men shall dream dreams: And on my servants and on my handmaidens I will pour out in those days of my Spirit; and they shall prophesy: And I will shew wonders in heaven above, and signs in the earth beneath; blood, and fire, and vapour of smoke: The sun shall be turned into darkness, and the moon into blood, before that great and notable day of the Lord come: And it shall come to pass, that whosoever shall call on the name of the Lord shall be saved.

After Pentecost, the apostles were indwelt with the Holy Spirit and began speaking in foreign languages. Peter likened this to what the prophet Joel said would happen during the 70th Week. Therefore, Peter establishes the fact that believers will be indwelt with the Holy Spirit during the 70th Week in the same way that they were after Pentecost. Thus, we can conclude that the Holy Spirit will be on the earth during the 70th Week and will indwell believers in the same way that the apostles were indwelt. In fact, the scripture passages above indicate that not only will the Holy Spirit be here and indwell believers, but He will manifest His power in a greater way than He is being manifested today, working signs, wonders, and miracles through believers.

So who is the restrainer that is removed before the antichrist is revealed? I suggest that the restrainer is the Archangel Michael. Consider these two passages:

> And there was war in heaven: Michael and his angels fought against the dragon; and the dragon fought and his angels, And prevailed not; neither was their place found any more in heaven. And the great dragon was cast out, that old serpent, called the devil, and satan, which deceiveth the whole world: he was cast out into the earth, and his angels were cast out with him. And I heard a loud voice saying in heaven, Now is come salvation, and strength, and the kingdom of our God, and the power of his Christ: for the accuser of our brethren is cast down, which accused them before our God day and night. And they overcame him by the blood of the Lamb, and by the word of their testimony; and they loved not their lives unto the death. Therefore rejoice, ye heavens, and ye that dwell in them. Woe to the inhabiters of the earth and of the sea! for the devil is come down unto you, having great wrath, because he knoweth that he hath but a short time. And when the dragon saw that he was cast unto the earth, he persecuted the woman which brought forth the man child. And to the woman were given two wings of a great eagle, that she might fly into the wilderness, into her place, where she is nourished for a time, and times, and half a time, from the face of the serpent. (Rev. 12:7–14)

> And at that time shall Michael stand up, the great prince which standeth for the children of thy people: and there shall be a time of trouble, such as never was since there was a nation even to that same time. (Dan. 12:1)

After the war in heaven, satan will be thrown down to earth and will indwell the antichrist and begin persecuting the saints during the great tribulation. This is when the restraining power of Michael the archangel will be removed. Marvin Rosenthal describes it like this:

> Speaking of the one who will hinder the antichrist, Paul said, "only he who now hindereth will continue to hinder until he be taken out of the way" (2 Thess. 2:7). The word hindereth means to hold down, and the phrase taken out of the way

means to step aside. Therefore, the one who had the job of hindering the antichrist will step aside; that is, he will no longer be a restraint between the antichrist and those the antichrist is persecuting.

... Further, Daniel has already said that Michael will stand up during "a time of trouble, such as never was since there was a nation even to that same time." The unprecedented time of trouble can only refer to the Great Tribulation. Since Daniel is told that this great trouble relates to his people—and his people are the Jews—this can only be "the time of Jacob's Trouble" (Jer. 30:7), which is a synonym for the Great Tribulation. It is at that time that the archangel Michael will stand up.

But what does the Hebrew word for stand up (*amad*) mean? Rashi, one of Israel's greatest scholars ... understood stand up to literally mean [to] stand still. The meaning, according to one of Israel's greatest scholars, would be to stand aside or be inactive. Michael, the guardian of Israel, had earlier fought for her (Dan. 10:13, 21), but now this one "who standeth for the children of thy people" would stand still or stand aside. He would not help; he would not restrain; he would not hold down.

The Midrash, commenting on this verse, says, "The Holy One, Blessed be He, said to Michael, 'You are silent? You do not defend my children.'"[37]

So when "the restrainer" Michael removes his restraining power, then the antichrist will be revealed and the great tribulation will begin. The great tribulation and rule of the antichrist begins after the Abomination of Desolation. Thus, 2 Thessalonians 2:6–7 does not support a pre-trib rapture, but shows that the rapture will occur after the great tribulation.

Rapture in Revelation 4?

Finally, another very weak argument put forth by pre-trib adherents is that they say that the raptured saints are clearly seen in Revelation 4 and 5: "And I beheld, and I heard the voice of many angels round about the throne and the beasts and the elders: and the number of them was ten thousand times ten thousand, and thousands of

---

[37] *Pre-Wrath Rapture of the Church*, 257–258.

thousands" (Rev. 5:11). The scene depicted in Revelation 4 and 5 occurs before the seals are opened. Therefore, they conclude, the rapture occurs before the 70th Week.

They also claim that Revelation 4:1 is the trumpet that sounds at the rapture and John who went up to heaven at the time is symbolic of the rapture: "After this I looked, and, behold, a door was opened in heaven: and the first voice which I heard was as it were of a trumpet talking with me; which said, Come up hither, and I will shew thee things which must be hereafter." Scripture does not support these assertions. First, scripture tells us that the voice only *sounds* like a trumpet, not that a trumpet is sounding. If it were a trumpet sounding, scripture would have said that. Secondly, nowhere does it mention any saints in this scene besides the 24 elders. All listed as being present in this scene are angels, beasts, and the 24 elders. That is it. One cannot assume that the 100 trillion are made up of raptured saints. God tells us who is present, and to conclude otherwise is an assumption that is not supported by the text. Therefore, scripture in no way supports the notion that raptured saints are present in Revelation 4 and 5.

The raptured saints do, however, appear in scripture in Revelation 7:

> After this I beheld, and, lo, a great multitude, which no man could number, of all nations, and kindreds, and people, and tongues, stood before the throne, and before the Lamb, clothed with white robes, and palms in their hands . . . And one of the elders answered, saying unto me, What are these which are arrayed in white robes? and whence came they? And I said unto him, Sir, thou knowest. And he said to me, *These are they which came out of great tribulation,* and have washed their robes, and made them white in the blood of the Lamb. Therefore are they before the throne of God, and serve him day and night in his temple: and he that sitteth on the throne shall dwell among them. (Rev. 7:9–15) [italics mine]

These are the raptured saints, not the elders, beasts, and angels of Revelation 4 and 5.

Where Is the Church?

Another argument used by pre-trib adherents is that they say that the word "church" is not used in any of the passages in Revelation after the first seal is opened because the church has been raptured. I admit that the word "church" is not mentioned in any of the Revelation passages after the first seal is opened. But one cannot assume that because the word "church" is not mentioned that it has been raptured. 2 Timothy, Titus, 2 Peter, 1 John, 2 John, and Jude all do not use the word "church." But clearly, all those books were written to people who were part of the church and were not raptured. Revelation contains several references to Christians being present during the 70th Week: Rev. 8:3; 13:7,10; 14:12; 17:6; 18:24. So just because the word "church" is not used in Revelation after the opening of the first seal, you cannot assume that it is because the church has been raptured.

In fact, I believe that there is a reason that the word "church" is not used; it is because the church age has ended and the 70th Week has begun. This is the same reason that gatherings of believers were not called a "church" during the 69 weeks. During the time of the ministry of the Lord Jesus Christ, a called-out assembly of believers followed Him. What did He call this group of believers? Did He call them or refer to them as a church? No, He called them "disciples" or "saints." Why did He not refer to them as a church? The answer is simple: because the historical church period had not yet begun. The called-out assembly of believers was not called a church until after Pentecost.

Jesus did use the word "church" in two instances: Matthew 16:18 and 18:17; but it was in reference to the church that was soon to be. So I contend that the reason Jesus did not refer to the called-out assembly of believers that followed Him as "church" is because they were in the 69th week—the historical church period had not begun. I also contend that the reason that believers are not referred to as "church" in Revelation is because the historical church period has ended and the 70th Week has begun.

Too Many Scriptural Contradictions

A pretribulation rapture view requires that the return of Christ is imminent. As we have shown certain signs must occur before the Day of the Lord and the rapture occurs. Some of those signs will not occur until after the sixth seal has been opened during the 70th Week of Daniel; therefore, the rapture will not occur before that time and cannot occur until the signs are fulfilled *during* the 70th Week. Thus there is no doctrine of immanency. Since the pre-trib rapture view contradicts this scriptural fact, it cannot be correct.

The pre-trib rapture belief necessitates that the wrath of God begins with the first seal. Scripture is clear that the wrath of God does not start until after the sixth seal is opened. Again the pre-trib rapture belief contradicts this fact.

An exegesis of Revelation 3:10 shows that the Christian will be rescued out of the midst of the great tribulation. The pre-trib view says that the Christian will be rescued before the 70th Week starts. Again the pre-trib view contradicts scripture.

Many of the other tenents that the pre-trib rapture view stands on such as; the antichrist will be revealed before the rapture, no one knows the day or hour, etc. do not necessitate a pre-trib view. For instance pre-trib adherents state that the rapture occurs before the antichrist is revealed. An examination of the essential scripture passages shows that the antichrist is indeed revealed before the rapture but that the rapture occurs after the Abomination of Desolation. Again, this scriptural fact does not necessitate a pre-trib rapture. Pre-trib adherents state that if the rapture does not occur before the 70th Week, then you will know the "day and hour" of Christ's return. However, Christ can return to rapture his bride after the opening of the sixth seal during the 70th Week and you will still not know the "day and hour" of His return.

Thus, in light of the discussions above, the pre-trib rapture is not necessitated by scripture, and, furthermore, contradicts some scriptures and thus cannot be correct. The next time you hear someone say, "Hopefully we will be raptured before . . . ," realize that the rapture cannot occur until after the sixth seal is opened and that the pre-trib view is therefore not correct. I pray that all of God's children would be awakened to these facts.

Chapter 5
Why Does It Matter?

Why does it matter what you believe? Why be concerned with when the rapture will occur? Furthermore why should I risk my reputation in promoting this idea about the rapture after the sixth seal? In fact because I do not believe in a pre-trib rapture, some may consider me to be denying the faith, deceived by the devil, and even some of you may consider me to be a heretic. Let me share a little of my background with you. I became a Christian, by grace through faith, about 29 years ago. And for about 23 of those years, I was taught and believed in the pre-trib rapture theory. I have sat under some very influential and famous preachers and teachers, have read many pre-trib books, and have a Master of Divinity degree from a well-known conservative fundamental Christian university that teaches the pre-trib view. I have been a Bible teacher for 20 years and I have personally preached and taught the pre-trib theory for many years. I may also lose all of my current ministry positions for not believing the pre-trib view and for writing this book. The point is that, even though I have been taught this view for many years, and even taught it myself for many years, and could suffer in loss of finances and relationships because I do not hold this view anymore, I count it but loss for the cause of Christ because I want to be pleasing to God and adhere to what the scriptures alone teach and not what a theological system dictates. And the scriptures show that the rapture will not occur until after the sixth seal is opened.

Another reason I am writing this book is that, since many Christians adhere to the pre-trib view, which is wrong, they are in grave danger of being caught off-guard to the coming sorrows of the 70th Week. I pray that this book would be used to awaken God's children to these truths so that they can be prepared for what lies ahead. It is not important what man-made theological position you hold. What *is* important is what the Word of God says. And the scriptures clearly tell us that the rapture occurs after the sixth seal is opened.

Here is a summary of the pertinent facts that lead us to that conclusion:

1. The rapture occurs at the Day of the Lord event (1 Thess. 4:15-5:2, 2 Thess. 2:1–2).

2. The moon must be turned to blood before the Day of the Lord occurs (Joel 3:30).

3. The moon is turned to blood at the sixth seal (Rev. 6:12).

These are three undisputable scriptural facts that can only lead to one conclusion—the rapture occurs at the Day of the Lord after the sixth seal is opened.

This rapture view has been termed the "pre-wrath" rapture view. It is the only view that agrees with *all* of the prophetic scriptures. In contrast, the pre-trib view contradicts some very critical prophetic scriptures, such as the moon must be turned to blood, the antichrist revealed, and the great falling away all must occur before the Day of the Lord/rapture event. It has been shown that these events all occur during the 70th Week of Daniel and not before. Thus, the pre-trib rapture view does not agree with all of scripture.

Even Walvoord, a strong pre-trib promoter, says this about the pre-trib theory: "The fact is that neither posttribulationism nor pretribulationism is an explicit teaching of the Scriptures. The Bible does not, in so many words, state either."[38] So Walvoord himself admits that the pre-trib rapture view is not an explicit teaching of scripture.

In fact, if you study the writings of the early church fathers, there is overwhelming evidence to show that the vast majority believed that Christians would not be raptured until after the persecution of the antichrist, which we know would place the rapture after the Abomination of Desolation. H. L. Nigro, in *Before God's Wrath: The Bible's Answer to the Timing of the Rapture,* has an appendix devoted to key passages from the early church writings.

Here are just four of the earliest quotes:

---

[38] Walvoord, John F. *The Rapture Question*, 1st ed. Findlay, OH, 1957, p.148.

O unreasoning men! understanding not what has been proved by all these passages, that two advents of Christ have been announced: the one, in which He is set forth as suffering, inglorious, dishonored, and crucified; but the other, in which He shall come from heaven with glory, when the man of apostasy, who speaks strange things against the Most High, shall venture to do unlawful deeds on the earth against us the Christians, who, having learned the true worship of God from the law, and the word which went forth from Jerusalem by means of the apostles of Jesus, have fled for safety to the God of Jacob and God of Israel....
—Justin Martyr, Dialogue with Trypho [150-165 AD]

Those, therefore, who continue steadfast, and are put through the fire, will be purified by means of it. For as gold casts away its dross, so also will ye cast away all sadness and straitness, and will be made pure so as to fit into the building of the tower. But the white part is the age that is to come, in which the elect of God will dwell, since those elected by God to eternal life will be spotless and pure. Wherefore cease not speaking these things into the ears of the saints. This then is the type of the great tribulation that is to come.
—The Pastor of Hermas [160 AD]

It therefore behooves us, who inquire much concerning events at hand, to search diligently into those things which are able to save us. Let us then utterly flee from all the works of iniquity, lest these should take hold of us; and let us hate the error of the present time, that we may set our love on the world to come: let us not give loose reins to our soul, that it should have power to run with sinners and the wicked, lest we become like them. The final stumbling block (or source of danger) approaches.... We take earnest heed in these last days; for the whole [past] time of your faith will profit you nothing, unless now in this wicked time we also withstand coming sources of danger, as becometh the sons of God. That the Black One may find no means of entrance, let us flee from every vanity, let us utterly hate the works of the way of wickedness. Take heed, lest resting at our ease, as those who are the called [of God], we should fall asleep in our sins, and the wicked prince, acquiring power over us, should thrust us away from the kingdom of the Lord.

—The Epistle of Barnabas
[100-120 AD]

Watch for your life's sake. Let not your lamps be quenched, nor your loins unloosed; but be ye ready, for ye know not the hour in which our Lord cometh. But often shall ye come together, seeking the things which are befitting to your souls: for the whole time of your faith will not profit you, if ye be not made perfect in the last time. For in the last days false prophets and corrupters shall be multiplied, and the sheep shall be turned into wolves, and love shall be turned into hate; for when lawlessness increaseth, they shall hate and persecute and betray one another, and then shall appear the world-deceiver as Son of God, and shall do signs and wonders, and the earth shall be delivered into his hands, and he shall do iniquitous things which have never yet come to pass since the beginning. Then shall the creation of men come into the fire of trial, and many shall be made to stumble and shall perish; but they that endure in their faith shall be saved from under the curse itself. And then shall appear the signs of the truth; first, the sign of an out-spreading in heaven; then the sign of the sound of the trumpet; and the third, the resurrection of the dead; yet not of all, but as it is said: The Lord shall come and all His saints with Him. Then shall the world see the Lord coming upon the clouds of heaven.

—The Didache (The Teaching of the Twelve Apostles)
[100-120 AD]

Thus, it is apparent that the early Church fathers expected the Church to be persecuted by the antichrist during the end-times and then rescued via the rapture from the persecution they would undergo. This is what the pre-wrath view also states—that the church will be raptured after the opening of the sixth seal out of the great tribulation, which will be instilled at the hands of the antichrist.

Many modern-day "church fathers" have also believed that the church would be subject to persecution at the hands of the antichrist. One famous one was Spurgeon:

> In a recent article published by Dennis M. Swanson entitled "The Millenial Position of Spurgeon," he concludes that

> 'despite claims to the contrary, his [Spurgeon's] position was most closely identifiable with that of historic premillennialism in teaching the church would experience the tribulation, the Millennial Kingdom would be the culmination of God's program.' Later in the text, Swanson goes on to state that the 'Key features of historic premillennialism are twofold: (1) the kingdom will be the culmination of the church age and (2) the "rapture" will follow the tribulation, with the church going through the tribulation under the protection of God....Spurgeon fits most consistently in the "historic or covenantal premillennial system.' In other words, Spurgeon too, by definition, ignore[d] the doctrine of imminency of Jesus' return, seeing the church facing the persecution of antichrist before the return of Christ. In doing this he also 'rejects the pretribulation rapture of the church.[39]

So if the early church fathers—and even more modern-day "fathers"—did not believe in a pre-trib rapture, when did the pre-trib belief arise? There are three candidates to whom are credited with the origin of the pre-trib rapture theory: John Darby (one of the founders of the Plymouth Brethren movement), Edward Irving (thrown out of the Presbyterian Church and started the Apostolic Catholic Church), and finally Margaret MacDonald (a 15-year-old Catholic girl who was supposedly miraculously healed and given a vision of the "secret" rapture so popular with today's pretribulation rapture teachers.)

In summarizing the development of the pretrib doctrine, H. L. Nigro says this:

> The development of the pretribulation rapture is generally attributed to John Darby of the Plymouth Brethren, who formalized the theory around 1830. Prior to this time, the return of Christ was seen as a singular event. Jesus would return to earth once, to rapture His Church, to redeem lost Israel, and to judge the wicked and rebellious world, and this was seen either as a midtribulational or posttribulational event. Darby was the first to formally theorize that Jesus would return in two stages: first in spiritual form to rapture the Church, then in bodily form seven years later to judge the world. This allowed Jesus to return triumphantly at

---
[39] Van Kampen, Robert. *The Rapture Question Answered Plain & Simple.* P. 201–2

Armageddon while keeping the Church out of the 70th Week..[40]

So it is Darby to whom most attribute the pre-trib position. Another founder of the Plymouth Brethren had this to say about the teachings of Darby as elaborated on by Van Kampen:

> It should be noted, however, that Dr. Samuel P. Tregelles, the renowned conservative Greek scholar of the nineteenth century (the author of six separate works on translation), considered one of the founding fathers of the Plymouth Brethren Church, strongly disagreed with John Nelson Darby on the position when it first appeared in England. Dr. Tregelles believed in a face-value hermeneutic, and he knew the original languages like few others of his time. In his book *The Hope of Christ's Second Coming* (pp. 74-82), first published in 1864, he denounced the pre-tribulation Rapture position as being sentimental and emotional and without a thread of biblical support. He stated boldly that the pre-tribulation "doctrine of the coming of Christ [is] not taught in the Word of God....This whole system stands in distinct contradiction of what the Scripture reveals" (p. 32).[41]

At the best the pre-trib rapture theory had a dubious beginning and most likely gained in popularity because it was "easy believism" and a lot more pleasant to think about than enduring the sorrows and persecutions of the first five seals.

Even though the pre-trib position is a relatively new teaching and the early church fathers clearly expected the Church to enter the 70th Week and endure the persecution of the antichrist, and even though the pre-trib position is not an explicit teaching of scripture as admitted by Walvoord, and even though the pre-trib position contradicts some of scripture, some will still want to hold onto it. If that is the case with you, I ask you to go back over the scriptures and logic that have been presented. Here are the essential facts we need to keep in mind; Thessalonians equates the rapture with the Day of the Lord event. Joel and Acts says that the moon must be turned to blood before the Day of the Lord. In Revelation 6 we see the moon turned to blood after the

---

[40] H. L. Nigro, *Before God's Wrath: The Bible's Answer to the Timing of the Rapture.* p. 122.
[41] Van Kampen, Robert. *The Rapture Question Answered Plain & Simple.* P. 193,4

sixth seal is opened. These are scriptural facts. If you do not deny any of them, then sound logic dictates that the rapture must occur after the sixth seal is opened. Any other conclusion would be a denial of sound logic and create a contradiction to truth. I encourage you to adhere to what scripture and scripture alone says. We must be faithful and loyal to the Word of God above our *alma mater* or church. Adhere to what scripture teaches and scripture alone! To make it easier for you to understand these concepts I have summarized, compared, and analyzed the teachings of the various rapture theories and put them into a chart entitled "A Comparison of the Rapture Theories," which can be found at the end of this book.

Your Rapture Theology Matters

I am writing this book, not only because I want the truth to be known, but also because it is very dangerous to not have a correct view about the timing of the rapture. Since the rapture does not occur until the sixth seal, then a Christian must prepare for the first five seals. Without proper preparation, one could find themselves and their family in pretty desperate situations. As Jesus said "Lest coming suddenly he find you sleeping. And what I say unto you I say unto all, Watch." (Mark 13:36-37) How to properly prepare for the first five seals will be the subject of a later chapter. Furthermore, since the rapture will not occur until the sixth seal and the antichrist is revealed and comes to power before the rapture, then all alive at the time will most likely have to decide whether or not to take the mark. And if a person is deceived as a result of not knowing the truth about the prophetic time in which they are living, they will be more easily deceived during the 70th Week.

> And he causeth all, both small and great, rich and poor, free and bond, to receive a mark in their right hand, or in their foreheads. And that no man might buy or sell, save he that had the mark, or the name of the beast, or the number of his name. (Rev. 13:16–17)

Could You Be Deceived into Taking the Mark?

The decision of whether or not to take the mark of the beast will most likely come about after the Abomination of Desolation and shortly after the antichrist takes control of the world. This "mark" will most likely be a small computer chip implanted in the hand or forehead or an invisible tattoo made with RFID ink.[42] Such technology already exists and is being tested in humans now and is available for use now. The World Net Daily has pictures of chips, and even the process of implanting them, and explains how these implantable chips will be used for a cashless society.[43] Mexico has just recently announced that they are going to start implanting chips in children, and the military. Prince Charles is "chipped." The Department of Defense has just announced that all products sold to them must be "chipped." It is reported that half of all products sold in the U.S will be "chipped" by the end of 2004. Coke even had a promotion running in the summer of 2004 where they "chipped" some cans of soda and then would find them by satellite and the lucky winners would win a prize. The motto of this promotion was "You can win, but you can't hide."

The mechanics and technology of chipping or "taking the mark" are already in place. They even have chip mobiles ready to come to your neighborhood!

Having to decide whether or not to take the mark is not a good situation to be in if you do not recognize that you are actually in the 70th Week of Daniel or are not properly prepared for it. You will not be able to buy or sell without the mark, and if you do not realize that you are in the 70th Week because you falsely believe in a pre-trib rapture view, one could easily go along with what the government tells them and be deceived into following the antichrist and taking the mark and ending up in Hell. Of course no true Christian would take the mark.

> And the third angel followed them, saying with a loud voice, If any man worship the beast and his image, and receive his mark in his forehead, or in his hand. The same shall drink of the wine of the wrath of God, which is poured out without mixture into the cup of his indignation; and he shall be tormented with fire and brimstone in the presence of the holy angels, and in the presence of the Lamb. And the smoke of their torment ascendeth up for ever and ever: and they have no rest day nor night, who worship the beast and his image, and whosoever receiveth the mark of his name. (Rev. 14:9-11)

---

[42] http://www.informationweek.com/news/showArticle.jhtml;?articleID=196802844
[43] http://www.worldnetdaily.com/news/article.asp?ARTICLE_ID=35766

More Dangers of False Teaching

Another reason any false prophetic teaching, including pre-trib, is harmful is that, when the teaching proves to be erroneous, those under that teaching may lose their respect for the things of the Lord and fall away from Him. We know that before the rapture there will be a great falling away, as was discussed earlier. No doubt, the false teaching about the pre-trib rapture probably will, along with other things, be part of why people will fall away from the faith.

Do not be deceived the rapture will not occur before the final 7 years, the 70th Week, but will occur after the sixth seal is opened between the Abomination of Desolation and the end of the 70th Week. The rapture will be a time of great deliverance from the persecution of the antichrist and his followers. The Lord will descend to the clouds and will blow the trump of God and the dead in Christ will rise first and then those who are still alive at his coming will be caught up to the clouds with Him.

> For the Lord himself shall descend from heaven with a shout, with the voice of the archangel, and with the trump of God: and the dead in Christ shall rise first: Then we which are alive and remain shall be caught up together with them in the clouds, to meet the Lord in the air: and so shall we ever be with the Lord. Wherefore comfort one another with these words. (1 Thess. 4:16-18)

Oh what a glorious occasion that will be for all the saints who have been awaiting His return! "Looking for that blessed hope, and the glorious appearing of the great God and our Saviour Jesus Christ" (Titus 2:13). The entire world will see him. "Behold, he cometh with clouds; and every eye shall see him, and they also which pierced him: and all kindreds of the earth shall wail because of him. Even so, Amen" (Rev. 1:7). After the world is darkened at the sixth seal, the entire world will be able to see the Lord Jesus Christ shining brighter than the sun as He comes to rescue His children.

In heart-wrenching contrast, those not raptured will at least temporarily recognize their plight and flee from His presence for they will know that the wrath of God is about to be poured out upon the world:

And the kings of the earth, and the great men, and the rich men, and the chief captains, and the mighty men, and every bondman, and every free man, hid themselves in the dens and in the rocks of the mountains. And said to the mountains and rocks, Fall on us, and hide us from the face of him that sitteth on the throne, and from the wrath of the Lamb. For the great day of his wrath is come; and who shall be able to stand? (Rev. 6:15-17)

That is when they will have their epiphany concerning Christ. But it will be too late then. The view you hold concerning the rapture matters. An epiphany will come to all. The sooner you have yours the better.

CHAPTER 6
The Great Day of His Wrath is Come

The Day of the Lord has begun! Christians, having been rescued from the wrath to come via the rapture, are with God in heaven. The peoples of the world, after realizing their error in following the antichrist, will be in a fear stricken panic. They have seen Christ in the clouds, and they have had an epiphany and are scared to death. The big question is what will happen next?

After the rapture occurs, many other catastrophic events—all part of the Day of the Lord—will occur during this time. These events are succinctly listed in Revelation and will encompass the seventh seal and the trumpet and vial (or bowl) judgments. We will examine these events individually, so we can get a feel for what this time will be like.

The first judgment of the Day of the Lord is the seventh seal:

> And when he had opened the seventh seal, there was silence in heaven about the space of half an hour. And I saw the seven angels which stood before God; and to them were given seven trumpets. And another angel came and stood at the altar, having a golden censer; and there was given unto him much incense, that he should offer it with the prayers of all saints upon the golden altar which was before the throne. And the smoke of the incense, which came with the prayers of the saints, ascended up before God out of the angel's hand. And the angel took the censer, and filled it with fire of the altar, and cast it into the earth: and there were voices, and thunderings, and lightnings, and an earthquake. And the seven angels which had the seven trumpets prepared themselves to sound. (Rev. 8:1-6)

When the seventh seal is opened, the first thing that we notice is that there is a time of silence in heaven. This silence indicates to me that something very important and sobering is about to occur. It is plausible to theorize that there may also be a great silence in the hearts and minds of the people left on earth after the rapture, after having just seen Christ in the clouds and witnessing the disappearance of millions of people. I am sure that they will be pondering the events that just took place and the events that are about to unfold. The next thing we see is that fire is cast to the earth. This may indicate a meteor shower or horrific lightning storms. There is another earthquake and the seven trumpet judgments are permitted to begin.

Scripture tells us that this pouring out of wrath is the result of the prayers of the saints in connection with the persecution they have suffered at the hands of the antichrist and his followers (Rev. 6:10-11). God's vengeance is a just recompense for the wickedness that the world has committed. So the seventh seal consists of "fire" cast to the earth, a great earthquake, and seven more judgments known as the trumpet judgments.

The First Trumpet

The first trumpet judgment is found in Rev. 8:7:

> The first angel sounded, and there followed hail and fire mingled with blood, and they were cast upon the earth: and the third part of trees was burnt up, and all green grass was burnt up.

Several interpretations have been offered as to what this judgment entails, including a meteor shower, fire and brimstone literally falling from heaven, and severe thunderstorms with huge hail and catastrophic lightning. Although we cannot be sure, I feel that the language of the text lends itself to the latter interpretation. That is, the judgment consists of horrific thunderstorms with devastating hail and fire. One of the main reasons leading me to this conclusion is that the language in the passage is very similar to the language in Ex 9:22–23:

> And the Lord said unto Moses, Stretch forth thine hand toward heaven, that there may be hail in all the land of Egypt, upon man, and upon beast, and upon every herb of the field, throughout the land of Egypt. And Moses stretched forth his rod toward heaven: and the Lord sent thunder and hail, and the fire ran along upon the ground; and the Lord rained hail upon the land of Egypt.

We see here a local judgment on the land of Egypt consisting of horrific thunderstorms with devastating hail and fire. It is interesting to note that the hail caused fire to run upon the ground. This may be what is known as ball lightning, which has been observed frequently in modern times. This phenomena is caused by the air being supercharged with static electricity. I remember as a boy at scout camp a thunderstorm came across the bay toward where we were standing. As it approached, ball lightning eerily sizzled as it moved erratically about fifteen feet above our heads. It could have just as easily occurred on the ground. Another possible cause is electrically charged hail lying on the ground. While I feel the most likely scenario is horrific thunderstorms with hail, whatever this judgment is, it will result in one-third of all the trees on the earth being burnt up and all the grass being burnt up.

The Second Trumpet

The second trumpet judgment is described as a great mountain burning with fire cast into the sea. This is found in Rev. 8:8–9:

> And the second angel sounded, and as it were a great mountain burning with fire was cast into the sea: and the third part of the sea became blood; And the third part of the creatures which were in the sea, and had life, died; and the third part of the ships were destroyed.

This judgment is most likely a meteorite crashing into the ocean. A meteorite is a rock composed of various substances that falls to earth from outer space. As a meteor, which could vary in size from a piece of sand to what is described here as a great mountain, hits the earth's atmosphere, its outer layer catches on fire. Hence, the phrase "a great mountain burning with fire." Small meteors burn up before they reach the earth, but the larger ones make it to earth. When a huge meteorite slams into the ocean, due to the temperature difference between the ocean and the meteorite's burning outer layer and frozen core, the meteor will explode. If this is, in fact, what will occur during this judgment, the resulting explosion would dwarf any nuclear bomb explosion by many times. Scientists have calculated that a meteor of 1,700 meters in diameter would unleash an explosion equivalent to 100,000 to 1,000,000 megatons of TNT.[44] The heaviest and biggest meteors usually have iron in them, so the blood color referred to in the passage would probably be caused by the tiny bits of iron ore, which

---

[44] Morrison, Chapman, and Slovic. *The Impact Hazard.*

due to the huge explosion, would be scattered over large distances and will rust in sea water, turning it red or blood in color. Thus, the affected area would become poisonous and kill any sea life in that area, just as scripture describes. The explosion will also unleash huge tidal waves, and as a result, one-third of all ships in the world will be destroyed and most likely coastal communities would be impacted.

The Third Trumpet
The third trumpet judgment is another celestial event, described in Rev. 8:10-11:

> And the third angel sounded, and there fell a great star from heaven, burning as it were a lamp, and it fell upon the third part of the rivers, and upon the fountains of waters. And the name of the star is called Wormwood: and the third part of the waters became wormwood; and many men died of the waters, because they were made bitter.

The "great star from heaven, burning as it were a lamp" most likely describes a comet, which will explode near the surface of the earth or actually hit the earth. It is hotly debated as to what comets are made of. Some think they are made of frozen inert gases, such as ammonia. Others think they may be composed of plasma. Whatever they are composed of, when they explode over an area, they produce a devastating effect. It is thought that a comet of lesser degree than mentioned in this judgment did explode over Siberia in 1908. As pictures attest, the devastation was widespread. The result looked like a nuclear explosion, and there was evidence of the area becoming uninhabitable.

When the comet of the third trumpet enters the earth's atmosphere, it will burn brightly as a lamp. Thus, it will give off much light. The comet will probably be so bright that it will have the ability to make night look like day. The name of the comet is "Wormwood." Wormwood is a plant that grows in Europe and is used to make absinthe, an hallucinogenic liquor. Taking too much of it could bring death. Thus, the name Wormwood implies that the comet will be made up of poisonous substances. Upon exploding this comet will spew whatever poisonous material it contains over a large area, and as the scriptures say one-third of fresh water will become poisonous and, many men will die.

The Fourth Trumpet

The fourth trumpet judgment also involves the amount of one-third. This judgment removes one-third of all light. Look at what Rev. 8:12 says:

> And the fourth angel sounded, and the third part of the sun was smitten, and the third part of the moon, and the third part of the stars; so as the third part of them was darkened, and the day shone not for a third part of it, and the night likewise.

As a result of this judgment, the light of the sun, moon, and stars is diminished by one-third. This phenomenon could be caused by all the debri in the atmosphere from the explosions of the second and third trumpet judgments or it could be caused by some other astral phenomena. Whatever the cause, the earth will only receive one-third of the light that it would normally get. This would probably result in many plants dying and a great "ice age" descending upon the earth.

Let's Review

With the occurrence of the rapture, the Day of the Lord begins. After this event then the wrath of God will begin to be poured out upon the earth. It will start with fire being cast to the earth and a great earthquake at the seventh seal. Then a series of four horrific trumpet judgments are unleashed. These most likely consist of severe thunderstorms with killing hail and lightning, which destroys one-third of all the trees; a meteor exploding in the ocean which destroys one-third of all sea life and ships; an exploding comet which poisons one-third of freshwater, killing many; and a diminishing of one-third of the world's sunlight.

This, however, is nothing in comparison to the next three trumpet judgments, which are so severe that a special announcement is given before they occur.

> And I beheld, and heard an angel flying through the midst of heaven, saying with a loud voice, Woe, woe, woe, to the inhabiters of the earth by reason of the other voices of the trumpet of the three angels, which are yet to sound! (Rev. 8:13)

The triple woe is an indication that the last three trumpet judgments are going to be much more devastating and severe than the first four. Let's take a look.

The Fifth Trumpet
The fifth trumpet judgment is found in Rev. 9:1-12:

> And the fifth angel sounded, and I saw a star fall from heaven unto the earth: and to him was given the key of the bottomless pit. And he opened the bottomless pit; and there arose a smoke out of the pit, as the smoke of a great furnace; and the sun and the air were darkened by reason of the smoke of the pit. And there came out of the smoke locusts upon the earth: and unto them was given power, as the scorpions of the earth have power. And it was commanded them that they should not hurt the grass of the earth, neither any green thing, neither any tree; but only those men which have not the seal of God in their foreheads. And to them it was given that they should not kill them, but that they should be tormented five months: and their torment was as the torment of a scorpion, when he striketh a man. And in those days shall men seek death, and shall not find it; and shall desire to die, and death shall flee from them....And they had tails like unto scorpions, and there were stings in their tails: and their power was to hurt men five months. And they had a king over them, which is the angel of the bottomless pit, whose name in the Hebrew tongue is Abaddon, but in the Greek tongue hath his name Apollyon. One woe is past; and, behold, there come two woes more hereafter.

In the first verse, we see a star falling from heaven. This is an angel. We know this because the second part of the verse says that "he" is given a key to open up hell. Later in the passage we are told who this angel is: "And they had a king over them, which is the angel of the bottomless pit, whose name in the Hebrew tongue is Abaddon, but in the Greek tongue hath his name Apollyon." Abaddon and Apollyon are names for satan. So what happens here is that satan is thrown down to the earth and he opens the bottomless pit or hell, and the sun and air are darkened from the huge volume of smoke coming out of this pit. Literally, I believe this pit is a huge hole in the earth where lava and smoke spew out. This scenario is similar to what scientists describe as a super volcano. Scientists tell us that the largest super volcano in the world is located at Yellowstone. They say that if it erupts, it would open up a 20-mile x 40-mile hole in the earth. Recently, Yellowstone has been showing signs of increased activity, alarming some that a massive eruption may be looming.

The darkening of the sun and air by smoke is nothing in comparison to the most horrific thing coming out of the pit: demon locust creatures. These horrible-looking demon creatures will have power to afflict men for five months with so much pain that people wish that they could die, and even want to kill themselves, but the scripture says that death will flee from them.[45]

The Sixth Trumpet

The next woe, or horrific judgment, is the sixth trumpet found in Rev. 9:13-19:

> And the sixth angel sounded, and I heard a voice from the four horns of the golden altar which is before God, Saying to the sixth angel which had the trumpet, Loose the four angels which are bound in the great river Euphrates. And the four angels were loosed, which were prepared for an hour, and a day, and a month, and a year, for to slay the third part of men. And the number of the army of the horsemen were two hundred thousand thousand: and I heard the number of them. And thus I saw the horses in the vision, and them that sat on them, having breastplates of fire, and of jacinth, and brimstone: and the heads of the horses were as the heads of lions; and out of their mouths issued fire and smoke and brimstone. By these three was the third part of men killed, by the fire, and by the smoke, and by the brimstone, which issued out of their mouths. For their power is in their mouth, and in their tails: for their tails were like unto serpents, and had heads, and with them they do hurt."

---

[45] This is the first judgment that is listed in which those with the seal of God in their forehead will not be afflicted. This does not mean that no one will be spared from the other trumpet judgments, but this is the first one that specifically states an exemption. It is likely that the 144,000, who are sealed right after the sixth seal and the rapture (Rev. 7:4) will be spared from the trumpet judgments in their entirety. These are God's protected witnesses who are to proclaim the eternal gospel and the truth about the antichrist to all who will listen during the latter part of the 70th Week of Daniel..

This judgment is another attack by a demon force. This time, it is not demon locust creatures, but a demon army mounted on demonic horse creatures with lion's heads that spew out fire, smoke, and brimstone, and who have tails that are like serpents. This frightening demon army will kill one-third of all mankind left on the earth at that time. Some think that the phrase "which were prepared for an hour, and a day, and a month, and a year," indicates that this judgment will last for 13 months a day and an hour. I see that as a possibility, or the phrase could just be indicating that the judgment would start at a certain hour, month, day, and year.

After all of these occurrences and judgments the earth's population has been drastically reduced. The first five seals have eliminated at least one-third of the world's population. The sixth seal has reduced the world's population via the rapture by an untold amount. The first five trumpet judgments have also killed much of the world's population. These judgments consisting of the severe thunderstorms, the meteor, the comet, and the removal of one-third of sunlight have killed an unspecified amount of people. The water being made bitter from the comet explosion will its self kill many people, for it says; "and many men died of the waters, because they were made bitter." The fifth trumpet, the demon locusts, has not killed anyone, just tormented them. And now at the sixth trumpet the demon army kills one-third of all the people that are left on the earth at that time.

So let's say if we start with six billion people at the beginning of the 70th Week of Daniel, and subtract one-third for the first four seals, that leaves us with 4.5 billion. Then let's speculate and say we lose another billion from the first five trumpet judgments, which I feel is a conservative estimate, we are down to 3.5 billion. And then lose another one-third with the sixth trumpet that leaves the world's population at about 2.33 billion. And I believe this to be a conservative estimate.

The Seventh Trumpet

The final trumpet judgment is the most severe of all, and just like the seventh seal judgment, it is composed of seven more judgments known as the vial or bowl judgments. This last trumpet will come near the end of the 70th Week. We know this by several verses found in Revelation:

And sware by him that liveth for ever and ever, who created heaven, and the things that therein are, and the earth, and the things that therein are, and the sea, and the things which are therein, that there should be time no longer: But in the days of the voice of the seventh angel, when he shall begin to sound, the mystery of God should be finished, as he hath declared to his servants the prophets. (Rev. 10:6-7)

We notice here that it says there will "be time no longer," and it also says that, when the angel sounds the seventh trumpet, "the mystery of God should be finished." Thus, this last trumpet judgment comes near the end and will consist of seven bowl or vial judgments. The last bowl judgment, the battle of Armageddon, will be the end of the reign of the antichrist. Another verse that confirms this is Rev. 11:15: "And the seventh angel sounded; and there were great voices in heaven, saying, The kingdoms of this world are become the kingdoms of our Lord, and of his Christ; and he shall reign for ever and ever." So the final result of the seventh trumpet is the seven bowl judgments, which will culminate in the Lord defeating the gathered armies, the antichrist, the false prophet, and satan at the battle of Armageddon.

Some feel that the 70th Week will end at the seventh trumpet and Christ will descend to earth and begin reigning from Jerusalem at the sound of this trumpet. They believe this because of the language in Rev. 10:7 and 11:15, which respectively say "the mystery of God should be finished" and "the kingdoms of this world are become the kingdoms of our Lord." In both of these verses, the prophetic aorist form of the verb is used. Use of the prophetic aorist indicates that the event is so certain and imminent that it can be considered as already taking place, but that it has actually not yet occurred. So these verses do not indicate that at the sound of the seventh trumpet that Christ has begun to reign, only that it is so certain that it can be considered to have occurred. As a matter of fact, Dan. 7:11-14 indicates that Jesus will not begin His reign until after satan, the antichrist, and false prophet are thrown into hell, which we know happens after the battle of Armageddon (Dan. 7:11-14, Rev. 19:11-21)

The Bowl Judgments

These bowl judgments, which occur within the 70th Week of Daniel, will be very severe and extremely catastrophic. The first bowl judgment is a grievous sore or boil upon all who have the mark of the beast, as it says in Rev. 16:2: "And the first went, and poured out his vial upon the earth; and there fell a noisome and grievous sore upon the men which had the mark of the beast, and upon them which worshipped his image." The word "noisome" most likely refers to the cries of pain that will be uttered by those afflicted with the boils.

The second vial turns the sea into the blood of a dead man and all living things die in the sea. "And the second angel poured out his vial upon the sea; and it became as the blood of a dead man: and every living soul died in the sea (Rev. 16:3)." In the second trumpet judgment, we theorized that the sea will be turned to "blood" in color as a result of the discoloration of the sea from the exploding meteor. In this judgment, the verse suggests that the sea will *actually* be turned to blood, reminiscent of when Moses changed the Nile to blood before Pharaoh.[46] But not fresh blood but putrid decomposing blood as of a "dead man." As a result, all living things in the sea will die. I can imagine that the stench from the decayed blood and all of the dead sea creatures will encompass the globe and at the least would be nauseating.

The third vial turns all freshwater to blood: "And the third angel poured out his vial upon the rivers and fountains of waters; and they became blood" (Rev. 16:4). Again, for reasons mentioned above, this refers to all freshwater actually being turned into blood.

The fourth vial causes extreme heat to come over the earth. This could be caused by the sun becoming hotter or because the earth is now closer to the sun, due to possibly having a changed orbit. "And the fourth angel poured out his vial upon the sun; and power was given unto him to scorch men with fire. And men were scorched with great heat, and blasphemed the name of God, which hath power over these plagues: and they repented not to give him glory" (Rev. 16:8,9).

The fifth vial causes total darkness over the whole earth: "And the fifth angel poured out his vial upon the seat of the beast; and his

---

[46] For readers wondering why I see the second trumpet judgment as being a figure of speech while the second bowl as being literal is because, in the second trumpet, the exploding meteor will be pulverized and will spew its debris over a huge area, thus changing the sea to a blood color. This will be the natural result of that event, as an exploding meteor will naturally discolor the sea and will kill the sea creatures in that area. Whereas in the second bowl judgment, there is no natural causal agent. The text simply says that the sea will turn to blood. Thus, literal blood is the most natural way to read the text.

kingdom was full of darkness; and they gnawed their tongues for pain" (Rev. 16:10).

The sixth vial makes possible the seventh and final vial judgment by drying up the Euphrates River and allowing all the kings to gather for the battle of Armageddon after being deceived by the antichrist and the false prophet into fighting against Jesus, who will be returning to earth:

> And the sixth angel poured out his vial upon the great river Euphrates; and the water thereof was dried up, that the way of the kings of the east might be prepared. And I saw three unclean spirits like frogs come out of the mouth of the dragon, and out of the mouth of the beast, and out of the mouth of the false prophet. For they are the spirits of devils, working miracles, which go forth unto the kings of the earth and of the whole world, to gather them to the battle of that great day of God Almighty. (Rev. 16:12-14)

Still Deceived?

After witnessing Christ in the clouds and many disappearing in the rapture, and after experiencing all of these judgments, how can the world still be deceived? How will the antichrist be able to trick people into ignoring what the scriptures say and get them to gather to fight against God in the great battle of Armageddon? Here is a possible scenario: We know the antichrist—who I believe will claim to be the alien who started life on earth—will be able to perform miraculous signs and will probably trick people into believing that hostile aliens (namely, Jesus and the saints) have been responsible for all the recent disasters and are coming to take over the world. They will then rally the people of the world to fight against them to save the planet. This same scenario was portrayed in the popular movie "Independence Day," which depicted aliens trying to take over the earth and the people of the earth collaborating to defeat them.

R. A. Coombes comments beautifully in this regards:

> The UFO phenomenon seems to be, from all indications, nothing less and nothing more than, activity promulgated by the satanic/rebel forces that are preparing to embroil humanity in a war against the Creator-God of the Universe. And how will these satanic forces do this? By deceiving people into believing that they are good aliens and that Jesus

and the saints—who will be returning to earth from "outer space"—are bad aliens whom the world should fight against.[47]

Whatever deceptions they use, unfortunately the world will ignore the scriptures and believe the deceiving spirits and gather for the great battle of Armageddon. Thus, we come to the final judgment.

> And the seventh angel poured out his vial into the air; and there came a great voice out of the temple of heaven, from the throne, saying, It is done. And there were voices, and thunders, and lightnings; and there was a great earthquake, such as was not since men were upon the earth, so mighty an earthquake, and so great. And the great city was divided into three parts, and the cities of the nations fell: and great Babylon came in remembrance before God, to give unto her the cup of the wine of the fierceness of his wrath. And every island fled away, and the mountains were not found. And there fell upon men a great hail out of heaven, every stone about the weight of a talent: and men blasphemed God because of the plague of the hail; for the plague thereof was exceeding great. (Rev. 16:17-21)

This last and final judgment starts with the greatest earthquake that the world has ever experienced. This earthquake is so great that every mountain and island are now gone! If all the mountains and islands are gone, surely there will be no buildings left, either. As a result, Jerusalem, the great city, is divided into three parts. At the time of this earthquake the end-times Babylon will receive its final judgment and sink into the ocean. This is also the day that the famed battle of Armageddon will take place. This is the day that the armies will gather in the valley of Armageddon to destroy Israel that has been hidden in "Bozrah."[48] Then the Lord will descend with all the saints and totally destroy the armies that are gathered against Him.

---

[47] Coombes, R.A. *America, The Babylon*, p. 101
[48] Where is Israel during this time? For the last 3.5 years of the 70th Week, Israel will be living in the wilderness after having fled at the Abomination of Desolation. "And the woman fled into the wilderness, where she hath a place prepared of God, that they should feed her there a thousand two hundred and threescore days." (Rev 12:6) Scripture indicates that they will have fled to Edom to a place called Bozrah (Micah 2:12–13). Edom is modern day Jordan. The word "Bozrah" means "sheep pen." A sheep pen was an enclosure, usually constructed of rocks that only had one way in and out. The shepherd would sleep at the entrance, and acted as the door and

Isaiah 63:1-4 tells of this event:

> Who is this that cometh from Edom, with dyed garments from Bozrah? this that is glorious in his apparel, traveling in the greatness of his strength? I that speak in righteousness, mighty to save. Wherefore art thou red in thine apparel, and thy garments like him that treadeth in the winefat? I have trodden the winepress alone; and of the people there was none with me: for I will tread them in mine anger, and trample them in my fury; and their blood shall be sprinkled upon my garments, and I will stain all my raiment. For the day of vengeance is in mine heart, and the year of my redeemed is come.

Notice in the beginning of the passage that the Lord's garments are stained red from blood. This is as a result of the treading of the winepress of God, the destruction of the armies at Armageddon. This is also recorded in Rev. 19:13: "And he was clothed with a vesture dipped in blood: and his name is called The Word of God." Revelation 16 tells us that the Lord will defeat these armies with severe thunder and lightning storms that will be unleashed upon the valley of Megiddo with 100-pound hailstones, resulting in the armies of the world being crushed in the "winepress of God." The valley is literally filled up to the horses' bridles with blood.

Yet another account shows that Jesus, the righteous judge, is the one who delivers the judgment by the sword of His mouth as He returns to earth to rule and reign and set up His Millennial Kingdom:

> And out of his mouth goeth a sharp sword, that with it he should smite the nations: and he shall rule them with a rod of iron: and he treadeth the winepress of the fierceness and wrath of Almighty God. (Rev 19:15)

---

would protect the sheep. This is what Jesus alluded to in John 10:7: "Then said Jesus unto them again, Verily, verily, I say unto you, I am the door of the sheep." Thus, Israel will have fled to a "sheep pen" to be protected and God will protect and sustain Israel during the Day of the Lord. Some think that this sheep pen could be a place in Jordan called Petra. It is a natural rock enclosure with only one way in and out. Petra—a city carved out of rock—has enough room for 250,000 people. It even has a 5000-seat amphitheatre. This is the most likely place that Israel will be protected and sustained for the 3.5-year attack of the antichrist.

> And the remnant were slain with the sword of him that sat upon the horse, which sword proceeded out of his mouth: and all the fowls were filled with their flesh. (Rev 19:21)

Here is some additional detail on this battle and the destruction that will ensue:

> Come near, ye nations, to hear; and hearken, ye people: let the earth hear, and all that is therein; the world, and all things that come forth of it. For the indignation of the Lord is upon all nations, and his fury upon all their armies: he hath utterly destroyed them, he hath delivered them to the slaughter. Their slain also shall be cast out, and their stink shall come up out of their carcases, and the mountains shall be melted with their blood. And all the host of heaven shall be dissolved, and the heavens shall be rolled together as a scroll: and all their host shall fall down, as the leaf falleth off from the vine, and as a falling fig from the fig tree. For my sword shall be bathed in heaven: behold, it shall come down upon Idumea, and upon the people of my curse, to judgment. The sword of the Lord is filled with blood, it is made fat with fatness, and with the blood of lambs and goats, with the fat of the kidneys of rams: for the Lord hath a sacrifice in Bozrah, and a great slaughter in the land of Idumea. And the unicorns shall come down with them, and the bullocks with the bulls; and their land shall be soaked with blood, and their dust made fat with fatness. For it is the day of the Lord's vengeance, and the year of recompences for the controversy of Zion. And the streams thereof shall be turned into pitch, and the dust thereof into brimstone, and the land thereof shall become burning pitch. It shall not be quenched night nor day; the smoke thereof shall go up for ever: from generation to generation it shall lie waste; none shall pass through it for ever and ever. (Isa. 34:5-10)

So Israel who has been protected in the wilderness at Bozrah, when they see the armies gathered against them, will call out to the Lord Jesus Christ for deliverance and the Lord will respond and do battle for them. The battle of Armageddon will totally destroy the armies that are gathered against Israel.

At their defeat the antichrist, and the false prophet will be hurled into the lake of fire; satan will be thrown into the bottomless pit:

> And I saw heaven opened, and behold a white horse; and he that sat upon him was called Faithful and True, and in righteousness he doth judge and make war. His eyes were as a flame of fire, and on his head were many crowns; and he had a name written, that no man knew, but he himself. And he was clothed with a vesture dipped in blood: and his name is called The Word of God. And the armies which were in heaven followed him upon white horses, clothed in fine linen, white and clean. And out of his mouth goeth a sharp sword, that with it he should smite the nations: and he shall rule them with a rod of iron: and he treadeth the winepress of the fierceness and wrath of Almighty God. And he hath on his vesture and on his thigh a name written, KING OF KINGS, AND LORD OF LORDS…And I saw the beast, and the kings of the earth, and their armies, gathered together to make war against him that sat on the horse, and against his army. And the beast was taken, and with him the false prophet that wrought miracles before him, with which he deceived them that had received the mark of the beast, and them that worshipped his image. These both were cast alive into a lake of fire burning with brimstone. And the remnant were slain with the sword of him that sat upon the horse, which sword proceeded out of his mouth: and all the fowls were filled with their flesh. (Rev. 19:11-21)
>
> And I saw an angel come down from heaven, having the key of the bottomless pit and a great chain in his hand. And he laid hold on the dragon, that old serpent, which is the devil, and satan, and bound him a thousand years, And cast him into the bottomless pit, and shut him up, and set a seal upon him, that he should deceive the nations no more, till the thousand years should be fulfilled: and after that he must be loosed a little season. (Rev 20:1-4)

Thus, the Day of the Lord, which started with the coming of Christ to the clouds to receive His own at the rapture, is a time in which God pours out His wrath upon the earth. This wrath is contained in the seventh seal and the seven trumpet and seven bowl judgments and culminates with the return of Christ to the earth at the battle of Armageddon. Fortunately the story does not end here, after the great battle the blessings of the Day of the Lord period will begin to be poured out during the Millennium and beyond. We will discuss these events in the next chapter.

CHAPTER 7
The Millennium and Beyond

Have you ever tried to imagine what it would have been like to have been one of the disciples, and to have been able to spend time with, talk to, and interact with Jesus? I have and I think it must have been fantastic! Some day that will be a reality for all God's children, we will be able to dwell with the Lord. That is the greatest aspect of the greatly anticipated Millennium kingdom—God dwelling with man. Right after the battle of Armageddon, Jesus will set up His Millennial Kingdom. Several events will take place during this time of transition. At this point, we will examine the order in which the events after the battle of Armageddon occur and concern ourselves with a more exact timing in the next chapter.

Let's start this discussion with what happens after Armageddon. Immediately after the battle of Armageddon, the Lord will come from Bozrah to Jerusalem. Zechariah 14 speaks of this battle and then shows the Lord returning to Jerusalem:

> Behold, the day of the Lord cometh, and thy spoil shall be divided in the midst of thee. For I will gather all nations against Jerusalem to battle; and the city shall be taken, and the houses rifled, and the women ravished; and half of the city shall go forth into captivity, and the residue of the people shall not be cut off from the city. Then shall the Lord go forth, and fight against those nations, as when he fought in the day of battle. And his feet shall stand in that day upon the mount of Olives, which is before Jerusalem on the east, and the mount of Olives shall cleave in the midst thereof toward the east and toward the west, and there shall be a very great valley; and half of the mountain shall remove toward the north, and half of it toward the south. And ye shall flee to the valley of the mountains; for the valley of the mountains shall reach unto Azal: yea, ye shall flee, like as ye fled from before the earthquake in the days of Uzziah king of Judah: and the Lord my God shall come, and all the saints with thee. And it shall come to pass in that day, that the light shall not be clear, nor dark: But it shall be one day which shall be known to the Lord, not day, nor night: but it shall come to pass, that at

evening time it shall be light. And it shall be in that day, that living waters shall go out from Jerusalem; half of them toward the former sea, and half of them toward the hinder sea: in summer and in winter shall it be. And the Lord shall be king over all the earth: in that day shall there be one Lord, and his name one. All the land shall be turned as a plain from Geba to Rimmon south of Jerusalem: and it shall be lifted up...And men shall dwell in it, and there shall be no more utter destruction; but Jerusalem shall be safely inhabited. And this shall be the plague wherewith the Lord will smite all the people that have fought against Jerusalem; Their flesh shall consume away while they stand upon their feet, and their eyes shall consume away in their holes, and their tongue shall consume away in their mouth...And it shall come to pass, that every one that is left of all the nations which came against Jerusalem shall even go up from year to year to worship the King, the Lord of hosts, and to keep the Feast of tabernacles. (Zech 14:1-16)

This lengthy passage brings out several important facts. First we see the nations gathering against Israel, and from our discussion in the last chapter, we saw that Israel has been hidden and protected by God in Bozrah (Petra). Then, as the armies descend upon her, Jesus comes to the rescue of Israel and destroys the gathered armies. After the battle, He stands on the Mount of Olives, which splits and a great valley is formed. At this time, living waters will flow out of Jerusalem and the Lord will be anointed king over all the earth and all the land be turned into a plain and lifted up. The living waters are mentioned in Ezekiel and are seen to be coming from the throne of God and will bring blessings to the whole earth:

Afterward he brought me again unto the door of the house; and, behold, waters issued out from under the threshold of the house eastward...Then he brought me, and caused me to return to the brink of the river. Now when I had returned, behold, at the bank of the river were very many trees on the one side and on the other. Then said he unto me, These waters issue out toward the east country, and go down into the desert, and go into the sea: which being brought forth into the sea, the waters shall be healed. And it shall come to pass, that every thing that liveth, which moveth, whithersoever the rivers shall come, shall live: and there shall be a very great

> multitude of fish, because these waters shall come thither: for they shall be healed....And by the river upon the bank thereof, on this side and on that side, shall grow all trees for meat, whose leaf shall not fade, neither shall the fruit thereof be consumed: it shall bring forth new fruit according to his months, because their waters they issued out of the sanctuary: and the fruit thereof shall be for meat, and the leaf thereof for medicine. (Ez 47:1-12)

In the passage above, the prophet Ezekiel sees a vision of this great river of life. It has as its source the house of the Lord and goes "out toward the east country, and goes down into the desert, and goes into the sea." This indicates that the river of life will flow into the Dead Sea and restore and purify its waters and then flow to all the earth. Zechariah tells us that the river will divide into two parts. One part of the river will flow toward the Dead Sea and the other to the Mediterranean. "And it shall be in that day, that living waters shall go out from Jerusalem; half of them toward the former sea, and half of them toward the hinder sea: in summer and in winter shall it be." (Zech14:8) It also was noted by Ezekiel that there were trees for food and medicine that grow along side this river.

> And by the river upon the bank thereof, on this side and on that side, shall grow all trees for meat, whose leaf shall not fade, neither shall the fruit thereof be consumed: it shall bring forth new fruit according to his months, because their waters they issued out of the sanctuary: and the fruit thereof shall be for meat, and the leaf thereof for medicine. (Eze. 47:12)

The river will also bring life and healing with it. Remember that after the bowl judgments, all living things in the ocean were destroyed. This river will restore life wherever it flows, and will bring an abundance of fish.

So when Jesus returns to Jerusalem after the battle of Armageddon, the river of life will start flowing from the throne of God. This implies that the throne is there and further implies that the temple has been restored, because the temple is the place of God's throne.

Ezekiel shows us these exact things in his description of the millennial temple:

> Afterward he brought me to the gate, even the gate that looketh toward the east: And, behold, the glory of the God of Israel came from the way of the east: and his voice was like a noise of many waters: and the earth shined with his glory...and I fell upon my face. And the glory of the Lord came into the house by the way of the gate whose prospect is toward the east. So the spirit took me up, and brought me into the inner court; and, behold, the glory of the Lord filled the house. And I heard him speaking unto me out of the house; and the man stood by me. And he said unto me, Son of man, the place of my throne, and the place of the soles of my feet, where I will dwell in the midst of the children of Israel for ever, and my holy name, shall the house of Israel no more defile, neither they, nor their kings, by their whoredom, nor by the carcases of their kings in their high places. (Ezek 41:1-7)

After Armageddon, the Lord will rebuild the temple occupy the throne and the waters of life will start flowing. The temple that was built and occupied by the antichrist would have surely been destroyed by the great earthquakes, and it will be the Lord, Himself, that will rebuild it:

> And speak unto him, saying, Thus speaketh the Lord of hosts, saying, Behold the man whose name is The Branch; and he shall grow up out of his place, and he shall build the temple of the Lord: Even he shall build the temple of the Lord; and he shall bear the glory, and shall sit and rule upon his throne; and he shall be a priest upon his throne: and the counsel of peace shall be between them both. (Zech 6:12,13)

Scripture also tells us that the day after Armageddon, the day that Jesus takes the throne, the first resurrection will be complete:

> And I saw thrones, and they sat upon them, and judgment was given unto them: and I saw the souls of them that were beheaded for the witness of Jesus, and for the word of God, and which had not worshipped the beast, neither his image, neither had received his mark upon their foreheads, or in their hands; and they lived and reigned with Christ a thousand years. But the rest of the dead lived not again until

the thousand years were finished. This is the first resurrection. Blessed and holy is he that hath part in the first resurrection: on such the second death hath no power, but they shall be priests of God and of Christ, and shall reign with him a thousand years. (Rev. 20:4-6)

Here we see a description of the last phase of the "first resurrection" where those who will become Christians after the rapture and were martyred will be resurrected. These saints will join the saints who were resurrected with Christ at His first coming and those resurrected at the rapture. All three of these groups comprise the "first resurrection" as expounded upon by Rev. Charles Cooper:

> Consequently, we are able to posit that John's *resurrection to life* and his *first resurrection* both refer to a general multi-phased resurrection of the righteous. It stretches from the resurrection of Christ and those raised with Him (Matt. 24:52-53), to those raised at the Rapture/Parousia (1 Cor. 15:23), to those beheaded martyrs raised in close proximity to the beginning of the millennium (Rev. 20:4-5). This is the first resurrection.[49]

These first resurrection saints will rule and reign with Christ for a thousand years in the Millennial Kingdom. A theocracy—a government under the direction of God will reign over the earth from Jerusalem. This kingdom will be the final world kingdom in which the Lord Jesus Christ Himself will be the sovereign king of the entire world. He will not be like any earthly king or president as we know, but He will be perfect in all aspects and will have a perfect government. There will be one religion—namely, the worship of the one true God: the Father, Son, and Holy Spirit. And the saints will have the privilege to rule and reign with Him in this great kingdom. "And hath made us kings and priests unto God and his Father; to him be glory and dominion for ever and ever. Amen." (Rev 1:6) The saints will also receive rewards at what is commonly referred to as the Bema Seat judgment:

> For other foundation can no man lay than that is laid, which is Jesus Christ. Now if any man build upon this foundation

---

[49] Cooper, Charles. *What is the First Resurrection.* http://www.solagroup.org/articles/faqs/faq_0012.html

> gold, silver, precious stones, wood, hay, stubble; Every man's work shall be made manifest: for the day shall declare it, because it shall be revealed by fire; and the fire shall try every man's work of what sort it is. If any man's work abide which he hath built thereupon, he shall receive a reward. If any man's work shall be burned, he shall suffer loss: but he himself shall be saved; yet so as by fire. (1 Cor. 3:11-15)

We also see this in Rev. 11:17–18:

> Saying, We give thee thanks, O Lord God Almighty, which art, and wast, and art to come; because thou hast taken to thee thy great power, and hast reigned. And the nations were angry, and thy wrath is come, and the time of the dead, that they should be judged, and that thou shouldest give reward unto thy servants the prophets, and to the saints, and them that fear thy name, small and great; and shouldest destroy them which destroy the earth.

After the Bema seat judgment comes the "sheep and goat" judgment. This judgment is for all the gentiles who survived the 70th Week of Daniel.

> When the Son of man shall come in his glory, and all the holy angels with him, then shall he sit upon the throne of his glory: And before him shall be gathered all nations: and he shall separate them one from another, as a shepherd divideth his sheep from the goats: And he shall set the sheep on his right hand, but the goats on the left. Then shall the King say unto them on his right hand, Come, ye blessed of my Father, inherit the kingdom prepared for you from the foundation of the world: For I was an hungered, and ye gave me meat: I was thirsty, and ye gave me drink: I was a stranger, and ye took me in: Naked, and ye clothed me: I was sick, and ye visited me: I was in prison, and ye came unto me…Then shall he say also unto them on the left hand, Depart from me, ye cursed, into everlasting fire, prepared for the devil and his angels: For I was an hungered, and ye gave me no meat: I was thirsty, and ye gave me no drink: I was a stranger, and ye took me not in: naked, and ye clothed me not: sick, and in prison, and ye visited me not…And these shall go away into everlasting punishment: but the righteous into life eternal. (Matt. 25:31-46)

After the judgment of the nations, it will be Israel's turn for judgment. Fortunately for Israel, all who survive the 70th Week—although this will only be one-third—will be saved:

> And it shall come to pass, that in all the land, saith the Lord, two parts therein shall be cut off and die; but the third shall be left therein. And I will bring the third part through the fire, and will refine them as silver is refined, and will try them as gold is tried: they shall call on my name, and I will hear them: I will say, It is my people: and they shall say, The Lord is my God. (Zech 13:8–9)

God through the Apostle Paul also tells us that all who are left of Israel will be saved:

> For I would not, brethren, that ye should be ignorant of this mystery, lest ye should be wise in your own conceits; that blindness in part is happened to Israel, until the fulness of the Gentiles be come in. And so all Israel shall be saved: as it is written, There shall come out of Sion the Deliverer, and shall turn away ungodliness from Jacob: For this is my covenant unto them, when I shall take away their sins. (Rom. 11:25-27)

Ezekiel, in his passage about the restored temple, indicates that Israel will be saved on the eighth day. (We will discuss when the eighth day occurs and a more exact chronology of these events in the next chapter.)

> Seven days shalt thou prepare every day a goat for a sin offering: they shall also prepare a young bullock, and a ram out of the flock, without blemish. Seven days shall they purge the altar and purify it; and they shall consecrate themselves. And when these days are expired, it shall be, that upon the eighth day, and so forward, the priests shall make your burnt offerings upon the altar, and your peace offerings; and I will accept you, saith the Lord God. (Ez 43: 25-27)

At this time, the Lord will place David as king over Israel:

> And say unto them, Thus saith the Lord God; Behold, I will take the children of Israel from among the heathen, whither they be gone, and will gather them on every side, and bring them into their own land: And I will make them one nation in the land upon the mountains of Israel; and one king shall be king to them all.... I will save them out of all their dwelling places, wherein they have sinned, and will cleanse them: so shall they be my people, and I will be their God. *And David my servant shall be king over them*; and they all shall have one shepherd: they shall also walk in my judgments, and observe my statutes, and do them. And they shall dwell in the land that I have given unto Jacob my servant, wherein your fathers have dwelt; and they shall dwell therein, even they, and their children, and their children's children for ever: *and my servant David shall be their prince for ever.* Moreover I will make a covenant of peace with them; it shall be an everlasting covenant with them: and I will place them, and multiply them, and will set my sanctuary in the midst of them for evermore. My tabernacle also shall be with them: yea, I will be their God, and they shall be my people. And the heathen shall know that I the Lord do sanctify Israel, when my sanctuary shall be in the midst of them for evermore. (Ezek 37:21-28—emphasis mine)

After this time the saints of God will partake of the marriage supper of the lamb in the millennial Jerusalem.

> And in this mountain shall the Lord of hosts make unto all people a Feast of fat things, a Feast of wines on the lees, of fat things full of marrow, of wines on the lees well refined. And he will destroy in this mountain the face of the covering cast over all people, and the vail that is spread over all nations. He will swallow up death in victory; and the Lord God will wipe away tears from off all faces; and the rebuke of his people shall he take away from off all the earth: for the Lord hath spoken it. And it shall be said in that day, Lo, this is our God; we have waited for him, and he will save us: this is the Lord; we have waited for him, we will be glad and rejoice in his salvation" (Isa. 25:6-9)

The Millennium, the greatest time on earth, will then have begun. Here are a few passages that describe the greatness of the Millennium.

The wolf also shall dwell with the lamb, and the leopard shall lie down with the kid; and the calf and the young lion and the fatling together; and a little child shall lead them. And the cow and the bear shall feed; their young ones shall lie down together: and the lion shall eat straw like the ox. And the sucking child shall play on the hole of the asp, and the weaned child shall put his hand on the cockatrice' den. They shall not hurt nor destroy in all my holy mountain: for the earth shall be full of the knowledge of the Lord, as the waters cover the sea. And in that day there shall be a root of Jesse, which shall stand for an ensign of the people; to it shall the Gentiles seek: and his rest shall be glorious" (Isa. 11:6-10)

And I will rejoice in Jerusalem, and joy in my people: and the voice of weeping shall be no more heard in her, nor the voice of crying. There shall be no more thence an infant of days, nor an old man that hath not filled his days: for the child shall die an hundred years old; but the sinner being an hundred years old shall be accursed. And they shall build houses, and inhabit them; and they shall plant vineyards, and eat the fruit of them. They shall not build, and another inhabit; they shall not plant, and another eat: for as the days of a tree are the days of my people, and mine elect shall long enjoy the work of their hands. They shall not labour in vain, nor bring forth for trouble; for they are the seed of the blessed of the Lord, and their offspring with them. And it shall come to pass, that before they call, I will answer; and while they are yet speaking, I will hear. The wolf and the lamb shall feed together, and the lion shall eat straw like the bullock: and dust shall be the serpent's meat. They shall not hurt nor destroy in all my holy mountain, saith the Lord. (Isa. 65: 19-25)

We see here that the earth will be restored to Garden of Eden conditions. The earth will be full of the knowledge of the Lord. Peace will rule the world, and even the animals will not attack each other or humans; nor will they be afraid of humans. People will live to very old ages probably like before the flood. The crops and trees will yield abundantly. This will be a truly fantastic time. The blessings of God will abound to all.

The Christian is to set their hope and affections on these things:

> If ye then be risen with Christ, seek those things which are above, where Christ sitteth on the right hand of God. Set your affection on things above, not on things on the earth. For ye are dead, and your life is hid with Christ in God. When Christ, who is our life, shall appear, then shall ye also appear with him in glory. (Col 3:1-4)

This truly unique time will last for 1,000 years as described in Rev. 20:1-4.

> And I saw an angel come down from heaven, having the key of the bottomless pit and a great chain in his hand. And he laid hold on the dragon, that old serpent, which is the devil, and satan, and bound him a thousand years, And cast him into the bottomless pit, and shut him up, and set a seal upon him, that he should deceive the nations no more, till the thousand years should be fulfilled: and after that he must be loosed a little season. And I saw thrones, and they sat upon them, and judgment was given unto them: and I saw the souls of them that were beheaded for the witness of Jesus, and for the word of God, and which had not worshipped the beast, neither his image, neither had received his mark upon their foreheads, or in their hands; and they lived and reigned with Christ a thousand years.

Some Christians reject the fact that there will be a literal Millennial reign, and or believe that we are in it now and Christ will return after the Millennium, but it is easily seen by these verses that the 1000-year reign will be literal and that it has not started because the conditions described have not occurred since the garden of Eden.

After the 1000-year reign, satan will be let loose for seven years to "try" those that live on the earth. During the Millennium, the people who lived through the 70th Week of Daniel will repopulate the earth. This new population will be given a choice as to whether they want to follow God or satan. Unfortunately, some will follow satan and be deceived into thinking that they can defeat God and will be annihilated in one final battle.

> And when the thousand years are expired, satan shall be loosed out of his prison, And shall go out to deceive the nations which are in the four quarters of the earth, Gog, and

> Magog, to gather them together to battle: the number of whom is as the sand of the sea. And they went up on the breadth of the earth, and compassed the camp of the saints about, and the beloved city: and fire came down from God out of heaven, and devoured them. And the devil that deceived them was cast into the lake of fire and brimstone, where the beast and the false prophet are, and shall be tormented day and night for ever and ever. (Rev. 20:7-10)

After this final battle will be the second resurrection and the great white throne judgment. Then, the Lord will create a new heaven and a new earth:

> And I saw a great white throne, and him that sat on it, from whose face the earth and the heaven fled away; and there was found no place for them. And I saw the dead, small and great, stand before God; and the books were opened: and another book was opened, which is the book of life: and the dead were judged out of those things which were written in the books, according to their works. And the sea gave up the dead which were in it; and death and hell delivered up the dead which were in them: and they were judged every man according to their works. And death and hell were cast into the lake of fire. This is the second death. And whosoever was not found written in the book of life was cast into the lake of fire. And I saw a new heaven and a new earth: for the first heaven and the first earth were passed away; and there was no more sea." (Rev. 20:11- 21:1)

After these events, the New Jerusalem, adorned as a bride, will descend out of heaven.

> I John saw the holy city, new Jerusalem, coming down from God out of heaven, prepared as a bride adorned for her husband. And I heard a great voice out of heaven saying, Behold, the tabernacle of God is with men, and he will dwell with them, and they shall be his people, and God himself shall be with them, and be their God. And God shall wipe away all tears from their eyes; and there shall be no more death, neither sorrow, nor crying, neither shall there be any more pain: for the former things are passed away. And he that sat upon the throne said, Behold, I make all things new. (Rev. 21:2-5).

This is where the saints of all time will live after the Millennium—in the New Jerusalem. And yes, Old Testament saints will live there too:

> By faith he sojourned in the land of promise, as in a strange country, dwelling in tabernacles with Isaac and Jacob, the heirs with him of the same promise: For he looked for a city which hath foundations, whose builder and maker is God. But now they desire a better country, that is, an heavenly: wherefore God is not ashamed to be called their God: for he hath prepared for them a city. (Heb 11:9,10,16)

From what we see above, the best part about this great city is that the Lord Jesus Christ will dwell there. We also notice that this city will truly be heaven on earth, for there will be no crying, pain, tears, or dying. It will also be a city of great beauty:

> And there came unto me one of the seven angels which had the seven vials full of the seven last plagues, and talked with me, saying, Come hither, I will shew thee the bride, the Lamb's wife. And he carried me away in the spirit to a great and high mountain, and shewed me that great city, the holy Jerusalem, descending out of heaven from God, Having the glory of God: and her light was like unto a stone most precious, even like a jasper stone, clear as crystal; And had a wall great and high, and had twelve gates, and at the gates twelve angels, and names written thereon, which are the names of the twelve tribes of the children of Israel: On the east three gates; on the north three gates; on the south three gates; and on the west three gates. And the wall of the city had twelve foundations, and in them the names of the twelve apostles of the Lamb...And the building of the wall of it was of jasper: and the city was pure gold, like unto clear glass. And the foundations of the wall of the city were garnished with all manner of precious stones...And the twelve gates were twelve pearls: every several gate was of one pearl: and the street of the city was pure gold, as it were transparent glass. And I saw no temple therein: for the Lord God Almighty and the Lamb are the temple of it. And the city had no need of the sun, neither of the moon, to shine in it: for the glory of God did lighten it, and the Lamb is the light thereof.

> And the nations of them which are saved shall walk in the light of it: and the kings of the earth do bring their glory and honour into it. And the gates of it shall not be shut at all by day: for there shall be no night there. And they shall bring the glory and honour of the nations into it. And there shall in no wise enter into it any thing that defileth, neither whatsoever worketh abomination, or maketh a lie: but they which are written in the Lamb's book of life. (Rev. 21:9-27)

O what a beautiful sight! And just think, if you are a Christian, you will be able to live there for all eternity.

The next thing we notice about this city is that it is a city of light. "Having the glory of God: and her light was like unto a stone most precious, even like a jasper stone, clear as crystal" (Rev. 21:11). It shines brightly, for the glory of God is there. "God is light and in Him there is no darkness at all" (1 John 1:5).

When Saul saw the Lord Jesus on the road to Damascus, the Lord appeared in His glory and Saul saw a bright light, so bright that it blinded him.

> And as he journeyed, he came near Damascus: and suddenly there shined round about him a light from heaven. (Acts 9:3).

> At midday, O king, I saw in the way a light from heaven, above the brightness of the sun, shining round about me and them which journeyed with me. (Acts 26:13)

If we were to look at God with our human eyes, we, too, would be blinded. God emanates a very bright light, so bright that our eyes cannot even look upon Him. What happens to a crystal when a very bright light is shined upon it? As the light passes through it, the crystal changes and enhances the light. The crystal then emits its own light, commonly known as a laser light. So by subjecting a gemstone to a very bright light, the gemstone will emit a laser. Thus, the New Jerusalem will, because of the bright light of Christ, display a huge laser light show. Hence the phrase "and her light was like unto a stone most precious."

Next, we see that this great city has a very high wall with 12 gates of giant pearls and with an angel at each gate. These gates are three on a side, with the names of the 12 tribes of Israel written upon each one. The city also has 12 foundations, each a precious gemstone and each with the name of an apostle on it. The shape of the great city is a cube; with length, width, and height all equal to 12,000 furlongs. A furlong is approximately one-eighth of a mile. Thus, the city would be about 1500 miles long, high, and wide. The volume of this city would then be 3,375,000,000 cubic miles. That is a huge city.

Let's try to understand just how big this city is. For illustration purposes let's think of this city as a building with stories. And let's say that each story is 10 feet high. That would yield approx. 528 stories per mile of height. Thus, this city would be a building with 792,000 stories. In comparison the tallest building in the world, the Taipei 101, has only 101 stories. Now try to imagine this building being 1,500 miles wide and 1,500 miles long. This great city will dwarf the greatest human accomplishment a million times over. Let's try to think of its size another way. If you could explore one square mile of a story of this city a day, it would take you 225,000 days, or approximately 616.5 years to explore a single story. To explore all 792,000 stories, it would take you 488,188,000 years! Let's consider another scenario; let's increase the distance between levels from 10ft to a mile, then there would be 1500 levels yielding a total area of 3,375,000,000 billion square miles. This would be 75 times the area of the habitable land area on the earth!

One of the most famous and talked about aspects of this city, which has been used quite frequently in describing heaven, are the streets of gold: "and the street of the city was pure gold, as it were transparent glass" (Rev. 21:21). The gold in this city is not like any gold on earth. This gold is pure and transparent. We are also told that this heavenly city does not have a temple. A temple is a place where God dwells. In Old Testament days, the glory of God dwelt in the earthly temple. For the Christian, his body is a temple, for the Lord indwells all true believers. In this city, "the Lord God Almighty and the Lamb are the temple of it" (Rev. 21:22). That is because God lives there with the saints. What a privilege that will be!

God not only lives there, but He also illuminates the city with a light equal to or greater than the sun: "And the city had no need of the sun, neither of the moon, to shine in it: for the glory of God did lighten it, and the Lamb is the light thereof" (Rev. 21:23) The light of this city is so bright that "the nations of them which are saved shall walk in the light of it" and the light will be shining continuously, 24 hours a day. During this great time the nations will bring presents and gifts to the city: "And the kings of the earth do bring their glory and honour into it. And the gates of it shall not be shut at all by day: for there shall be no night there. And they shall bring the glory and honour of the nations into it" (Rev. 21:24-26).

This city will be pure and perfect. There will be no sin within its walls, and only the saints of God can enter. "And there shall in no wise enter into it any thing that defileth, neither whatsoever worketh abomination, or maketh a lie: but they which are written in the Lamb's book of life" (Rev. 21:9-27). The blessings of God will be poured out upon the earth from here. There will be a river of pure water of life that will go forth from this city to all the earth. Along side of this river will be special trees. These trees, which grow alongside this river, are the famed "trees of life" which, were once in the Garden of Eden and are now found here. The trees bear 12 different fruits continually, and the leaves of the trees will be used for medicine for the world.

> And he shewed me a pure river of water of life, clear as crystal, proceeding out of the throne of God and of the Lamb. In the midst of the street of it, and on either side of the river, was there the tree of life, which bare twelve manner of fruits, and yielded her fruit every month: and the leaves of the tree were for the healing of the nations. (Rev. 21:2-5)

The new heaven and new earth will be the place where we will live with the Lord for all eternity. We will dwell with God and experience His greatness forever. Since we have established a clear picture of the things that will happen before, during, and after the 70th Week of Daniel, and in what order, we will now turn our attention to America in end-times prophecy.

CHAPTER 8
O America

O beautiful for spacious skies, for amber waves of grain, for purple mountain majesties above the fruited plain! America! America! God shed his grace on thee and crown thy good with brotherhood from sea to shining sea! America is the greatest most blessed nation in all the earth. Where does America fit in the prophetic scheme of things? Is America mentioned in the Bible? Will it have a role to play in the end-times scenario? Many say that America is not mentioned in the Bible. I disagree and strongly believe that America *has* been prophesied about in the Bible and that it will play a major role in the end times. How could the greatest nation in the world, the only super power, not have a role to play? Of course, it will. America has been mentioned many times in scripture. The clearest mention is found in Revelation 18. This chapter describes the end-times Babylon and the judgment that it will receive. I believe America is the end-times Babylon talked about in this chapter. Let us examine this chapter to find out why I believe America is the end-times Babylon, and what will happen to her.

The main reason why I — along with many others — believe that America is the Babylon talked about in Revelation 18 is because of several verses that, when considered collectively, lead us to conclude that America is the only country that fulfills all of the parameters listed in the verses. Let us examine what the scriptures say about this modern day end-times Babylon and see how they undeniably point to America.

1. End-times Babylon is a great nation that receives judgment for its many sins.

> And he cried mightily with a strong voice, saying, Babylon the great is fallen, is fallen, and is become the habitation of devils, and the hold of every foul spirit, and a cage of every unclean and hateful bird. (Rev. 18:2)

2. This nation is a superpower and has world dominance and importance. It has also spread its corruption to the world.

> For all nations have drunk of the wine of the wrath of her fornication, and the kings of the earth have committed fornication with her. (Rev. 18:3)

3. The merchants of the world are made rich through trading with this nation. This nation consumes huge amounts of goods.

> And the merchants of the earth are waxed rich through the abundance of her delicacies. (Rev. 18:3)

> And the merchants of the earth shall weep and mourn over her; for no man buyeth their merchandise any more: The merchandise of gold, and silver, and precious stones, and of pearls, and fine linen, and purple, and silk, and scarlet, and all thyine wood, and all manner vessels of ivory, and all manner vessels of most precious wood, and of brass, and iron, and marble, And cinnamon, and odours, and ointments, and frankincense, and wine, and oil, and fine flour, and wheat, and beasts, and sheep, and horses, and chariots, and slaves, and souls of men. (Rev. 18:11–13)

4. This nation is proud and arrogant and considers herself to be invincible and the greatest nation on earth.

> How much she hath glorified herself, and lived deliciously, so much torment and sorrow give her: for she saith in her heart, I sit a queen, and am no widow, and shall see no sorrow. (Rev. 18:7)

5. This nation is typified by an extravagant lifestyle.

> And saying, Alas, alas, that great city, that was clothed in fine linen, and purple, and scarlet, and decked with gold, and precious stones, and pearls! (Rev. 18:16)

6. Other nations are controlled by her and given great riches by her.

> And the kings of the earth, who have committed fornication and lived deliciously with her. (Rev. 18:9)

7. This nation is a coastal nation, with deepwater ports and much international trade.

> And every shipmaster, and all the company in ships, and sailors, and as many as trade by sea, stood afar off. (Rev. 18:17)

8. This nation has defenses in the heavens.

> Though Babylon should mount up to heaven, and though she should fortify the height of her strength, yet from me shall spoilers come unto her, saith the Lord. (Jer. 51:53)

Which nation is the only one in the world that meets all those qualifications? America! We are the greatest country in the world. We are the only remaining super power. We dominate world politics and dictate much of what happens in other countries through whom and what we fund in those countries. We have the largest Gross National Product (GNP) in the world, far surpassing all other countries. We buy huge amounts of goods from other countries. In fact, the economy of many countries would collapse without our trade dollars. We are a proud and arrogant people and feel that we are invincible and that we are the greatest nation in the world. America, as a whole, lives in luxury compared to the rest of the world. America has many deepwater ports, and the vast majority of goods entering this country come by way of ship. And, yes, we now are the only country that has offensive and defensive weapons in space.[50,51] The only country that meets all of the qualifications above is America.

Yes, America is described in Revelation 18 as the end-times Babylon. R.A. Coombes, in his book *America the Babylon*, sums it up like this:

> So if not America, what nation will be the 'mystery Babylon' spoken of in Revelation, chapters 17 and 18? I submit that

---

[50] Floyd, Charles. *Dark Matter*. The Moscow Times. April, 9 2004. http://context.themoscowtimes.com/stories/2004/04/09/120.html
[51] Wolf, Jim. *U.S. Deploys Satellite Jamming System*. Science Reuters.

there is no other nation that could or will, and that therefore America must be the "super" nation mentioned in Revelation…..Empirical data suggests that it is America, not Rome, or London, nor some resurrected Iraqi empire, nor the United States of Europe. Textually, from the scriptures, there is overwhelming evidence that is ironclad in its data pointing only to the identity of 'mystery Babylon' as being that of the United States of America. Revelation chapters 17 and 18 give us 65 major identifying data points, which are identifying markers, that point out the identifying characteristics that point out the identity of this 'Babylon', and what its future will be.[52]

It is also interesting that, at this time in history, America, as a result of the Iraq war, has conquered and is in control of ancient Babylon. Even though Iraq has been officially handed over to the Iraqis, we are still in control, and many have deemed the government now in place as a puppet government. Ancient Babylon was a world power that encompassed the ancient "mystery" religions, hedonism, and materialism. America also embraces the ancient "mystery religions," hedonism, and materialism, and in many ways is similar to ancient Babylon, and ironically, now controls the land it once occupied.

Some think that the end-times Babylon mentioned in Revelation 18 is Rome. They base their reasoning on Rev. 17:9: "And here is the mind which hath wisdom. The seven heads are seven mountains, on which the woman sitteth." Through the centuries, Rome has been called the city of seven hills; thus, they make the connection that end-times Babylon is Rome. But Rome does not meet the qualifications of the great nation that has control over the world during the end-times as outlined above.

Here is what author Stewart Best said about this:

> Rome is usually pointed at as being Babylon the city, if a literal city is even recognized. Rome, however, *does not* come close to being able to fulfill the parameters of God for the identification of the city, Babylon. It fails in almost all aspects. Because it does not meet the requirements of God, Rome cannot be the "great city" Babylon. This is not to say

---

[52] Coombes R. A. *America, The Babylon: America's Destiny Foretold in Biblical Prophecy*. P. 26.

that Rome is not important in prophecy, for it is - it plays a major role and is part of the Babylonian system!

The argument goes that Rome is a city-state, and the Vatican is in reality a nation, which it is, but beyond that fact, it utterly fails all of the parameters for Babylon the Great. Babylon the Great is a large nation, with many cities. It has many huge warm water seaports, a huge military, a space program, etc. Rome does not fulfill any of these. Therefore, believe God and not man.[53]

Here is what another author has to say about the Rome/Babylon connection:

> Some Bible expositors make a big deal of the fact that Revelation 17 refers (verse 9) to the seven heads of the Beast as "seven hills". (Rome was apparently built on seven hills.) A momentary allusion to Rome was appropriate at the time, but everything else in the same chapter makes it clear that even the hills are not literal hills, but rather "seven kings". So there are circles within circles here (as there are is so many prophecies) that are easily missed if one becomes obsessed with only one aspect of a prophecy.[54]

So if one pays close attention to the language of Revelation 17 and 18, one can easily see that Rome does not meet the qualifications of end-times Babylon; nor does ancient Babylon itself, located in Iraq.

Still not convinced that America is the end-times Babylon? Here are some verses that prove it conclusively.

> Your *mother* shall be sore confounded; she that bare you shall be ashamed: behold, the *hindermost* of the nations shall be a wilderness, a dry land, and a desert. Because of the wrath of the Lord it shall not be inhabited, but it shall be wholly desolate: every one that goeth by Babylon shall be astonished, and hiss at all her plagues. (Jer. 50:12,13 — emphasis mine)

---

[53] Best, Stewart. Is America Babylon? http://www.markswatson.com/BAB.htm
[54] http://cust.idl.net.au/fold/New_studies/The%20Blood%20of%20the%20Saints.html (No longer online.)

These verses in Jeremiah speak of the destruction that end-times Babylon will receive. It refers to end-times Babylon as having "a mother." What country has a "mother?" America! Its "mother" is England. Consider the words of Author Stewart Best again:

> This latter day Babylon has a mother, which is also a nation. This mother was responsible for "birthing" this mighty Babylon of the End Times. If Iraq is Babylon as some try to claim, who is the mother of Iraq? If you read this verse carefully, it says that the mother nation preceded Babylon, gave birth to her, watches her rise to full power, and watches her die in fire. Again, who is the mother of Iraq? Iraq has none.
>
> Who is the mother of Rome, which is often presented as Babylon? Rome is not a nation, but a city. Further, she has no mother. Who is the mother of the EC, which is often presented as Babylon, the Revived Roman Empire? In point of fact, she will have no mother, and further, Babylon the Great is always shown as a single nation from her birth to her rise to full power and glory. The EC does not qualify. Each parameter must be fulfilled. You cannot pick and choose that which you wish to present to prove your case.
>
> However, America has a mother. This mother was directly responsible for her birth. That mother preceded her. England has been around awhile. England gave birth to America, and England is still around, and England will watch America burn. England is further confirmed as the mother of Babylon the Great by Daniel the Prophet in Daniel 7:4 (the lion). Ezekiel also mentions it in Ezekiel 38/39 as "Tarshish", who gives birth to "young cubs". Tarshish is a cryptic reference to England and her young cubs are America, Canada, Australia, New Zealand, etc. Daniel refers to her as a lion. The national symbol of England is a lion. The eagle wings on top the lion is America, her daughter. America's national symbol is the eagle with outstretched wings.[55]

America is the country with "a mother" and America meets the other scriptural qualifications. Thus, the clear scriptural interpretation is that America is the end-times Babylon.

---

[55] Best, Stewart

More Indications

There are more indications that America is the end-times Babylon, as well. For example, at the gateway to our nation stands the Statue of Liberty. Free Masons in Paris gifted it to America in 1886. They commissioned fellow Mason Augusste Bertholdi, who was seeking a commission to create a robed statue of the goddess Isis, the Egyptian Queen of Heaven, holding a torch. Her connection to Babylon is easily seen in the next quote.

> The Babylonian heritage of the "Statue of Liberty" should come as no real surprise to God's people. Her identity is written in her shape. She stands on a base patterned after the Babylonian stepped-pyramids, or zigurrats, of old — which themselves were designed by the "tower" woman Semiramis and her architects. She stands literally on a base patterned after the tower of Babel! She wears a turreted crown, like Rhea, Cybele, Diana, and the pagan goddesses who were counterparts of Semiramis. She stands as a universal symbol of "liberty," apart from the laws and commandments of God. She represents the "emanicpation" of mankind, and "immigration" and "unity" and the coming together of many races to become one universal mankind, all peoples coming together to one land, uniting the nations as "one," with one language.
>
> In her poem "The New Colossus," Emma Lazarus calls the "Statue of Liberty" the "Mother of Exiles." But the truth is, she is the "Mother of harlots and abominations of the earth" (Rev. 17:5).[56]

Arguments against America as Babylon

Even though the evidence points to America as being end-times Babylon, some reject this hypothesis, citing Rev. 17:6 and 18:24:

> And I saw the woman drunken with the blood of the saints, and with the blood of the martyrs of Jesus: and when I saw her, I wondered with great admiration.

---

[56] Dankenbring, William F. *Is the Statue of Liberty Pagan?* http://yahushua.net/babylon/liberty/pagan_statue.htm

> And in her was found the blood of prophets, and of saints, and of all that were slain upon the earth.

They assert that America cannot be end-times Babylon because she has not participated in murdering Christians. I assert, however, that America *is* guilty of the murder of many Christians and Jews and will be guilty of even more in the near future.

> We can assert that America already is and has slaughtered millions of innocent victims. The wholesale death of the American Indians by US forces from the 1700's forward along with all of the aborted babies. Then of course we assert that the US leadership (Illuminati leaders) ordered fellow Illuminist, Adolf Hitler and his "illuminated" Nazi's to kill the Jews and create the Holocaust of World War 2. In addition to that, US leaders ordered fellow Illuminist Joe Stalin to purge Russia of not just Jews but also millions of Christians during the 1930's, 40's and 50's. But that's not all, these same Illuminist leaders also ordered Illuminist Mao Tse-Tung and his Red Chinese army to slaughter up to as many as 70 million innocent men, women and children, of whom many were Chinese Christians.[57]

Mr. Coombes, in the referenced article, lists several supporting documents for his claims. I assert that, as the future leader of the New World Order, America will also be the one responsible for the martyrdom of Jews and Christians during the 70th Week of Daniel. As a matter of fact, the U.S. Senate has just passed legislation that paves the way for Christians to be arrested for hate crimes for preaching anything negative about any race, religion, sexual gender or "sexual orientation."[58]

Not only is end-times Babylon talked about in Revelation 18, but is also talked about in Revelation 17 and other parts of scripture such as in Jeremiah 50–51 and several chapters in Isaiah as detailed by R.A. Coombes:

> Babylon as a city and nation is perhaps the most mentioned gentile city/state/nation in the Bible. Only those cities in Israel, such as Jerusalem receive greater mention. There are

---

[57] Coombes R.A. *USA to Outlaw Christianity.* Alpha Omega Report.
[58] http://www.rense.com/general57/ywe.htm

approximately 359 direct references to the name Babylon in the Old Testament. Of these references, many are simply tied to historical accounts of events in past history. However, the 2 major prophets of the Old Testament, Isaiah and Jeremiah received from God information about a future Babylon yet to come. This future Babylon is separate and distinct from the Babylon of their day. The message of the prophets is that a latter-day Babylon would arise that would carry on the 'spirit' of the old Babylon. Hence, these two prophets present significant data concerning the identity of the future Babylon and its destiny. The prophets explain what will happen to this later Babylon along with data on who will be involved, where it will take place, when and how...along with why it takes place. These two prophets account for more than 80 direct references to this future city/state/nation. 64 of those are found in two chapters of Jeremiah. Those chapters are chapters 50 and 51. Isaiah accounts for two dozen more in chapters 13, 14, 18 and 47. These chapters provide a substantial insight into what happens to this latterday Babylon of the future.[59]

Jeremiah 50 and 51 is a large section of scripture concerning end-times Babylon that describe its destruction. I will not list them in full here, but I would encourage you to read them. Here are a few key verses from the text.

> Because of the wrath of the Lord it shall not be inhabited, but it shall be wholly desolate: every one that goeth by Babylon shall be astonished, and hiss at all her plagues. Put yourselves in array against Babylon round about: all ye that bend the bow, shoot at her, spare no arrows: for she hath sinned against the Lord. Shout against her round about: she hath given her hand: her foundations are fallen, her walls are thrown down: for it is the vengeance of the Lord: take vengeance upon her; as she hath done, do unto her. Cut off the sower from Babylon, and him that handleth the sickle in the time of harvest: for fear of the oppressing sword they shall turn every one to his people, and they shall flee every one to his own land. (Jer. 50:13-16)

---

[59] Ibid. p.47

> How is the hammer of the whole earth cut asunder and broken! How is Babylon become a desolation among the nations! I have laid a snare for thee, and thou art also taken, O Babylon, and thou wast not aware: thou art found, and also caught, because thou hast striven against the Lord. (Jer. 50:23,24)
>
> Behold, I am against thee, O thou most proud, saith the Lord God of hosts: for thy day is come, the time that I will visit thee. And the most proud shall stumble and fall, and none shall raise him up: and I will kindle a fire in his cities, and it shall devour all round about him. (Jer. 50:31,32)
>
> As God overthrew Sodom and Gomorrah and the neighbour cities thereof, saith the Lord; so shall no man abide there, neither shall any son of man dwell therein. Behold, a people shall come from the north, and a great nation, and many kings shall be raised up from the coasts of the earth. They shall hold the bow and the lance: they are cruel, and will not shew mercy: their voice shall roar like the sea, and they shall ride upon horses, every one put in array, like a man to the battle, against thee, O daughter of Babylon. (Jer. 50:40-42)

These verses paint a gloomy picture of the end-times Babylon and the destruction that it will receive. How do we know that Jeremiah chapters 50 and 51 are talking about the end-times Babylon? One of the main reasons is that ancient Babylon was not destroyed in the way described in the passages above. Consider again the words of Mr. Coombes.

> The future-Babylon prophecies of Isaiah and Jeremiah have over the centuries been misunderstood and misapplied. Until recently, many commentators considered many of the prophecies to have already occurred. It does seem that some of the predicted results do apply to the ancient Babylon. Those results speak of Babylon becoming a desert, where desert animals live and no man resides there. In reality, ancient Babylon—the city, has been deserted for nearly a thousand years. It did *not occur in the manner described in the future prophecies!* Furthermore, the old national empire of Babylon has remained inhabited by man, yet the prophecies speak of no habitation for the nation/state as well as the city. Additionally, the events in question indicate that

the demise of this Babylon will occur in ... one...that's 1...1 hour. Yes, that is 60 minutes of time...for complete annihilation of not just a city but also a city/state/nation. That never occurred for ancient Babylon. She just slowly dissolved into nothingness. Therefore, the prophecies of Isaiah and Jeremiah are indeed still for the future.[60]

Here is one of the prophecies that show that ancient Babylon was not destroyed in this manner. "The sea is come up upon Babylon: she is covered with the multitude of the waves thereof." (Jer. 51:42) Was ancient Babylon covered with waves? Did the sea come up upon it? No! Ancient Babylon was not destroyed in that way. Thus, these scriptures have to be talking about the end-times Babylon.

In Isaiah 18, we have further proof that the end-times Babylon is different from ancient Babylon:

> Woe to the land shadowing with wings, which is beyond the rivers of Ethiopia: That sendeth ambassadors by the sea, even in vessels of bulrushes upon the waters, saying, Go, ye swift messengers, to a nation scattered and peeled, to a people terrible from their beginning hitherto; a nation meted out and trodden down, whose land the rivers have spoiled! (Is 18:1,2)

Once again, notes Coombes:

> Finally, we have Isaiah 18:2, where we find a reference to the future Babylon's location as being beyond the land and rivers of Cush. This 'rivers of Cush' reference is relating to the Tigris and Euphrates rivers of Mesopotamia. *Therefore, we find the verse trying to tell us that future Babylon is BEYOND the old Babylon by a great distance !!! The implication is that the future Babylon is nowhere close, geographically, and requires a long sea voyage to get there from anywhere in the then known world.*[61]

If America is the end-times Babylon, which I am convinced that it is, then as you can see from these passages, America-Babylon is slated for destruction. America has lifted her fist in the face of God. Our sins have reached unto heaven. The murders, especially of babies,

---

[60] Ibid. p. 48.
[61] Ibid. p. 61.

the sexual perversions, the child abuse, the pornography, the drug abuse, the witchcraft that this country is involved in, are deplorable. The worst sins are yet future, however, in which America will be instrumental in bringing about the New World Order and persecuting Jews and Christians. As a result, God's judgment will come upon America swiftly and decisively.

America, as a whole, has shown God in recent years that it does not want Him. The nation has removed prayer from school, defamed the sanctity of marriage, and is removing the scriptures such as the Ten Commandments from being displayed publicly. America is shaking its fist in God's face and saying "We do not want you!" Unfortunately, that is what we will get. God has begun and will continue to remove His blessings and hand of protection from our nation. 9/11 was just the start, and we can see from the language employed in Revelation 18 that America will eventually suffer a terrible destruction.

> And he cried mightily with a strong voice, saying, Babylon the great is fallen, is fallen, and is become the habitation of devils, and the hold of every foul spirit, and a cage of every unclean and hateful bird. (Rev. 18:2)

> Therefore shall her plagues come in one day, death, and mourning, and famine; and she shall be utterly burned with fire: for strong is the Lord God who judgeth her." (Rev. 18:8)

> Standing afar off for the fear of her torment, saying, Alas, alas, that great city Babylon, that mighty city! for in one hour is thy judgment come. (Rev. 18:10)

Two-Stage Destruction

I do not know exactly to the last detail how the destruction of America will play out, but I do see the destruction occurring in two stages. My study of the related biblical passages has led me to believe that the first part of the judgment will involve an attack coming from the North by an invading army. Scriptures in Jeremiah and Revelation tell us that the attack is likened to what happened to Sodom and Gomorrah and will involve a sudden destruction with fire and a destroying wind that will happen in one hour. The noise of the destruction will move the earth; and the shipmasters will not want to come near us for fear. I ask, for fear of what? What type of destruction is swift, involves smoke, wind, fire, burning, moves the earth, and will cause shipmasters to not want to come near? This is most likely referring to nuclear weapons being unleashed against America in an "all out" attack.

Here is what Lt. Colonel Thomas E. Bearden, writing in his book, *Fer De Lance*, updated for 2002, said about the possibility and vulnerability of America burning:

> If attacked, our ground forces will be as vulnerable as sitting ducks, out on the hot sandy desert with no place to hide. America's cities and outmoded ABM systems will not protect us...we can expect to be attacked on all sides, with nuclear bombs, neutron bombs, EMPs, and the longitudinal electromagnetic interferometer waves that will come down upon us as fire from heaven. America will burn ...

I am sorry to say that whether you believe it or not, America as a nation is due to be judged in the 70th Week of Daniel by what looks to be an all-out nuclear attack. We will discuss the timing of this attack in the next chapter. After this first judgment, America will be totally decimated.

> Your mother shall be sore confounded; she that bare you shall be ashamed: behold, the hindermost of the nations shall be a wilderness, a dry land, and a desert. Because of the wrath of the Lord it shall not be inhabited, but it shall be wholly desolate: every one that goeth by Babylon shall be astonished, and hiss at all her plagues. (Jer. 50:12-13)

> Therefore the wild beasts of the desert with the wild beasts of the islands shall dwell there, and the owls shall dwell therein: and it shall be no more inhabited for ever; neither shall it be dwelt in from generation to generation. As God overthrew Sodom and Gomorrah and the neighbour cities thereof, saith the Lord; so shall no man abide there, neither shall any son of man dwell therein. (Jer. 50:39,40)

These verses indicate that, as a result of the first attack, America will become uninhabitable and likened to a desert.

The second and final judgment upon America will come near the end of the 70th Week as recorded in Revelation 16:

> And the great city was divided into three parts, and the cities of the nations fell: and great Babylon came in remembrance before God, to give unto her the cup of the wine of the fierceness of his wrath. And every island fled away, and the mountains were not found. And there fell upon men a great hail out of heaven, every stone about the weight of a talent: and men blasphemed God because of the plague of the hail; for the plague thereof was exceeding great." (Rev. 16:19-21)

> And a mighty angel took up a stone like a great millstone, and cast it into the sea, saying, Thus with violence shall that great city Babylon be thrown down, and shall be found no more at all. (Rev. 18:21)

So we see that this second judgment will occur at the return of Christ at the end of the 70th Week and will result in America not being found any more. This final destruction will probably occur as a result of the horrendous earthquake that will shake the world, causing every island to disappear and every mountain to be leveled, and America will sink into the ocean and be covered over by the waves forever:

> The sea is come up upon Babylon: she is covered with the multitude of the waves thereof. (Jer. 51:42)

> Thus with violence shall that great city Babylon be thrown down, and shall be found no more at all. (Rev. 18:21)

O America, I wish it were not true. Your sins have reached unto heaven and you will be smitten. The country that we love so dear, that was founded upon Christian principles and used to stand for righteousness, now promotes wickedness and will receive her just deserts. The scriptures will be fulfilled; America will be destroyed. If we repent — The only hope for America — I believe God would spare America just as He spared Nineveh when that city repented. The most grievous sin, abortion, needs to stop immediately! We also need to stop the pornography, the illicit sex, the flow of liquor, the drugs, the gambling, the witchcraft, and the flow of raw sewage coming out of the cesspool of Hollywood. America needs to stop its sin now! If we repent, maybe the Lord will have mercy upon us. But the scriptures tell us that America, like Sodom and Gomorrah, will not repent but will suffer the full blow of God's wrath. God hath numbered thy kingdom, and finished it. Thou art weighed in the balances, and art found wanting. You will receive your just reward.

O beautiful for spacious skies, for amber waves of grain, for purple mountain majesties above the fruited plain! America! America! God shed his grace on thee and you refused His Grace and will be engulfed by sea to shining sea! O America! O America! How I wish it were not true. I pray that many would be brought to repentance before it is too late.

Chapter 9
The Fourth Beast

Have you ever heard the term "New World Order?" That is the term given to the coming one world government. Former President Bush made reference to the NWO in several speeches. *The Washington Times* recently reported on the fact that President George Bush called for just such a New World Order while giving a speech in Canada:

> HALIFAX, Nova Scotia — President Bush yesterday challenged international leaders to create a new world order, declaring pre-September 11 multilateralism outmoded and asserting that freedom from terrorism will come only through pre-emptive action against enemies of democracy.[62]

In his inauguration speech, President Bush also acknowledged that the United States is going forward with the plan set about to bring in the "new order of the ages" or in other words the New World Order.[63] This coming one world government, NWO, was foreseen by Daniel thousands of years ago in a vision.

> After this I saw in the night visions, and behold a fourth beast, dreadful and terrible, and strong exceedingly; and it had great iron teeth: it devoured and brake in pieces, and stamped the residue with the feet of it: and it was diverse from all the beasts that were before it; and it had ten horns. I considered the horns, and, behold, there came up among them another little horn, before whom there were three of the first horns plucked up by the roots: and, behold, in this horn were eyes like the eyes of man, and a mouth speaking great things. (Dan 7:7-8)

> Then I would know the truth of the fourth beast…Thus he said, The fourth beast shall be the fourth kingdom upon earth,

---

[62] Curl, Joseph, *Bush Calls for Global Cooperation*. Washington Times, December 2, 2004.
[63] Bush transcript, Fox News;
http://www.foxnews.com/printer_friendly_story/0,3566,144976,00.html

> which shall be diverse from all kingdoms, and shall devour the whole earth, and shall tread it down, and break it in pieces. And the ten horns out of this kingdom are ten kings that shall arise: and another shall rise after them; and he shall be diverse from the first, and he shall subdue three kings. And he shall speak great words against the most High, and shall wear out the saints of the most High, and think to change times and laws: and they shall be given into his hand until a time and times and the dividing of time. But the judgment shall sit, and they shall take away his dominion, to consume and to destroy it unto the end. And the kingdom and dominion, and the greatness of the kingdom under the whole heaven, shall be given to the people of the saints of the most High, whose kingdom is an everlasting kingdom, and all dominions shall serve and obey him. (Dan 7:19-27)

The apostle John also saw a vision of the end times demonic world kingdom in Revelation 13.

> And I stood upon the sand of the sea, and saw a beast rise up out of the sea, having seven heads and ten horns, and upon his horns ten crowns, and upon his heads the name of blasphemy. And the beast which I saw was like unto a leopard, and his feet were as the feet of a bear, and his mouth as the mouth of a lion: and the dragon gave him his power, and his seat, and great authority. And I saw one of his heads as it were wounded to death; and his deadly wound was healed: and all the world wondered after the beast. And they worshipped the dragon which gave power unto the beast: and they worshipped the beast, saying, Who is like unto the beast? who is able to make war with him? And there was given unto him a mouth speaking great things and blasphemies; and power was given unto him to continue forty and two months. And he opened his mouth in blasphemy against God, to blaspheme his name, and his tabernacle, and them that dwell in heaven. And it was given unto him to make war with the saints, and to overcome them: and power was given him over all kindreds, and tongues, and nations. And all that dwell upon the earth shall worship him, whose names are not written in the book of life of the Lamb slain from the foundation of the world. (Rev 13:1-8)

This most dreadful world empire represented by the fourth beast will be controlled by the devil himself, of which the antichrist will be the leader for the last 3.5 years of the 70th Week. The NWO, the final world kingdom, will be the supreme entity on the earth during the end-times, and this final world kingdom will directly and indirectly affect many people's lives. They will be responsible for much of what occurs on the earth during the 70th Week and directly responsible for the first 5 seals. I feel it is necessary for people to know about the NWO so that people would not be caught off guard by their actions. The more you know about the NWO, the more you can help others avoid the great deception that is coming and that is already at work in the world today.

What Is the New World Order?

Throughout the ages many people—starting with Adam and Eve—have been deceived into following satan and doing his bidding. For the last couple of hundred years, satan has gathered a group of people whose goal has been to take over the world and form a one-world government. This group of people could best be called "the illuminati." And can refer to any group which has "seen the light" and been "illuminated" in the satanic way described above. This would include high level Masons, Theosophists, Knights Templar, satanists, pagans, and New Age adherents. All of these groups are very similar in belief.[64]

Here is a quote from New Age adherent and promoter David Spangler that shows the satan/Illuminati/New Age connection.

---

[64] Hitler was an illuminati who masqueraded as a Christian and was part of a satanic group called the Thule Society. Here is what he said: "I got Illumination...from the Freemasons....There is one dangerous element...I have copied from the Freemasons. They form a sort of priestly nobility. They have developed an esoteric doctrine....imparted through the medium of symbols and mysterious rites in degrees of initiation...by working on the imagination through magic and symbols of a cult — all this is the dangerous element that I have taken over. Don't you see that our party must be of this character?.... An order, the hierarchical Order of a secular priesthood." (*Morals and Dogma.* p.60.) Beware of leaders who proclaim to be Christians but their actions speak differently, especially if they have associations with the illuminati or veiled satanic groups and especially if they make statements like "we all worship the same God." Christians are to obey the government (Rom 13:1) and "honor the king" (I Pet 2:17). But that does not mean that Christians should blindly follow leaders or the government in disobeying the Lord.

> Lucifer is the angel of man's inner light....Lucifer, like Christ, stands at the door of man's consciousness and knocks....If man says, 'Come in,' Lucifer becomes....the being who carries...the light of wisdom....Lucifer is literally the angel of experience. He is an agent of God's love...and we move into a new age...each of us in some way is brought to that point which I term the Luceriferic initiation....It is one that many people now, and in the days ahead, will be facing, for it is an initiation into the New Age.[65]

In recent years, Illuminati have risen to the top of world and national politics. Here is a list of a few of the reported modern day Illuminati groups: The Carnegies, The CFR, The Bilderbergers, The Rothschilds, and the Tri Lateral Commission. Illuminati are in key world positions and control much of what happens in the world. Listen to what Jim Searcy has to say about the power and control of the Illuminati:

> Do not think for a moment you are going to vote the Illuminati out of office. They control the major and minor political parties. They control the process of government, they control the process of information flow, they control the process of creating money and finally they control Christendom. (However, God controls the hearts of His people.) In short, the Illuminati are generational satanic bloodlines which have gained the most power. A generational satanist described the Illuminati as "satan's elite." The Illuminati is the secret occult oligarchies which rule the world. God Himself has told us that the whole world lies in the power of the wicked one. Indeed a small group of satanic families control their nation and the world from behind the scenes. They have satanic power through their secret societies and exercise this power from behind the scenes.[66]

By their own admission, Illuminati also control the major media outlets;

---

[65] Ibid. p.140
[66] Searcy Jim. *The Who, What, and Why of the Illuminati.*

> We are grateful to *The Washington Post, The New York Times, Time Magazine* and other great publications whose directors have attended our meetings and respected their promises of discretion for almost forty years. It would have been impossible for us to develop our plan for the world if we had been subjected to the lights of publicity during those years. But, the world is now more sophisticated and prepared to march towards a world government. The supranational sovereignty of an intellectual elite and world bankers is surely preferable to the national auto-determination practiced in past centuries. —David Rockefeller, Baden-Baden, Germany 1991, Master Conspiring Globalist

Much research has been done about the Illuminati and the coming New World Order. The Conspiracy Archive, for example, has written a great article giving an overview of the Illuminati and its players.[67] There are also a myriad of books available on the subject.

Former satanist Doc Marquis had this to say about how satan has deceived the illuminati into joining with him to take over the world.

> According to their religious philosophy, the Illuminati believe: that in the beginning, Lucifer was equal to GOD in all things. However, as the millenniums rolled by, GOD became jealous of Lucifer's equality, and had him, and all those who followed him, thrown out of heaven. Right now, the Illuminati are convinced that they are summoning up enough of "the force," so that at the Battle of Armageddon, they'll kill GOD and the Holy Spirit, and put Lucifer on the throne where they feel he rightfully belongs.[68]

And yes, one day God will allow satan and his cohorts to take over the world at least, temporarily. They will take over the world during the last 3.5 years of the 70th Week, when the antichrist is given authority over all nations, tribes, and kingdoms. "And there was given unto him a mouth speaking great things and blasphemies; and power was given unto him to continue forty and two months." (Rev 13:5) Of course they will not kill God, as they believe. They will be utterly decimated at the battle of Armageddon (Rev. 19:20).

---

[67] http://www.conspiracyarchive.com/NWO/Illuminati.htm
[68] "Let's Talk Illuminati 2000," http://hometown.aol.com/ncscia/politics/

This coming New World Order has an intricate plan to take over the world. Its plan was first voiced by Masonry in the 1700s as detailed by historian Bernard Fay.

> Masonry, having thus ensured the political unity of England, started a new task: to try to unify political principles and customs throughout the world…. In a century when the conflicting religious denominations had reached a dead-lock, the only way for humanity to achieve unity was through freemasonry.[69]

So we can see that the Masons were the first ones to actively promote this. We will briefly discuss Masonry to try and understand what and who they are. But before we do that, let me say that within Masonry, there is an organization within an organization and the vast majority of Masons know nothing about its real meaning or purpose. Here is what David Bay, director of Cutting Edge ministries, has to say about this double organization: "One organization is deliberately lied to and misled with false interpretations, while the inner organization knows the spiritual Truth of Freemasonry, and embraces it with heart, soul, and mind."[70]

Masons themselves admit that there is a double organization. Here is what Mason Manly P. Hall said about this:

> Freemasonry is a fraternity within a fraternity—an outer organization concealing an inner brotherhood of the elect…the one visible and the other invisible. The visible society…devote themselves to ethical, educational, fraternal, patriotic, and humanitarian concerns. The invisible society is a secret and most august fraternity whose members are dedicated to the service of a mysterious *arcannum arcandrum.*[71]

Albert Pike, who was a highly revered Mason, reveals the purpose for this double organization:

---

[69] Cuddy, Dennis. p.20, Now is the Dawning of the New Age New World Order. 2000, Hearthstone publishing, Oklahoma City.
[70] Bay, David. Freemasonry—Two Organizations, One Visible, The Other Invisible. Cutting Edge Newsletter.
[71] Hall, Manly. Lectures on Ancient Philosophy. P. 433.

> Masonry, like all Religions, all mysteries, Hermeticism, and Alchemy, conceals its secrets from all except the Adepts and Sages, or the Elect, and uses false explanations and misinterpretations of its symbols to mislead those who deserve only to be misled; to conceal the Truth, which it calls light, and draw them away from it.[72]

Pike was a genius and was able to read and write in 16 different languages, and was the grand commander of North American Freemasonry from 1859-1891. He was also an avowed satanist and was known to have a bracelet in which he used to summon satan. Pike's teachings revealed much about the true meaning of Masonry. In 1858, in a speech entitled "The Meaning of Masonry," Pike stated, "There is no....independent and self existent Evil principle in rebellion against God....Evil is merely apparent; and all is in reality good and perfect."[73] In 1871, Pike published *Morals and Dogma,* detailing aspects of Masonry in which he revealed the true goal of Masonry:

> Masonry is a search after light: the search leads us directly back, as you see, to the Kabalah....Kabalah alone consecrates the alliance of the Universal Reason and the Divine Word....Everything scientific and grand in the religious dreams of all Illuminati... is borrowed from the Kabalah; all Masonic associations owe to it their secrets and their symbols.... Liberty of thought, Equality of all men in the eye of God, universal fraternity! A new doctrine, a new religion; the old primitive truth uttered once again... For the initiates, this [the devil] is not a person but a Force, created for good, but which may serve for evil. It is the instrument of Liberty or Free Will.... Lucifer, the Son of the Morning! Is it he who bears the Light, and with its splendors intolerable, blinds feeble, sensual, or selfish souls? Doubt it not... Masonry is a worship... Every Masonic lodge is a temple of religion; and its teachings are instruction in religion .... The world will soon come to us for its Sovereigns and Pontiffs. We shall constitute the equilibrium of the universe, and be rulers over the masters of the world.[74]

---

[72] Pike, Albert. Morals and Dogma. P. 103.
[73] Ibid, p.33
[74] Ibid, p.33-34

Masonry is basically another form of satan worship in which the devotee tries to become an "illumined one," where satan is a force that can be used for good or evil. But remember Pike's first comment. "Evil is merely apparent; and all is in reality good and perfect." Thus, if you combine the two, then in Masonry thinking, satan becomes a force for good and only apparent evil, which in reality is good and perfect. We know different, but that is what Masonry doctrine teaches. Notice also that this article brings out the meaning of the word "Illuminati"; it is those who have searched after the "light," which is satan, and have found it. Thus, Masons can be considered to be "Illuminati." In fact a group in Paris originally called Illuminati changed their name to Adepts in 1772 and then Freemasons in 1778.

Deceitful Takeover

The Illuminati have a plan to take over the world, and they have been methodically following their plan. Their plan, involving America as a key player, was first conceived on May 1, 1776.[75]

> I was reminded of a similar occasion when five men went into a cave near Ingolstadt, Bavaria, on May 1st, 1776. It was Dr. Adam Weishaupt, who with four other men, met in the cave at the behest of the Rothschild banking cartel to bring forth a conspiratorial plan to take over the world and present it one day to their god Lucifer. In that cave, these five men consulted with an invisible force that they called the controlling unknown. This "force" gave them the plan to recruit members of their new organization, which would become known as the Illuminati. They would conceal themselves by hiding in the high levels of the Masonic Lodge until they could foment revolutions and three world wars until their objective was achieved.[76]

George Washington, in a letter in which he wrote to Reverend G. W. Snyder in 1798, acknowledged the Illuminati plan and their connection with Free Masonry.

Mount Vernon, September 25, 1798.

---

[75] Cutting Edge News Article, #1756
[76] http://lasttrumpetnewsletter.org/2009/02_09.html

Sir: Many apologies are due to you, for my not acknowledging the receipt of your obliging favour of the 22d. Ulto, and for not thanking you, at an earlier period, for the Book you had the goodness to send me.

I have heard much of the nefarious, and dangerous plan, and doctrines of the Illuminati, but never saw the Book until you were pleased to send it to me. The same causes which have prevented my acknowledging the receipt of your letter have prevented my reading the Book, hitherto; namely, the multiplicity of matters which pressed upon me before, and the debilitated state in which I was left after, a severe fever had been removed. And which allows me to add little more now, than thanks for your kind wishes and favourable sentiments, except to correct an error you have run into, of my Presiding over the English lodges in this Country. The fact is, I preside over none, nor have I been in one more than once or twice, within the last thirty years. I believe notwithstanding, that none of the Lodges in this Country are contaminated with the principles ascribed to the Society of the Illuminati.

With respect I am &c

George Washington [77]

I have heard much of the nefarious and dangerous plan and doctrines of the Illuminati. It was not my intention to doubt the doctrines of the Illuminati and the principles of Jacobinism had not spread in the United States. On the contrary no one is more satisfied of this fact than I am.
　　　—George Washington, *The Writings of George Washington*

It was even reported that John F Kennedy was going to expose the Illuminati plan and was assassinated for it.[78]

Unfortunately, Illuminati have used America in the past and will use her in the future to play a large role in bringing about the New World order. Want some evidence? Take a look at the back of a dollar bill. In the two circles are depicted both sides of The Great Seal. The

---

[77] Fitzpatrick, John Clement. *The writings of George Washington* from the original manuscript George Washington. p.453
[78] Rainbowlt, p.16

pyramid is on one side of the Great Seal and the eagle on the other. The great seal is used to authenticate official U.S. documents.

Ever wonder what these symbols mean? The Cutting Edge has analyzed these mysterious symbols and what they reveal.

    The Pyramid represents the past. Note that the capstone of this pyramid is not in place, thus denoting an unfinished situation. This unfinished situation was planned to remain in effect until the Old World Order was destroyed and replaced with The New World Order.

    1.   Annuit Coeptis - "Announcing The Birth"
    2.   Novus Ordor Seclorum - "New World Order"
    3.   Capstone - Eye of Horus [Theocracy of Egyptian Mysticism] = Eye of satan or Lucifer
    4.   MDCCLXXVI on the bottom layer of stones = 1776 [May 1, Beltaine, Second High-Holy Day of the Year] On May 1, 1776, a New World Order was born when the Masters of the Illuminati was founded, whose foundation would be built upon depravity and rebellion. Its leader would be satan.
    5.   Thirteen Layers to the Pyramid = The number, '13' is the occult number of Depravity and Rebellion.[79]

    Here is another quote that not only brings out the meaning of the pyramid side of the seal but also the other side.

---

[79] Cutting Edge News Article, #1756

This is the Illuminati's pyramid symbol. There are "**13**" stacks of bricks on the 'all seeing eye' pyramid. The official national seal of the United States contains "**13**" arrows, "**13**" letters, "**13**" laurel leaves, "**13**" berries, "**13**" stars above the eagle in the form of a hexagram, "**13**" stripes on the shield. The "**9**" tail feathers indicate the "**9**" additional degrees of the York Rite of Freemasonry. Then the American eagle with 32 feathers on one wing and "**33**" on the other. There are "**33**" steps on the side of the pyramid representing the "**33**" degrees of Freemasonry.[80]

Here is what Alice Bailey who was the head of the House of Theosophy for many years and who's husband was a 33rd degree Mason said about the "all seeing eye" of satan depicted on the dollar bill.

> The Masonic movement …is the home of the Mysteries, and the seat of initiation. It holds in its symbolism the ritual of Diety, and the way of salvation is pictorially preserved in its work. The methods of Diety are demonstrated in its Temples, and under the All-seeing Eye the work can go forward. It is a far more occult organization than can be realized, and it is intended to be the training school for the coming advanced occultists.[81]

The seal also has a link to the coming third temple.

> We correctly link the symbolism of the All-Seeing Eye of Lucifer hovering over the unfinished pyramid on the back of the Dollar Bill to the coming prophesied Third Temple on the Temple Mount in Jerusalem! The Masons have been steadfastly determined since 1782 to seize control of the Temple Mount so they could resurrect Solomon's Temple for use by their Masonic Christ!
>
> Since this was the plan in 1782 when the Seals were created, the Masons made sure that the symbolism of the unfinished pyramid directly tied into their plan to rebuild Solomon's

---

[80] Rainbowlt, p.14
[81] Bailey, Alice. <u>Externalisation of the Hierarchy.</u> P.511

Temple. When the Masonic Christ (Antichrist) is planned to be the "Living Stone" to top off the unfinished pyramid![82]

So we can see that the symbol on the back of a dollar bill is an Illuminati symbol depicting the forthcoming New World Order, implying that America will play a large role in its formation. There are some "official" explanations concerning the meaning of the symbols on the Great Seal, but these are merely attempts to mask their true meaning.

Notice what happens when you draw a six-pointed star as depicted below. The points of the star point to the letters "MASON." Is that by coincidence or design? I have calculated the odds that the six points align with the letters "MASON" to be at least 380,000 to one.

It is also interesting to note that if you take the date of 1776 that appears in Roman numerals across the bottom of the pyramid as "MDCCLXXVI" and place each letter at the vertices of three successive triangles some interesting numbers appear.

---

[82] http://www.cuttingedge.org/detail.cfm?ID=1984

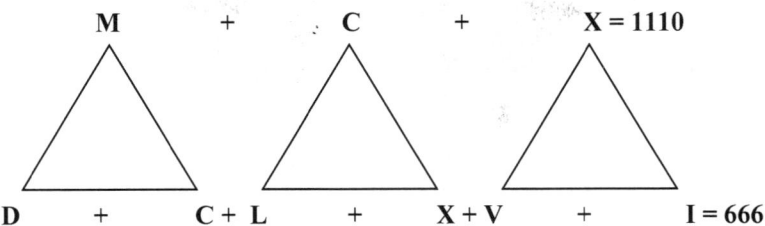

This may be pure coincidence, or it may be some veiled Illuminati message giving some information about the antichrist and or the establishment of the NWO. We know that 666 is the number of the antichrist, I can only speculate as to what the 1110 means, but it may be in reference to the timing of WWIII or another prophetically important event. It is interesting to note that in Babylon, they used a sexagesimal number system, and converting 1110 from a sexagesimal into a centesimal system, we get 1110 x 0.60 = **666**.[83]

The History of the Seal

The history of the seal is equally interesting and shows an Illuminati connection:

> Even though it was officially voted into creation by a meeting of Freemason Continental Congressmen in 1782, the symbol was hidden from public view for fear the American people would recognize it as being the satanic symbol it truly was.

> However, in 1935, the Guiding Spirit of President Roosevelt and Agriculture Secretary Wallace told them the time had arrived to put this symbol on the back of the One Dollar Silver Certificate, for the people had moved far, far away from their Christian roots and awareness of both the Bible and the "wiles" and "strategies" of satan.[84]

Henry Wallace, a friend of President Roosevelt, was also a prominent Freemason, and in 1934, he wrote about the significance of the Great Seal.

---

[83] http://www.greatdreams.com/political/invasion_of_america.htm
[84] Ibid,

> It will take a more definite recognition of the Grand Architect of the Universe before the apex stone [capstone of the pyramid] is finally fitted into place and this nation in the full strength of its power is in position to assume leadership among the nations in inaugurating 'the New Order of the Ages.'[85]

Not only is the great seal a symbol that links America to the Illuminati[86], but so is the architectural design of Washington D.C. We will not delve into that topic here, but here is the link to a Web site that expounds upon that topic.[87]

Thus from the above discussion, and realizing that America is the most powerful nation in the world, it is obvious that America will play a large role in bringing about the New World Order and "finishing the pyramid."

Writing about the coming NWO takeover of the United States, one Illuminati defector has indicated that each region of the United States has a designated "nerve center" or power base for regional activity. Each region has military compounds and bases hidden in remote, isolated areas or on large private estates used to train Illuminati in military techniques, hand-to-hand combat, crowd control, use of arms, and other aspects of military warfare. These are seen as necessary because the Illuminists believe that our government, as we know it, as well as the governments of most nations around the world, are destined to collapse.

These will be planned collapses, and they will occur in the following ways:

> The Illuminati has planned first for a financial collapse that will make the great depression look like a picnic. This will occur through the maneuvering of the great banks and financial institutions of the world, through stock manipulation, and interest rate changes. Most people will be indebted to the federal government through bank and credit card debt, etc. The governments will recall all debts

---

[85] Wallace, Henry A., 1934. Statesmanship and Religion. New York, Round Table Press, Inc, pp 78-79.
[86] If you would like to see some more evidence of the NWO on our money Google "twenty dollar bill twin towers"
[87] http://www.theforbiddenknowledge.com/chapter3/index.htm

> immediately, but most people will be unable to pay and will be bankrupted. This will cause generalized financial panic, which will occur simultaneously worldwide, as the Illuminists firmly believe in controlling people through finances....
>
> Next there will be a military takeover, region by region, as the government declares a state of emergency and martial law. People will have panicked, there will be an anarchical state in most localities, and the government will justify its move as being necessary to control panicked citizens. The cult trained military leaders and people under their direction will use arms as well as crowd control techniques to implement this new state of affairs. ...Military bases will be set up, in each locality (actually, they are already here, but are covert). In the next few years, they will go above ground and be revealed. Each locality will have regional bases and leaders to which they are accountable. The hierarchy will closely reflect the current covert hierarchy.[88]

Just recently a top Russian economic scholar predicted that the U.S. will break up into 6 regions.[89] They are even starting to prep our military to see who may or may not go along with this plan. Some military personnel have recently been given a questionnaire that included some very interesting questions.

> One of the subscribers to this newsletter recently sent me a questionnaire that was administered to him by a female brigadier general at Camp Lejuene. There were a total of 46 questions with four possible answers to each one: strongly disagree, disagree, strongly agree, and no opinion. Item number 45 reads as follows: "I would swear to the following code: I am an United Nations fighting person. I serve in the forces which maintain world peace and every nation's way of life. I am prepared to give my life in their defense." Item number 46 says: "The U.S. Government declares a ban on the possession, sale, transportation, and transfer of all non-sporting firearms. A thirty (30) day amnesty period is

---

[88] Makow, Henry. Illuminati Defector Speaks of Pervasive Conspiracy. http://www.rense.com/general30/Illuminatidefector.htm
[89] http://www.telegraph.co.uk/news/worldnews/northamerica/usa/3521671/US-will-collapse-and-break-up-Russian-analyst-predicts.html

permitted for these firearms to be turned over to local authorities. At the end of this period, a number of citizen groups refuse to turn over their firearms. Consider the following statement: I would fire upon U.S. citizens who refuse or resist confiscation of firearms banned by the U.S. government.[90]

The Larger Scheme

The New World Order will be a global effort; America will only play a part in this diabolical scheme. In the coming New World Order, the Illuminati plan and scripture indicates that the world will be divided up into 10 "spheres of influence." These 10 planned spheres of influence or super nation states are as follows:

1. North America
2. Western Europe
3. Japan
4. Australia, South Africa, and the rest of the market economy of the developed world.
5. Eastern Europe, including Russia
6. Latin America
7. North Africa and the Middle East
8. Tropical Africa
9. South and Southeast Asia
10. China[91]

Some of these "super states" already exist and some are in the process of being formed. With the formation of NAFTA, the planned building of a U.S./Canadian/Mexican highway,[92] the planned Amero,[93] and the linking of the U.S. and Canadian armies,[94] super nation #1 is beginning to be formed. I believe that these 10 super nation states are what the ten horns represent in the vision given to Daniel and John.

After this I saw in the night visions, and behold a fourth beast, dreadful and terrible, and strong exceedingly; and it

---

[90] Meyer, David. Last Trumpet Newsletter July 2004. http://www.lasttrumpetministries.org/2004/July2004.html
[91] Cutting Edge News Article #1002
[92] http://www.youtube.com/watch?v=DAs7XZVgKhI&feature=related
[93] http://www.youtube.com/watch?v=6hiPrsc9g98
[94] http://www.chuckbaldwinlive.com/c2008/cbarchive_20080226.html

had great iron teeth: it devoured and brake in pieces, and stamped the residue with the feet of it: and it was diverse from all the beasts that were before it; and it had ten horns. I considered the horns, and, behold, there came up among them another little horn, before whom there were three of the first horns plucked up by the roots: and, behold, in this horn were eyes like the eyes of man, and a mouth speaking great things. (Dan 7:7,8)

And I stood upon the sand of the sea, and saw a beast rise up out of the sea, having seven heads and ten horns, and upon his horns ten crowns, and upon his heads the name of blasphemy. (Rev. 13:1)

I saw a woman sit upon a scarlet coloured beast, full of names of blasphemy, having seven heads and ten horns... And the angel said unto me, Wherefore didst thou marvel? I will tell thee the mystery of the woman, and of the beast that carrieth her, which hath the seven heads and ten horns....And the ten horns which thou sawest are ten kings, which have received no kingdom as yet; but receive power as kings one hour with the beast. These have one mind, and shall give their power and strength unto the beast....And the ten horns which thou sawest upon the beast, these shall hate the whore, and shall make her desolate and naked, and shall eat her flesh, and burn her with fire. For God hath put in their hearts to fulfil his will, and to agree, and give their kingdom unto the beast, until the words of God shall be fulfilled. And the woman which thou sawest is that great city, which reigneth over the kings of the earth. (Rev. 17:3-18)

In the latter vision, I believe the whore riding upon the beast represents America/Babylon symbolically. The beast represents the seventh world kingdom, the New World Order. The ten horns represent the 10 "super nation" states that the world will be divided up into as indicated above. America will be the leading/controlling nation, the 10 spheres of influence under the leadership of the antichrist will eventually turn against America and "burn her with fire" and give the kingdom over to the antichrist. This is also reflected in the Daniel passage where it indicates that the "little horn" will "pluck up" three of the horns or will destroy three super nation states.

Why will the NWO turn against America, the very country that was so instrumental in bringing the NWO about? Here is what white magic occultist David Icke said about that.

> The United States may be the world superpower today and that's precisely what the Illuminati planned for it to be in the agenda for the centralization of global control....
>
> But while America is being used now as the vehicle to impose this current stage of the fascist agenda it is not meant to continue as the superpower. In fact, destroying that status and breaking the spirit of America is fundamental in the installation of the Illuminati global dictatorship.
>
> The reason is this: a world government (dictatorship) and a superpower do not go together. The Illuminati dictatorship is meant to be the only superpower and for that to happen the United States must be brought into line.[95]

This is typical of how satan works. He will come to someone and promise them and give them all kinds of things, use them to do his will, and then destroy them.

For any Illuminati or occultists who may be reading this book, let me set the record straight. satan was never equal with God. He was created as the greatest angel, he chose to rebel against God, was defeated and will eventually be locked up in Hell forever. The devil knows this, and he hates God and hates all men because they are made in God's image. His objective is to take as many people to Hell with him as possible, and he will stop at nothing to achieve his goals. Hell is a place of burning and torment that will last forever, there will be no "partying" there as satan has told some of his followers. If you have fallen prey to the devil's deception, flee from him and fall on your knees before God and receive the Lord Jesus Christ as your Savior before it is too late. No one is too sinful to receive the love and forgiveness of the Lord Jesus Christ. "And it shall come to pass, that whosoever shall call on the name of the Lord shall be saved" (Acts 2:21).

---

[95] Icke, David. *The Plan is to Use America to Break America.*

How Will the Plan Unfold?

How will the culmination of this plan produce the New World Order with the antichrist as the world ruler? The framework of this plan was given to Albert Pike on January 22, 1870. This plan was kept secret for many years, but was revealed by former Illuminati, Doc Marquis, in his book *Secrets of the Illuminati*. Marquis tells us that Pike received this plan from a "guiding spirit." In other words, he received this plan for the establishment of the New World Order from satan or one of his demons. The major components of the plan entailed the fighting of three world wars.

The First World War was designed to overthrow czarist Russia and establish communism.[96] The Second World War was to be started by Britain and Germany and had as its eventual goal the strengthening of Russia into a superpower.[97] As we know from history, both objectives were fulfilled. Officially, some claim Pike's letter is a fake. However the contents of the letter were revealed to the public just after WWI, and the fact that WWII fulfilled the plan in the letter is proof that it is authentic.

The Third World War is supposed to be triggered by war between Judaism and Islam and will eventually spread to the whole world. Listen to what Albert Pike said about WWIII:

> The third World War must be formented by taking advantage of the differences caused by the 'agentur' of the 'Illuminati' between the political Zionists and the leaders of Islamic World. The war must be conducted in such a way that Islam and political Zionism mutually destroy each other. Meanwhile the other nations, once more divided on the issue will be constrained to fight to the point of complete physical, moral, spiritual and economical exhaustion...Then everywhere, the citizens, obliged to defend themselves against the world minority of revolutionaries, will exterminate those destroyers of civilization, and the multitude, disillusioned with Christianity...will receive the true light through the universal manifestation of the pure doctrine of Lucifer, brought finally out in public view.[98]

---

[96] "Who Was Albert Pike?" http://www.threeworldwars.com/albert-pike.htm
[97] Ibid
[98] *Who Was Albert Pike?*

Another illuminati writer, H.G. Wells, has further detailed that WWIII will start from an event that occurs in Basra. He was given this information from a demonic Guiding Spirit in 1933 in which he wrote about in his book entitled, *"The Shape of Things To Come."*

> "...the plan for the 'Modern World-State' (New World Order) would succeed in its third attempt (WWIII) and would come out of something that would occur in Basra, Iraq."

In light of their plans we can see that WWIII will probably be triggered by the Middle East conflict and in light of the planned destruction will involve nuclear weapons. Although there are too many details to go into here, what readers should take from this is that satan has planned three world wars to establish the New World Order. Their plan also calls for the possibility of using nuclear weapons to kill many people "... a very short but very deadly global war using nuclear weapons upon select population concentrations was contemplated and to tell you the truth, was not ruled out ..."[99] The ultimate goal of WWIII is to usher in the New World Order with the antichrist as the ruler of the world. According to former Illuminati satanist, Doc Marquis, once World War III begins the antichrist will arise on the world scene in 13 weeks (91 days). Here is another interesting tidbit; The book *Atlas Shrugged* is reported to be an illuminati fictional novel which portrays their plan to take over the world written in code. The timetable presented in the book ends with this "When the lights of New York City go out for the last time, we will have the World!" WWIII could be the event to turn the lights off in NYC for it would surely be a target of such an attack.

Tying It Back to the Seals

Some think that this Illuminati-planned WWIII will occur after the Abomination of Desolation and before the rapture at the sixth seal. There are several verses which lead me to a different conclusion. I believe that WWIII will start before the Abomination of Desolation. Look at Matt. 24:4-9:

> And Jesus answered and said unto them, Take heed that no man deceive you. For many shall come in my name, saying, I am Christ; and shall deceive many. And ye shall hear of wars

---

[99] Cooper, Behold a Pale Horse. p. 167, 177

and rumours of wars: see that ye be not troubled: for all these things must come to pass, but the end is not yet. For nation shall rise against nation, and kingdom against kingdom: and there shall be famines, and pestilences, and earthquakes, in divers places. All these are the beginning of sorrows. Then shall they deliver you up to be afflicted, and shall kill you: and ye shall be hated of all nations for my name's sake.

Notice the timing of events in this passage: deception, wars, and rumors of wars with nation arising against nation and kingdom against kingdom, famines, pestilences, and earthquakes. I believe the nation arising against nation and kingdom against kingdom is in reference to WWIII. All these events are called "the beginning of sorrows." Then, after these sorrows, the persecution of believers occurs. As we mentioned before, the chronological order of these events mirrors the events listed in the first five seals. Thus this passage places the great wars of nation arising against nation and kingdom arising against kingdom before the persecution of believers (Seal 5) and the pestilences and famines (Seal 3). Thus, the great wars listed here would either have to occur during Seal 1 or 2. Thus, I conjecture that the nation arising against nation and kingdom arising against kingdom is the Illuminati planned WWIII and will start during Seal 1 or 2, probably Seal 2.[100]

God commands Israel to flee into the wilderness at the Abomination of Desolation and when she is surrounded by armies.

---

[100] Some have cited Luke 21:12-24 as evidence that WWIII occurs after the Abomination of Desolation. One reason that they surmise this is because the passage says; "But before all these, they shall lay their hands on you, and persecute you, delivering you up to the synagogues, and into prisons, being brought before kings and rulers for my name's sake." Thus, they assert that the things mentioned above all happen after Seal 5. If you just take the Luke passage alone, that is a logical conclusion, but taking into account the Matthew and Mark passage, which places the "nation arising against nation" before the Abomination of Desolation, this creates a contradiction. Scripture cannot contradict scripture; thus there has to be another interpretation for the Luke passage. The other interpretation is that the persecution that would happen before all these sorrows is the persecution that the first century Christians endured. Here is what Ryrie has to say about this in his *Study Bible*. "Luke 21-7 *when ...will these things happen?* There is a dual perspective in Christ's answer—the destruction of Jerusalem in A.D. 70 and the tribulation days just prior to his Second Coming." So I believe that the persecution that will occur before the great wars mentioned in the Luke passage is in reference to the persecution that the first century Christians endured.

The fact that they are told to flee at these two events infers that the events occur at the same time.

> When ye therefore shall see the Abomination of Desolation, spoken of by Daniel the prophet, stand in the holy place, (whoso readeth, let him understand:) Then let them which be in Judaea flee into the mountains: (Matt. 24:15,16)

> And when ye shall see Jerusalem compassed with armies, then know that the desolation thereof is nigh. Then let them which are in Judaea flee to the mountains; and let them which are in the midst of it depart out; and let not them that are in the countries enter thereinto. (Luke 21:20,21)

This military takeover by the antichrist will leave Israel ravished.

War of Gog-Magog

There is another end-times war we need to examine. This war, recorded in Ezekiel 38–39 and other parts of scripture, is often called the War of Gog-Magog. In this war, the nations identified as Gog and Magog will attempt destroy Israel and will suffer a terrible defeat. The identity of these nations is debated, and ranges from Northern Egypt and Libya to Russia, but the consensus seems to be that this will be a Muslim/Russian attack against Israel.

When will this war take place? This war will most likely start after the antichrist takes over the world and will be a reigniting of WWIII after the false peace of the antichrist breaks down. There are several verses in Ezekiel that show that the final destruction of this war will occur on the day of the Lord. Ezekiel 38:18-20, for example, says that on the day of the destruction of Gog and Magog, there will be a great shaking in all the earth.

> And it shall come to pass at the same time when Gog shall come against the land of Israel, saith the Lord God, that my fury shall come up in my face. For in my jealousy and in the fire of my wrath have I spoken, surely in that day there shall be a *great shaking in the land of Israel*. So that the fishes of the sea, and the fowls of the heaven, and the beasts of the field, and all creeping things that creep upon the earth, *and all the men that are upon the face of the earth, shall shake at*

my presence, and the mountains shall be thrown down, and the steep places shall fall, and every wall shall fall to the ground.

This great earthquake coincides precisely with one of the events of the sixth seal and the Day of the Lord. "And I beheld when he had opened the sixth seal, and, lo, there was a great earthquake; and the sun became black as sackcloth of hair, and the moon became as blood" (Rev. 6:12). The passage goes on to further describe this earthquake, which is so severe that all the mountains and islands are moved out of their places. This coordinates precisely with the Ezekiel passage above that says "and the mountains shall be thrown down, and the steep places shall fall, and every wall shall fall to the ground."

There is another event listed in Ezekiel concerning the Gog – Magog war that shows that this war culminates with the Day of the Lord event. Consider this verse from Eze. 39:4: "Thou shalt fall upon the mountains of Israel, thou, and all thy bands, and the people that is with thee: I will give thee unto the ravenous birds of every sort, and to the beasts of the field to be devoured." This passage tells us that "ravenous birds of every sort" will eat the defeated armies of the Gog-Magog war. Where else do we see birds eating the flesh of dead bodies? Jesus spoke about it in Luke 17:34-37 and Matt 24:25-28 in connection with the rapture:

> I tell you, in that night there shall be two men in one bed; the one shall be taken, and the other shall be left. Two women shall be grinding together; the one shall be taken, and the other left. Two men shall be in the field; the one shall be taken, and the other left. And they answered and said unto him, Where, Lord? And he said unto them, Wheresoever the body is, thither will the eagles be gathered together.

> Behold, I have told you before. Wherefore if they shall say unto you, Behold, he is in the desert; go not forth: behold, he is in the secret chambers; believe it not. For as the lightning cometh out of the east, and shineth even unto the west; so shall also the coming of the Son of man be. For wheresoever the carcase is, there will the eagles be gathered together.

The three passages above describing the birds eating the flesh of dead bodies links the end of the Gog – Magog war, the rapture, and of kingdoms, the beauty of the Chaldees' excellency, shall be as when God overthrew Sodom and Gomorrah. It shall never be inhabited, neither shall it be dwelt in from generation to generation: neither shall the Arabian pitch tent there; neither shall the shepherds make their fold there. But wild beasts of the desert shall lie there; and their houses shall be full of doleful creatures; and owls shall dwell there, and Satyrs shall dance there. And the wild beasts of the islands shall cry in their desolate houses, and dragons in their pleasant palaces: and her time is near to come, and her days shall not be prolonged.

Putting all of these verses together tell us that the destruction of end-times Babylon will occur after the Abomination of Desolation, after the sixth seal is opened, and as part of the wrath of God. We know that God's wrath starts after the rapture at the Day of the Lord. Therefore we can place the destruction of end-times Babylon/America to occur after the rapture. It is possible that this destruction occurs at the same time that Gog and Magog are destroyed.

Another interesting verse that we should consider, which may connect the Gog-Magog war with the destruction of end-times Babylon, is Eze. 39:6. It says: "And I will send a fire on Magog, and among them that dwell carelessly in the isles: and they shall know that I am the Lord." This verse indicates that God will not only allow Gog and Magog to be destroyed by fire, but also those that dwell carelessly in the isles.

Isaiah 47:1-9 also talks about the destruction to end-times Babylon and makes the connection with the "careless dwellers."

> Come down, and sit in the dust, O virgin daughter of Babylon, sit on the ground: there is no throne, O daughter of the Chaldeans: for thou shalt no more be called tender and delicate...for thou shalt no more be called, The lady of kingdoms...And thou saidst, I shall be a lady for ever: so that thou didst not lay these things to thy heart, neither didst remember the latter end of it. Therefore hear now this, thou that art given to pleasures, *that dwellest carelessly*, that sayest in thine heart, I am, and none else beside me; I shall not sit as a widow, neither shall I know the loss of children: But these two things shall come to thee *in a moment in one day*, the loss of children, and widowhood: they shall come

upon thee in their perfection for the multitude of thy sorceries, and for the great abundance of thine enchantments.

This passage refers to the inhabitants of end-times Babylon as those "that dwell carelessly." This may connect the destruction that end-times Babylon/America will receive after the rapture, with the Gog/Magog war.

Putting It All Together

Let's put all the pieces of the puzzle together and come up with a comprehensive "most probable" picture of major end times events. The 70th Week of Daniel may begin silently—without the occurrence of a major event—or it may begin with the signing of the peace treaty. The first four seals will be opened sometime during the 70th Week before the abomination of desolation. With the opening of the first seal the NWO starts to take over the world, seals 2, 3, and 4 unleash WWIII, economic collapse, famine, death, etc. on the world. As a result of these tribulations the world will lay in ruins with ¼ of its population now dead. The antichrist/false Messiah comes onto the scene with the solutions to the world's problems, including a peace treaty, and if the Illuminati plan is followed, this will occur 91 days after WWIII starts. He will then perform the Abomination of Desolation, at which Israel is commanded to flee. He will then take over the world on day 1260 and institute the mark of the beast, and begin persecuting Jews and Christians (Seal 5). A short time later the temporary peace will break down and WWIII will be reignited and the Gog-Magog war will begin. The rapture will occur just prior to the end of this war, which will begin the Day of the Lord period. This war will destroy three of the 10 spheres of influence — namely, Russia and her allies (the king of the North), Egypt and her allies (the king of the South), and America/Babylon. The antichrist will then be the supreme ruler of the world, with no one to stand in the way of his dictatorship. See the chart entitled "The Afflictions of the 70th Week" for a pictorial representation of this data.

Knowing that WWIII may shortly come to pass should you flee? There are two places mentioned in end-times biblical prophecy in which God tells people to leave; end-times Babylon and Judea:

> Flee out of the midst of Babylon, and deliver every man his soul: be not cut off in her iniquity; for this is the time of the

Lord's vengeance; he will render unto her a recompence. (Jer. 51:6)

We would have healed Babylon, but she is not healed: forsake her, and let us go every one into his own country: for her judgment reacheth unto heaven, and is lifted up even to the skies. (Jer. 51:9)

My people, go ye out of the midst of her, and deliver ye every man his soul from the fierce anger of the Lord. (Jer. 51:45)

And I heard another voice from heaven, saying, Come out of her, my people, that ye be not partakers of her sins, and that ye receive not of her plagues. (Rev. 18:4)

When ye therefore shall see the Abomination of Desolation, spoken of by Daniel the prophet, stand in the holy place, (whoso readeth, let him understand:) Then let them which be in Judaea flee into the mountains. (Mt 24:15,16)

God commands His people to leave end-times Babylon and Judea. If our timing of the destruction of end times Babylon is correct, then Christians will be raptured when this occurs. Therefore this verse is in reference to Jews and does not apply to Christians. The other place God tells people to flee is Judea. In the Mt. 24 passage above God tells the Jews to flee to the wilderness when the Abomination of Desolation occurs. This is when they are commanded to flee into the wilderness for 3.5 years while the gentiles, under the leadership of the antichrist, will be in control of Jerusalem. So if my analysis is correct concerning the timing of the Gog-Magog war and the destruction of America — that they will both occur after the Abomination of Desolation — then Jews should not only flee Judea after the Abomination of Desolation, but they should also flee from America. In regards to when and if one should flee we must also consider the second seal which suggests worldwide destruction and will most likely entail the beginning rounds of WWIII. Even though this first round of action in WWIII will not be as catastrophic as the second I would imagine that large population centers would be likely targets and a move to a more rural setting away from the big cities may be prudent.

Concerning the topics of WWIII, the Gog-Magog war, and the destruction of end-times Babylon and associated events: putting them in a timeline has been one of the most challenging things that I have wrestled with so far. There are many theories regarding these future events. Am I confident that I have put all the pieces of this part of the end-times puzzle together correctly? No, I am not, for as scripture says "For now we see through a glass, darkly; but then face to face: now I know in part; but then shall I know even as also I am known" (1 Cor. 13:12). There will be many events that will come into play during the end-times, to put them all together correctly is a daunting task that has bewildered many a more scholarly man than myself for years. What I have tried to do is take an honest and hard look at what all the scriptures teach—not just a select few—and come up with a scenario in which none of the many scriptures are contradicted. What I have just outlined before you is the result.

Am I confident that there will be a WWIII, Gog-Magog war, and destruction of end-times Babylon? Yes, I am. And with all of the recent events transpiring in the Middle East, and the world, it is not hard to imagine how the present hostilities could escalate into these prophesied wars especially if you take into account that it is looking like the ongoing Middle East conflict may soon involve nuclear weapons. In fact, the peace treaty of prophecy, the treaty of death that will divide the land, may be a prerequisite to start these wars. The "Road Map" originally proposed by President Bush calls for Israel retreat to its 1949 Armistice borders and to have the land for the Palestinians be "contiguous," which would effectively divide Israel into two sections. Mr. Netanyahu himself has also agreed to this two state solution. Consider what a Cutting Edge has to say about this initiative.

> Once the IDF repositions its forces as this plan dictates, the nation of Israel becomes a series of separated enclaves, and that is a military tactician's nightmare. Arafat's Palestinian paramilitary forces could attack key targets from within, forcing the IDF to fight in separated locations. Syria and Egypt would also be tempted to jump into the fray to take advantage of this unbelievable Israeli self-inflicted wound.[101]

---

[101] Cutting Edge news article #1864

Once Israel retreats to its 1949 borders and is divided, it will be very vulnerable to attack. Sometime after that is when the Muslim world, in accordance with Illuminati plans, will attack. Then, in response, Israel will retaliate with nuclear weapons, decimating the Arabs.

Scriptures mention one such outcome of this attack in Jer. 49:24: "The burden of Damascus. Behold, Damascus is taken away from being a city, and it shall be a ruinous heap." Damascus is the oldest city still in existence. But as the result of this future war, it will be a ruinous heap, which is indicative of a nuclear attack. This verse clearly establishes the fact that several passages in Jeremiah are in reference to end-times events, because Damascus is still in existence today and has never been a "ruinous heap" in its history. So the peace treaty may serve to set the stage for these wars including WWIII, which according to the Illuminati plan will usher in the antichrist.

The One World Religion

Not only is there a plan to produce a one-world government with the antichrist as the leader, but there is also a plan to produce a one-world religion. This plan, as heralded by the Illuminati, is entitled the New Jerusalem Covenant project. Bill Lambert, director of the New England House of Theosophy, presented this plan in August of 1991. A Cutting Edge News writer took notes on his speech. Here are some excerpts from his notes:

> Step one – Three global conferences must be held in order to give birth to the New World Order system.
>
> Step two – General fear of war needed to be instituted and maintained in order to provide the pressure needed to move the parties into this plan.
>
> Step three – International control over Jerusalem Religious areas and subsequent combined worship center for Jews, Christians, and Muslims.
>
> Step four – Roman Catholic Pope travels to Jerusalem to dedicate this new worship center, proclaiming that all religions of the world are now one. He is their head and the New World order religion is now official.

Step five – Antichrist will come to the world scene, after the world war has been fought to produce him."[102]

The three global conferences were held in August/September of 2000. These conferences consisted of a Global religious conference, a Global business meeting and a global political conference. The illuminati looked upon these conferences as birthing ceremonies for their New World Order.[103][104] The general fear of war, as outlined in step 2, has been maintained for a long time in the Middle East. Step 3 was shockingly proposed by Shimon Peres in 2003, and is also backed by former Popes. Popes have also called for step 4, in fact in the Pope's 2004 new years address, he called for a one-world religion. As of now steps 3 – 5 are yet to be fulfilled. We will have to wait and see when they come about. So not only do the illuminati have a plan to take over the world but they also have a plan to establish a one-world religion with the pope as the head.

The Proof is in the Cards

We have discussed several aspects of the plan of the Illuminati to take over the world and usher in the antichrist as their leader. Their plans have helped us to gain insight into formulating a proper chronological scenario and understanding of prophetic events listed in scripture. We have also examined several events that will transpire during the antichrist's reign and we have seen that he and his kingdom will come to swift and decisive end. As you see the ultimate goal of their plan is to create a situation in which the world will readily accept the antichrist as the world ruler. After the decimation brought to the world — unleashed in the first 5 seals — through the power of satan and his evil cohorts, the world will be ready for a solution. They will be ready for someone to bring peace to a war torn world, for someone to restore the economy, for someone to put food back on the table. The antichrist will present himself as the savior, the messiah. Unfortunately, the world will be lured into his trap.

---

[102] Cutting Edge news article #1842.
[103] Ibid.
[104] It is interesting to note that a day and a year after the "birthing ceremonies" was the infamous 9/11 tragedy. The time span of "A day and a year" is significant to illuminati. This, among other things, is one of the indications that 9/11 was part of the illuminati plan to establish the NWO.

Many readers may think this is a fantastic scenario, but unlikely to occur. I want to present one last piece of evidence I hope will get your attention. In 1990, game inventor Steve Jackson of S. J. Games started working on an Illuminati role playing card game called "Illuminati – New World Order." This card game details events that the Illuminati want to bring about in order to establish the New World Order. He revised and published the game in 1995. White magic occultist David Icke has pulled out the most pertinent nine of the 100 cards in the game to tell the story, which was on his web site, for many years. Below is a description of those cards. Go to http://www.thecomingepiphany.com/BookArticles/Cardgame.html to view the cards as they appeared on his website.

Rewriting History: The first card depicts academic books being thrown in a trashcan. It represents the use of the public school system by the Illuminati to weaken and control people through false teachings such as evolution, abortion, acceptance of gay lifestyles, and so on.

Terrorist Nuke: This card depicts one of the World Trade Center buildings being destroyed by an explosion in the exact spot that one of the planes hit. The image on the card is an unmistakable representation of the 9/11 attack on the World Trade Center.

Pentagon: This card depicts the Pentagon on fire. It represents and was fulfilled on the 9/11 attack of the Pentagon.

Note: The three cards thus chosen by David Icke have been fulfilled and in the exact order as depicted.

Population Reduction: This card depicts a picture of New York City with black smoke over the whole city in the shape of a skull. It is a representation of one of the goals of the Illuminati, to reduce the population of the earth. They feel that there are too many people and want to clear the globe of the excess. They will accomplish this through wars, famine, pestilence, and terrorist actions.

Center for Disease Control: This card depicts a scientist creating viruses. It represents the notion that the CDC will be used in the future to inflict diseases upon a people group or the world.

Epidemic: This card depicts a pile of dead bodies, blackened from death, and some medical paraphernalia such as gloves and a mask. The word Quarantine is written over the picture. It represents plagues that the New World order will use to lessen the population.

Combined Disasters: This card depicts people running in fear due to buildings falling down around them. It represents the fact that they will combine several disasters at the same time to invoke great fear and thus create an atmosphere conducive for the acceptance of antichrist.

Goal: Kill for Peace: This card depicts hippies, one holding a peace sign, standing over a policeman, who is on all fours in a begging position. The Hippies are poised and ready to kill him. It represents the killing "for peace" that will happen to people who will not go along with the New World Order and its plans—namely, Christians and Jews. A peace sign is an upside down broken cross and also speaks of the destruction of Christianity and its followers at this time.

Tape Runs Out: This card depicts a reel-to-reel audiotape machine with the tape running out. Behind it is a picture of the world being split in half. Under the picture is written; "When the rapture comes…" This card represents the Day of the Lord and rapture of the church.

The order of these cards as presented by David Icke, which depicts "the story" is very interesting. Cards 1-3 have already been fulfilled, and in the exact order as depicted. Cards 4-8 parallel very closely the first five seals as recorded in Revelation. Seals 1-4, as we have already discussed, foretell war, famines, economic collapse, diseases, and so on, and parallels cards 4-7. The fifth seal involves the persecution of Jews and Christians, which parallels card 8. The last card in his list is the rapture. Note that he has placed the rapture occurring last in all these cards and immediately following the card that depicts the "killing for peace" initiative. This is exactly the order that the Bible gives us — the rapture after the first five seals. The existence of these cards should also help prove to you, if you do not believe it yet, that the Illuminati indeed have a plan to take over the world and are in the process of carrying it out.

There are two other noteworthy cards in the deck that I would like to mention. These cards refer to conservative talk show hosts being used by the Illuminati to mislead political conservatives into accepting the Illuminati agenda. These "weapons of mass instruction" give out 98.4% truth and 1.6% error. The problem is that since they give out so much truth, very few are discerning enough to detect the error. It is similar to rat poison: 99% food and 1% poison. This is one way that the Illuminati can get some of their programs such as NAFTA, GATT, Patriot Act I and II, and The Military Commissions Act passed without much conservative opposition. I am not suggesting that all talk show hosts fall into this category, but I admonish you to beware of them. They are smart enough to know about the conspiracy of the Illuminati. If they deny the existence of such a conspiracy, then I believe that it may be a sign that they are part of it. Unfortunately, some are so enamored with these talk show hosts because they promote conservatism that they cannot discern the truth about these individuals.

We have examined some aspects of the plan of the Illuminati to take over control of the world and institute the antichrist as the leader. It is readily seen how some of their plans will be fulfilled because we can see these plans as events foretold in the Bible. Some of their plans that are not foretold by the Bible may or may not come to pass. God is in ultimate control. How much of the plan God allows to occur is yet to be seen.

The knowledge of the illuminati and the NWO may cause you to feel hatred toward government. Scripture tells us that we are not to despise government (2 Pet 2:10). We are to pray for those in authority, even the illuminati, that we may lead a quiet and peaceable life (1 Tim 2:1-4). We are also commanded to honor the king, no matter who it is.

> Submit yourselves to every ordinance of man for the Lord's sake: whether it be to the king, as supreme; Or unto governors, as unto them that are sent by him for the punishment of evildoers, and for the praise of them that do well. For so is the will of God, that with well doing ye may put to silence the ignorance of foolish men: As free, and not using your liberty for a cloke of maliciousness, but as the servants of God. Honour all men. Love the brotherhood. Fear God. Honour the king. (1 Pet 2:13-17)

The Christian is commanded to obey the governing authorities (Rom 13:1) no matter how evil; we can only disobey the government when they tell us to do something directly against scripture or they perform an illegal action against us. So do not let the knowledge of these things cause you to hate the government and its leaders. God has allowed them to rule and reign for His purposes. We also need to realize that except for the grace of God "there go I." Respect, obey, and pray for them. For further discussions on this topic see the article entitled "To Obey or Not to Obey, That is the Question"

The prophetic one world government—The New World Order—is coming and many are working to bring it about. After the opening of the 5th seal, at the direction of the antichrist, the NWO will fiercely oppress and persecute Jews and Christians. Christians must prepare themselves for the troublous times that lie ahead. I hope you do not believe that all this stuff is just "wacko conspiracy theory nonsense." The evidence says, No!

> When we come into our kingdom, our orators will expound great problems which have turned humanity upside down in order to bring it, at the end, under our beneficent rule. Who will ever suspect, then, that all these peoples were stage-managed by us according to a political plan which no one has so much as guessed at in the course of many centuries?" [End of Protocol No. 13]

> Some even believe we [the Rockefellers] are part of a secret cabal working against the best interests of the United States, characterizing my family and me as 'internationalists' and of conspiring with others around the world to build a more integrated global political and economic structure--one world, if you will. If that's the charge, I stand guilty, and I am proud of it." (David Rockefeller's Memoirs)

Many world leaders are calling for the formation of a new world order and a new world currency. In economic and financial desperation, leaders around the globe are openly calling for the creation of a "New World Order," including prominent "old guard" members of the Trilateral Commission. Is the baby about to be born?[105]

A world currency moves nearer after Tim Geithner's slip. US Treasury Secretary Tim Geithner confessed on Wednesday that he had not read the plans by China's central bank governor for a "super-sovereign reserve currency" run by the International Monetary Fund, but nevertheless let slip that Washington was "open" to the idea. Whoops.[106]

The New World Order is coming whether you are ready or not! In the next chapter we will turn our attention to the coming leader of the NWO, the soon to be nefarious ruler of the world, the antichrist.

---

[105]http://www.rightsidenews.com/200901093251/editorial/chorus-call-for-new-world-order.html
[106]http://www.telegraph.co.uk/finance/economics/5051075/A-world-currency-moves-nearer-after-Tim-Geithners-slip.html

Chapter 10
The Son of Perdition

"I am God!" I expect to hear this statement coming out of the mouth of the man that will be the first and last human ruler of the entire world—the antichrist. And, believe it or not, many will believe his words and fall for his deception, and he will be heralded as the greatest man to ever live as he brings peace to a worn-torn, tumultuous world. Yes, there is coming a day when the world will cry out for someone to bring peace to the world and rule over them. After the chaos of the first four seals unfolds upon the earth—financial collapse, WWIII, famines, plagues, and death — and the desperation during the aftermath; the world will unfortunately turn to a man filled with satan to solve its problems — the false messiah, the son of perdition, the antichrist.

Since authority over the world will be given to him for the last 3.5 years of the 70th Week, his actions will affect every person living on the earth at that time. With the opening of the fifth seal, no one on earth will be able to buy or sell without taking his mark (Rev. 13:16,17) and he will wage war against Christians and Jews and they will suffer severe persecution at his hands: "And it was given unto him to make war with the saints, and to overcome them: and power was given him over all kindreds, and tongues, and nations." (Rev 13:7) Here is what the illuminati plan revealed in the *"Protocols of the Learned Elders of Zion"* say about his reign of despotism "and our kingdom will be distinguished by a despotism of such magnificent proportions as to be at any moment and in every place in a position to wipe out any ... who oppose us by deed or word."

We have briefly discussed the antichrist throughout the book, but since he will hold such a prominent position—the head of the NWO—and will affect so many, I believe that we should examine the biblical facts and other pertinent information about him. Exposing him may also help some avoid the trap of his deceptions.

What the Prophecies Reveal

One of the most prominent, easily recognized, and most likely public actions of the antichrist prophesied in scripture, which we have already discussed in detail, is that in the midst of the 70th Week, he will strengthen the seven-year peace treaty that was made with "the many."

> And he shall confirm the covenant with many for one week: and in the midst of the week he shall cause the sacrifice and the oblation to cease, and for the overspreading of abominations he shall make it desolate, even until the consummation, and that determined shall be poured upon the desolate. (Dan. 9:27)

Not only will he strengthen the peace treaty that will have already been in existence before he comes on the scene, but also this verse tells us another prominent action of the antichrist—that he will perform the abomination of desolation. This is when he will enter the temple and stop the sacrifices and proclaim to the entire world that he is god.

> Let no man deceive you by any means: for that day shall not come, except there come a falling away first, and that man of sin be revealed, the son of perdition; Who opposeth and exalteth himself above all that is called God, or that is worshipped; so that he as God sitteth in the temple of God, shewing himself that he is God. (2 Thess. 2: 3,4)

Of course this cannot happen until there is a temple, which will most likely be rebuilt during the first half of the 70th Week after the Dome of the Rock is destroyed by his henchmen. Daniel gives us more insights about the antichrist and his religious beliefs.

> Neither shall he regard the God of his fathers, nor the desire of women, nor regard any god: for he shall magnify himself above all. But in his estate shall he honour the God of forces: and a god whom his fathers knew not shall he honour with gold, and silver, and with precious stones, and pleasant things. Thus shall he do in the most strong holds with a strange god, whom he shall acknowledge and increase with glory: and he shall cause them to rule over many, and shall divide the land for gain. (Dan. 11:37-39)

Some interpret this verse to mean the antichrist will worship a god of forces/science and that he will set himself above all gods. The phrase "nor the desire of women" could refer to the fact that he will not worship a female god or could be in regards to his sexual orientation.

When will his reign begin? It will begin shortly after the abomination of desolation, at the midpoint of the 70th Week. His reign will last for 3.5 years. See the chart entitled "The 70th Week of Daniel"

> And there was given unto him a mouth speaking great things and blasphemies; and power was given unto him *to continue forty and two months.* (Rev. 13:5)

Another scripture that confirms his 3.5 year reign is found in Dan. 7:23-25.

> And he shall speak great words against the most High, and shall wear out the saints of the most High, and think to change times and laws: *and they shall be given into his hand until a time and times and the dividing of time.* (Dan. 7:23-25)

Note that this scripture also indicates that he will change "times and laws." Many think that this is an indication that the antichrist will change the way that time, days, and months will be accounted for.

Another verse confirming his 3.5-year reign and when it begins is Rev. 19:20, which tells us that at Armageddon the antichrist is thrown into the bottomless pit. Therefore, his reign must start 3.5 years before that, placing its beginning at day 1260.

Let's examine another fact about the antichrist. Scripture tells us that the antichrist will come from one of the old Roman Empire countries.

> And after threescore and two weeks shall Messiah be cut off, but not for himself: and the *people of the prince that shall come shall destroy the city* and the sanctuary; and the end thereof shall be with a flood, and unto the end of the war desolations are determined. (Dan. 9:26)

It was the Romans who destroyed Jerusalem in 70 AD. Thus, the "prince that shall come" will be from one of the countries that made up the Roman Empire, which stretched from modern-day Europe to the Middle East as far as Turkey. Even the recently constructed

European Parliament building suggests a link between the European Union—one of the 10 horns of the beast—and the antichrist. The building has 679 seats. Seat number 666—the number the Bible uses to identify the antichrist—remains unoccupied at this point in time.

Comments Ian Paisley:

> It is certainly a building of the Space Age. The seats of its massive hemicycle are designed like the crew seats in the Star Trek space machines. There are 679 of them – but wait for it! While these seats are allocated to Members, one seat remains unallocated and unoccupied. The number of that seat is 666. The relevant section of the seating-plan provided to each Member reads as follows:
>
> > 664 Thomas-Mauro
> > 665 Zissener
> > 666 -------
> > 667 Cappato
> > 668 Turco
>
> Revelation 13:18: "Here is wisdom. Let him that hath understanding count the number of the beast: for it is the number of a man; and his number is Six hundred threescore and six." That is 666. Today this scripture is being fulfilled before our very eyes. The antichrist's seat *will* be occupied. The world awaits his full and final development. The Lord will destroy him by the spirit of His mouth (the Word of God) and by the brightness of His coming (2 Thes. 2:8). The coming of the Lord draweth nigh."[107][108]

Some have even made the assertion that since America was born out of Europe, she could be considered a part or extension of the old Roman Empire and that the antichrist could come from America. I see this as a remote possibility, but believe that the antichrist will most likely arise from one of the actual old Roman Empire countries.

The quote above brings out another fact about the antichrist. His number is 666. All letters have number values associated with

---

[107] Paisley, Ian. *The Vacant Seat Number 666 in the European Parliament.* http://www.ianpaisley.org/article.asp?ArtKey=666
[108] I have recently been informed that seat #666 has been occupied.

them. Many believe that this verse indicates that the number values of the letters of his name must add up to 666. Though I see that as a possibility, it may be that his number could be in reference to something else, such as the parliament seat number, or it could even be the number of his mark. The mark will most likely be a computer chip planted under the skin in the hand or forehead. Everyone who receives the mark/chip will be given a unique number so that computer and satellite can track him or her. So it could be that the number of the chip that the antichrist receives himself could be #666. So it is uncertain as to which scenario or a combination thereof will come to pass. We will just have to wait and see.

Another prophecy that the antichrist will fulfill is that he will eventually rule the world from Jerusalem.

> But the court which is without the temple leave out, and measure it not; for it is given unto the Gentiles: and the holy city shall they tread under foot forty and two months. (Rev. 11:2)

> And he shall plant the tabernacles of his palace between the seas in the glorious holy mountain; yet he shall come to his end, and none shall help him. (Dan. 11:45)

Daniel 7 reveals to us that his reign will be a violent one, involving many wars. Not only will he attack Jews and Christians, but he will also subdue three kings and their countries/spheres of influence. As already discussed this will probably occur just after the rapture.

> And the ten horns out of this kingdom are ten kings that shall arise: and another shall rise after them; and he shall be diverse from the first, and he shall subdue three kings. And he shall speak great words against the most High, and shall wear out the saints of the most High, and think to change times and laws: (Dan. 7: 24,25)

Daniel 11 also tells us that he will participate in numerous military campaigns.

> And at the time of the end shall the king of the south push at him: and the king of the north shall come against him like a whirlwind, with chariots, and with horsemen, and with many ships; and he shall enter into the countries, and shall overflow and pass over. He shall enter also into the glorious land, and many countries shall be overthrown: but these shall escape out of his hand, even Edom, and Moab, and the chief of the children of Ammon. He shall stretch forth his hand also upon the countries: and the land of Egypt shall not escape. But he shall have power over the treasures of gold and of silver, and over all the precious things of Egypt: and the Libyans and the Ethiopians shall be at his steps. But tidings out of the east and out of the north shall trouble him: therefore he shall go forth with great fury to destroy, and utterly to make away many. (Dan. 11:40-44)

Here we see the antichrist involved in war with the king of the south (Egypt and her allies) and the king of the north (Russia and her allies). We have identified this particular military campaign as the Gog-Magog war.

Another prominent prophecy concerning the antichrist is that he will suffer a deadly wound to the head and be healed as described in Rev. 13:3.

> And I saw one of his heads as it were wounded to death; and his deadly wound was healed: and all the world wondered after the beast.

Most believe that this verse reveals that the antichrist will be wounded in the head, bringing him to the point of death or even actually dying. He will then be healed by satanic power, causing the entire world to "wonder" after him.

Not only will the true antichrist fulfill the biblical prophecies concerning him, but it is also interesting to note that the Illuminati are looking for their so-called "messiah" to fulfill certain of their prophecies, as well. One of those is revealed to us on the symbol of the Illuminati organization, the CFR. It shows the coming world ruler riding naked on a white horse with only one of his eyes showing. Many think this symbol foretells that the coming world ruler will be one-eyed and, at some fulfilling moment, will appear naked. There is even a scripture that some believe speaks of the coming antichrist as being one-eyed. "Woe to the idol shepherd that leaveth the flock! the sword shall be upon his arm, and upon his right eye: his arm shall be clean dried up, and his right eye shall be utterly darkened" (Zech. 11:17). Will the antichrist become blind or lose his eye as a result of the deadly wound he receives foretold in Revelation 13? We will have to wait and see.

Further light has been shed on Biblical prophecies that the antichrist will attempt—and appear—to fulfill, in order to deceive the world that he is their Messiah. These yet-to-be-fulfilled prophesies are listed in Peter Lemesurier's blasphemous book *The Armageddon Script* (p. 231).

1. The restored Messiah must reappear on Jerusalem's Mount of Olives at the time of the great earthquake.

2. He must enter Jerusalem from the east, escorted by a procession of rejoicing followers dressed in shining white.

3. Visiting the tomb of his spiritual ancestor, King David, he must emerge in suitably-perfumed royal robes as the great monarch returned.

4. Supported by a popular rising, he must proceed with his followers to the Temple mount, there to be enthroned, anointed and crowned King of the New Israel.

5. In token of his power, the cloud of the Divine presence must descend upon him amid thunders and lightnings.

This is what Illuminati are looking for their Messiah, the antichrist, to do. He will attempt to partially duplicate what Jesus will do when He returns to earth after Armageddon. And yes, I believe that the antichrist will fulfill these prophecies to the amazement of many. But these are not all the prophecies that the real Messiah must fulfill. Nor are they the way in which Jesus will fulfill them. These are only a select few that the antichrist will *appear* to fulfill through trickery and deceit.

The scriptures say that the antichrist will be given great—but limited—power and he will deceive many. "For there shall arise false

Christs, and false prophets, and shall shew great signs and wonders; insomuch that, if it were possible, they shall deceive the very elect" (Matt. 24:24). It is noteworthy that prophecy number three above states that the antichrist will be a descendant of David. There is a popular but blasphemous book called the *Da Vinci Code* which asserts that certain royal European bloodlines are descended from the supposed marriage between Mary Magdalene and Jesus.

> The premise is that Mary Magdalene stood pregnant with His baby as He was crucified, and that she was whisked away to safety immediately after the crucifixion. Later, as the story goes, Mary Magdalene gave birth to a girl, the alleged physical daughter of Jesus. Subsequently, the girl grew up and married and gave birth to another girl. This trend supposedly continued on with girl births always until this present time...there was and always will be a female descendant of Jesus until finally a male child is born of that bloodline. This male child is to be the ruler of the world.[109]

We know this coming "ruler of the world" to be the antichrist. This ridiculous theory is pure blasphemy, but is part of the intricate plan to trick the world into accepting the claims of the false messiah.

We have briefly examined the significant prophecies concerning the antichrist to help us understand what he is like and what he will do. In the past, there have been individuals who have been considered by many to be types of the antichrist. I believe it may help our understanding of the antichrist if we examine some of these past types.

Learning from History

To learn more about the coming antichrist, we can look to history. Many consider the historical figure Antiochus Epiphanes to be a type of the coming antichrist. Some of his actions are recorded in Dan. 11:28–33. Like the coming antichrist, Antiochus also committed a type of an abomination of desolation:

> That most blasphemous of all desecrations of the Jerusalem temple occurred in 168 B.C. when Antiochus ordered that

---

[109] Last Trumpet Newsletter. July 2006
http://www.lasttrumpetministries.org/2006/July2006.html

swine, the most ceremonially unclean of all animals, be offered on the temple altar of burnt offerings. And to make the sacrilege still worse, he insisted that those animals be offered to the pagan god Zeus. Because he had declared himself to be Theos Epiphanes (meaning; 'the manifest god'), and even more explicitly Zeus Epiphanes ('The manifestation of Zeus'), he was actually demanding worship of himself in place of almighty God.[110]

On Kislev 15, 168 BC, Antiochus erected an idol of Zeus, the supreme deity of the Greek pantheon, on the holy altar in the courtyard. Not surprisingly, it bore the face of Antiochus. On the birthday of Zeus (Kislev/December 25), Antiochus offered a pig on the altar. The pig was the ultimate abomination to the Jewish mind, strictly forbidden by the law of God. Antiochus sprinkled its blood in the Holy of Holies and poured its broth over the Holy scrolls before he cut them to pieces and burned them.[111]

Van Kampen has identified several parallels between Antiochus and the coming antichrist.

> First, under the guise of friendship and the promise of protection, both men make covenants with the nation of Israel
>
> Second, as in the days of Antiochus, many in Israel will again yield to this diabolical servant of satan after the signing of the covenant, again seeking to gain the favor of this powerful world ruler.
>
> Third, after making their treaties with Israel, while Israel lives under a false security, both men seek to conquer Egypt....
>
> Fourth, both men proclaim themselves to be gods and demand worship from their subjects, and those Jews who refuse become the primary target of their wrath.
>
> Fifth, Both tyrants have to contend with these groups of Jews who refuse to worship or serve them....[112]

---

[110] Van Kampen. P.148,9
[111] Howard. P. 163

Hitler was another type of antichrist, to whom satan promised to hand over the world. He was a great orator and charismatic leader who masqueraded as a Christian. He was a real wolf in sheep's clothing who attempted to take over the world and brought severe persecution and death upon the Jews and some Christians. He is the most recent example of a type of antichrist, and in fact, many including himself thought that he *was* the antichrist. Cutting Edge has written an excellent article showing many parallels between Hitler and the coming antichrist.[113] Judas was also a type of antichrist. Both he and the antichrist are given the same name—"son of perdition": "While I was with them in the world, I kept them in thy name: those that thou gavest me I have kept, and none of them is lost, but the *son of perdition*; that the scripture might be fulfilled" (Jn 17:12); "and that man of sin be revealed, *the son of perdition*" (II Thes 2:3). The phrase "son of perdition" means—by their own choice—that they are both damned to Hell. Even though these diabolical men were types of the antichrist, they were not *the* antichrist because they did not fulfill all the prophecies regarding him.

The Infernal Trio

The antichrist—indwelt by satan, whoever he is, will not be acting alone. He will have a powerful helper, the false prophet, who will join in the act and perform signs and wonders to deceive many into believing that the antichrist is who he says that he is.

> And I beheld another beast coming up out of the earth; and he had two horns like a lamb, and he spake as a dragon. And he exerciseth all the power of the first beast before him, and causeth the earth and them which dwell therein to worship the first beast, whose deadly wound was healed. And he doeth great wonders, so that he maketh fire come down from heaven on the earth in the sight of men. And deceiveth them that dwell on the earth by the means of those miracles which he had power to do in the sight of the beast. And he had power to give life unto the image of the beast, that the image of the beast should both speak, and cause that as many as

---

[112] Van Kampen. p.150
[113] http://www.cuttingedge.org/NEWS/n1017.html

would not worship the image of the beast should be killed. (Rev. 13:11-15)

Thus, the infernal trio of the antichrist, satan, and the false prophet will be able to accomplish many miraculous feats, either by technological means and or by satanic power. It has been documented that select satanic individuals can already exhibit certain powers, such as disappearing and reappearing at will in completely different dress and form, communicating by telepathy, and levitating. As a pair, the antichrist and false prophet will be a strong delusionary force. Unfortunately, many will choose to follow them into Hell. As we see, the main job of the false prophet is to get people to accept and worship the antichrist. With great demonic powers, the false prophet will work so-called "miracles" and even have the ability to bring fire—or, some think, lightning—out of the sky. At the end of the passage we even see that he has the power to give life to an image of the antichrist and cause it to speak. He is also given power to kill all that refuse to worship it.

Van Kampen interprets this portion of the passage in a very interesting way:

> The meaning of this passage, then is that after the world is commanded to build its own "images" or idols of antichrist, some form of spirit or life will be put within these "images," so "that the image of the beast might even speak and cause as many as do not worship the image of the beast to be killed" (Rev. 13:15)! Indeed, these idols will be different from all the idols the world has previously known.... In other words the idols and images will be indwelt by satan's demons, to form a worldwide monitoring system to enforce the worship of antichrist (whose likeness the images will bear), and to destroy any human being who refuses to comply with that worship....As Christians, therefore, it will be absolutely essential that we do not go near these images or enter any place where they are present—so that the images have no opportunity to "speak" and identify us, or to "cause [us who] do not worship the image of the beast to be killed."[114]

It appears that the false prophet may have the ability to do greater satanic signs than even the antichrist. Who will this false

---
[114] Van Kampen. P.239 - 42.

prophet be? He will be the leader of the one-world religion. Step four of the Illuminati's New Jerusalem Covenant project, referenced in the last chapter, entails the Pope dedicating a one-world religious system of which he is the head. Thus, if the Illuminati plan is fulfilled, a future pope will be the false prophet. This evil duo, along with the devil himself, will work their evil deeds right up to the end, still deluded into thinking that they will destroy God by taking over the world.

> And I saw three unclean spirits like frogs come out of the mouth of the dragon, and out of the mouth of the beast, and out of the mouth of the false prophet. 14. For they are the spirits of devils, working miracles, which go forth unto the kings of the earth and of the whole world, to gather them to the battle of that great day of God Almighty. Behold, I come as a thief. Blessed is he that watcheth, and keepeth his garments, lest he walk naked, and they see his shame. And he gathered them together into a place called in the Hebrew tongue Armageddon. (Rev. 16:13-16)

Their deceptions will be strong enough to deceive the armies of the world to gather outside of Jerusalem in the valley of Meggido and fight against God. And as already discussed, we know where the wicked trio of the dragon (satan), the beast (antichrist), and the lamb with horns (false prophet-Pope) will end up.

> And I saw the beast, and the kings of the earth, and their armies, gathered together to make war against him that sat on the horse, and against his army. And the beast was taken, and with him the false prophet that wrought miracles before him, with which he deceived them that had received the mark of the beast, and them that worshipped his image. These both were cast alive into a lake of fire burning with brimstone. (Rev. 19:19–21)

The armies that they gather together to fight against God will also be destroyed in the battle of Armageddon.

> And the angel thrust in his sickle into the earth, and gathered the vine of the earth, and cast it into the great winepress of the wrath of God. 20. And the winepress was trodden without the city, and blood came out of the winepress, even unto the

horse bridles, by the space of a thousand and six hundred furlongs. (Rev. 4:19–20)

So for the last 3.5 years before the return of the Lord, a man—filled with satan—will rule the world and will claim to be God. After the performing of the abomination of desolation and opening of the fifth seal, he will begin persecuting Jews and Christians. He will also engage in military conquests headquartered from Jerusalem. In his final battle—where he deceives the world to fight against God—he will finally come to an end.

Can We Know His Identity?
We know what prophecies the antichrist will fulfill and what he will be like, but do we know who he is? Is he alive today? There has been much speculation concerning the identity of the coming antichrist. There are people alive today who claim to know who the antichrist is, and there are some who have even claimed that title for themselves. Many have made assertions, such as the Pope, Prince Charles, Prince William, Maitreya, Obama, Bill Clinton, Solano, and many others. Some have written books presenting strong evidence as to who the antichrist is. Such as *The antichrist and a Cup of Tea,* which makes a strong case for Prince Charles. Another antichrist researcher firmly believes that prince William is the antichrist.[115] However, at this point in time—no matter how strong—all the evidence is just coincidental. I believe it unfair of me or anyone else to point a finger at someone and say they are the antichrist. Even people who believe they are may only be deceived themselves. I believe that the world will not know for sure who the antichrist is until he fulfills the prophecies concerning himself.

One particularly disturbing development is the rise of a charismatic leader called Maitreya, who is alive today and living in London. This man has not revealed his true identity to the world at this time. Many are asserting that he is the coming world ruler. If you examine some of his teachings, you will see they are claiming that Maitreya is God and will make himself known to the world on what is called "The Day of Declaration." Could that be the same as the day of the abomination of desolation? They also claim that he is descended from the "Masters of Wisdom, that group of advanced beings." These

---
[115] http://www.grailcode.net/

are who aliens claim to be; "advanced beings, ascended Masters of Wisdom of the Hierarchy." Will he claim to be God by saying that he was the alien who started life on this planet? I think that is a good possibility. As mentioned earlier in this book, I believe the antichrist and events associated with him will be the precipitating factor in the great falling away that will occur before the rapture. I feel strongly that, intertwined with all the occurrences listed above, will be actions of demons posing as aliens who have come to help our planet. The devil has been orchestrating a great deception at the hand of aliens, and by their own admission, they will be part of it. Here is a quote that reveals the greatest purpose of their deception.

> Aliens utilize standard New Age terminology when they communicate with their human "contactees." The best illustration of this is their teaching to the "contactees" that "the Ascended Masters of the Hierarchy" are preparing to intervene again in world History, to lead mankind to a higher level of consciousness. They will select a human person and endow him with superhuman powers and knowledge. This man will lead us to world government and world peace.[116]

Those versed in Bible knowledge can readily recognize this coming world ruler as the antichrist.

> Now, the time has come, the Aliens say, for them to intervene again in world history. This time they will intervene to save man from himself.... These Aliens will accomplish all this by raising up a man who will be imbued with a special level of consciousness.... of course, this man will be Maitreya the Christ, the Anti-Christ.[117]

While details on Maitreya and aliens go beyond the realm of this book, this is a name that readers should remember, for his teachings are blasphemous and, unfortunately, I am afraid many nominal Christians will fall for his deception, and the deception of others like him, and be engulfed by this satanic indoctrination that no doubt will precipitate the great falling away. So the answer of the question "Who is the antichrist?" We will not know until we see him

---

[116] When UFO'S Arrive. Cutting Edge Newsletter #1912.
[117] Ibid.

fulfill the prophecies concerning him. Is he alive today? With all the recent prophetic developments taking place in the world today I believe that he is most likely alive, willing and ready to come on the scene. Interestingly enough, in a speech to the U.N., The President of Iran, Mahmood Ahmadinejad, prayed for the 12th Imam, the Islamic Messiah, to come on the world scene.

> From the beginning of time, humanity has longed for the day when justice, peace, equality and compassion envelop the world. All of us can contribute to the establishment of such a world. When that day comes, the ultimate promise of all Divine religions will be fulfilled with the emergence of a perfect human being who is heir to all prophets and pious men. He will lead the world to justice and absolute peace.
>
> "0 mighty Lord, I pray to you to hasten the emergence of your last repository, the promised one, that perfect and pure human being, the one that will fill this world with justice and peace. 0 Lord, include us among his companions, followers and those who serve his cause."[118]

While Muslims will call him the 12th Imam, Hindus will call him "Maitreya", the Buddhists will call him the reincarnation of Buddha, Jews will call him Messiah, and deceived nominal Christians will call him Jesus, but true Christians will call him "antichrist".

The antichrist in a Nutshell

In summary the following is a list of information that the Bible reveals to us about the antichrist:

1. In the midst of the 70th Week, the antichrist will strengthen the peace treaty.

2. He will perform the abomination of desolation by stopping the sacrifice in the temple and proclaiming himself to be God.

3. He will subdue three kings/spheres of influence of the New World Order.

---

[118] http://www.cuttingedge.org/news_updates/nz2139.htm

4. He will be a great orator.

5. He will persecute and kill Jews and Christians.

6. He will rule the world from Jerusalem.

7. His number will be 666.

8. No one will be able to buy or sell unless he has his mark.

9. He will attack Egypt.

10. He will suffer a deadly wound and be healed.

11. He will rule the world for 1260 days, also described in the Bible as 42 months or three-and-one-half years.

Extra biblical sources tell us the following:

1. He will come on the scene 91 days after WWIII begins.

2. He will be an alleged descendant of David via the heretical and blasphemous assertion that Jesus and Mary Magdalene were married.

3. He will also be a descendant of the masters of the ages. Thus, he will be connected with "aliens."

4. He will appear on the Mount of Olives at the time of a great earthquake.

5. Dressed in white, he will lead a procession entering Jerusalem from the east.

6. He will proceed to the Temple Mount, where he will be crowned king of Israel.

7. He will be accompanied by displays of thunder and lightning.

"I am God! Bow down and worship me!" As already stated I expect to hear these words coming from the mouth of the antichrist. Many being deceived will not recognize him and will bow down and worship especially when they are faced with not being able to buy or sell unless they do so. If the peace treaty is signed in the near future, and if we live to the midpoint of the 70th Week, then we will see this man come to power and Jews and Christians will experience intense persecution at his hands. Regardless of what happens, we should not be afraid, for the Lord will take care of us.

Now that we have established a clear picture of the events and the major players during the end-times we will now turn our attention to developing a more exact chronology of the end.

Chapter 11
A Chronology of the End

10,9, 8, 7, 6, 5, 4, 3, 2, 1, 0, blast off! As a child I remember watching the launching of several Apollo mission rockets. One thing that stuck out in my mind was that the launches operated on a precise timeline. Nothing happened by chance, everything was done meticulously and precisely at the right time. God has a precise timeline too, a timeline of prophetic events in which nothing will happen by chance, but will occur precisely at the right time. Already having established a clear picture of the things that will happen before, during, and after the 70th Week of Daniel, and in what order, we will now turn our attention to examining a more exact timeline of the events associated with the end times. Let me warn you that this chapter and the next are a bit technical and can be a little overwhelming, so you may have to read through it more than once.

First let me establish the fact that no one knows the day or hour of Christ's return at the rapture. This is a doctrine and truth that the Lord Himself gave us:

> But of that day and hour knoweth no man, no, not the angels of heaven, but my Father only. But as the days of Noe were, so shall also the coming of the Son of man be. For as in the days that were before the flood they were eating and drinking, marrying and giving in marriage, until the day that Noe entered into the ark. And knew not until the flood came, and took them all away; so shall also the coming of the Son of man be. Then shall two be in the field; the one shall be taken, and the other left. Two women shall be grinding at the mill; the one shall be taken, and the other left. Watch therefore: for ye know not what hour your Lord doth come.

Even though no one knows the day or hour of the rapture there are scriptural truths that allow us to assign chronological parameters or timeframes for events within the 70th week including the beginning of the Day of the Lord and the rapture.

For instance, as already discussed, we know several events that will occur and will let us know that His return at the rapture is imminent:

1. The revealing of the antichrist and abomination of desolation.
2. The great falling away.
3. The appearance of the Two Witnesses.
4. The moon being turned to blood, sun darkened, great earthquake, etc.

All of the events listed above precede the rapture, and will be signs to all who heed them that the time of Christ's return to the clouds at the rapture is imminent. This is especially true of the sixth seal, which contains signs immediately preceding the rapture, where the sun is darkened and the moon is turned to blood, etc. When we see these signs, we know that the time is very near, even though we do not know exactly when it will occur. It is possible that the rapture could occur within hours, minutes, or even seconds after the events of the sixth seal. We also know that the rapture will occur sometime between the midpoint of the last 7 years—when the antichrist will take over the world, and the great tribulation begins—and Armageddon.

Other than these, are there any other scriptural truths that would allow us to further narrow down the time frame of events in the 70th week and the rapture? Yes I believe there is, and to help us answer that question, we first need to consider date parameters concerning the 69 weeks, and the 70th week. We will discuss the 69 weeks first. An examination of the chronology of the sixty-nine weeks will show us how precisely God's prophetic timing works. God told Daniel about the sixty-nine and seventieth weeks in a vision. That vision tells us that there will be seventy weeks of time from the decree to rebuild Jerusalem to when the most Holy is anointed.

> Seventy weeks are determined upon thy people and upon thy holy city, to finish the transgression, and to make an end of sins, and to make reconciliation for iniquity, and to bring in everlasting righteousness, and to seal up the vision and prophecy, and to anoint the most Holy. Know therefore and understand, that from the going forth of the commandment to restore and to build Jerusalem unto the Messiah the Prince

shall be seven weeks, and threescore and two weeks: the street shall be built again, and the wall, even in troublous times. And after threescore and two weeks shall Messiah be cut off, but not for himself: and the people of the prince that shall come shall destroy the city and the sanctuary; and the end thereof shall be with a flood, and unto the end of the war desolations are determined. (Dan 9:24-26)

Sixty-nine of the seventy weeks in that vision have already transpired. The passage says that the sixty-nine weeks would run from the decree to rebuild Jerusalem, including the wall and street, to "Messiah the prince." The decree to rebuild Jerusalem was recorded in Neh. 2:1-6:

> And it came to pass in the month Nisan, in the twentieth year of Artaxerxes the king, that wine was before him: and I took up the wine, and gave it unto the king. Now I had not been beforetime sad in his presence. Wherefore the king said unto me, Why is thy countenance sad, seeing thou art not sick? this is nothing else but sorrow of heart. Then I was very sore afraid, And said unto the king, Let the king live for ever: why should not my countenance be sad, when the city, the place of my fathers' sepulchres, lieth waste, and the gates thereof are consumed with fire? Then the king said unto me, For what dost thou make request? So I prayed to the God of heaven. And I said unto the king, If it please the king, and if thy servant have found favour in thy sight, that thou wouldest send me unto Judah, unto the city of my fathers' sepulchres, that I may build it. And the king said unto me, (the queen also sitting by him,) For how long shall thy journey be? and when wilt thou return? So it pleased the king to send me; and I set him a time.

We see here that the decree was issued in the month Nisan of the twentieth year of Artaxerxes. When did that occur? Over the years, many have debated the dating of the decree. There are several methods for dating the reigning years of kings. The most widely accepted year for the twentieth year of Artaxerxes and this decree is 444 B.C. Hoehner explains all of the various dating methods and how this date is arrived at in his work, *Chronological Aspects of the Life of Christ:*

In conclusion, the report to Nehemiah (1:1) occurred in Chislev (November/December) of 445 B.C. and the decree of Artaxerxes (2:1) occurred in Nisan (March/April) of 444 B.C. Therefore, Nisan 444 B.C. marks the *terminus a quo* of the seventy weeks of Daniel 9:24-27.[119]

Nehemiah does not specify the exact day of the month of the decree. However, in Hebrew narratives, when a date is given citing just a month, it is assumed that it is the first day of the month. In addition, it was traditional for Persian kings to issue decrees on the first day of the New Year. The Persian New Year started on Nisan 1. Thus having established that the decree to rebuild Jerusalem most likely went forth on Nisan 1, 444 B.C., which is March 3, 444 B.C. (Gregorian)[120], we can add sixty-nine weeks to that date and see what date we come to.

A "week" in this passage is referring to a period of seven years. Thus, we can calculate the following: 69 x 7 = 483 years. But we cannot just add 483 years to March 3, 444 B.C. because all years in the Bible coincide with a year length of 360 days, not the approximately 365.25 days that we now experience and on which our calendar is based. The Biblical 360-day year length is evidenced in the Genesis flood account, where the waters covered the earth for 150 days, which was equated to five months, (5 x 30 = 150), and also in Revelation where the antichrist is given authority to rule for 3.5 years, which is equated to 1,260 days (3.5 x 360 = 1260). It is theorized that the earth, as confirmed in Genesis, was originally on a 360-day rotation pattern. Many cultures indicate that, around 800 B.C., some great astronomical phenomena occurred to change the rotation from a 360-day rotation to our current approx. 365.25-day rotation. Therefore, to apply Biblical chronological information to our calendar system, we must convert any 360-day years to 365.25-day years.

Here is the calculation for the 69 weeks;

69 weeks x 7 years = 483 years x 360 days = 173880 days ÷ 365 = 476 years 140 days − 119 days (for leap years) + 4 days (for leap centuries) = **476 years 25 days.**

---

[119] Harold Hoehner, *"Chronological Aspects of the Life of Christ"* (Grand Rapids, MI 1977), p.128
[120] Ibid. p.138.

Thus, if we start with the decree to rebuild Jerusalem issued by Artaxerxes on March 3, 444 B.C. (Gregorian) and add 476 years and 25 days (69 weeks) you come to March 27, 33 A.D. (Gregorian)[121]. [Note: From this point forward, and as previously denoted, all dates will be given in Gregorian even though they will not be annotated as such. Also, in Hebrew reckoning, part of a day is counted as a whole day. Therefore, in our calculation, 3/3/444 B.C. was day one. This principle of inclusive reckoning will also be applied to all date calculations here in.]

So the 69 weeks ended on March 27, 33 A.D. What happened on March 27, 33 A.D.? That was Palm Sunday when Jesus Christ presented Himself as the Messiah and King of the Jews to the Jewish people and to the world—just as the prophecy foretold what would happen at the end of the 69 weeks. That fulfilled prophecy speaks significantly of the validity of the fact that Jesus was the Messiah, and that the Bible truly is God's Word. That day in the Hebrew calendar was 9 Nisan. The next day was 10 Nisan, when Jesus cleansed the temple and had His confrontation with the religious leaders. That day is also when the leadership decided to kill Jesus, as found in Mark 11:18: "And the scribes and chief priests heard it, and sought how they might destroy him: for they feared him, because all the people was astonished at his doctrine." Tradition tells us that Nisan 10 is also the day when the Jews would select the Passover lamb that would eventually be slaughtered between 3 PM and 5 PM on the afternoon before the start of Passover, which always occurred on Nisan 14. It just so happens that is exactly the date and time that Jesus died, about 3 PM. on Nisan 14, the afternoon before Passover in 33 AD.[122] After the crucifixion on Nisan 14, 33 A.D. (Friday April 1, 33 A.D.) Jesus stayed in the tomb until early Sunday morning when He rose from the dead. "Now when Jesus was risen early the first day of the week, he appeared first to Mary Magdalene, out of whom he had cast seven

---

[121] Let me show you how I calculated this for many do it wrong by not realizing that there is no year zero. 3/3/444 B.C. + **443 years** = 3/3/1 B.C. + **1 year** = 3/3/1 A.D. + **32 years, 25 days** = 3/27/33 A.D. (443 years + 1 year + 32 years, 25 days = 476 years, 25 days.)

[122] The chronology of the seventy weeks of Daniel pivots on the correct dating of Passover and the crucifixion. Many theories have been presented concerning the date of the crucifixion. I believe that the evidence clearly shows that Jesus was crucified on the Feast of Passover on Friday April 1st, 33 A.D. and He died at about 3 PM. A full discussion of the details associated with dating the crucifixion are addressed in the article entitled "The Date of the Crucifixion" at thecomingepiphany.com.

devils" (Mark 16:9). During the time Jesus was in the tomb, He fulfilled the Feast of Unleavened Bread in that His sinless body did not decay. Jesus rose from the dead on 16 Nisan (April 3, 33 A.D.) the exact day of the Feast of First Fruits. Paul alludes to this fact in his statement: "But now is Christ risen from the dead, and become the firstfruits of them that slept" (1 Cor. 15:20). The next feast fulfilled was the Feast of Weeks, better known as Pentecost. This feast occurred on Sunday, 6 Sivan (May 22, 33 A.D.), which was 50 days after the Feast of First Fruits. This feast was fulfilled with the pouring out of the Holy Spirit, which was accompanied with signs and wonders. Many contend that the historical church period began at Pentecost, and I agree with their assessment. Pentecost was the birthday of the Church. The exact alignment of these events show how precisely God controls prophetic events and how He aligned major prophetic events with the Spring feasts.

In summary; the seventy weeks of Daniel started with the issuing of the decree of Artaxerxes on March 3, 444 B.C. and ended sixty-nine weeks or 476 years and 25 days later on March 27, 33 A.D. at the triumphal entry. Then all 4 spring feasts were fulfilled, the last of which was Pentecost, which occurred on May 22, 33 A.D.—the start of the historical church period. Thus, it readily stands to reason that sixty-nine weeks have transpired for Israel and only one week is left, the 70th Week.

The Importance of the Feasts

As already has been alluded to, just as the spring feasts aligned with and were fulfilled by major prophetic events of the First Coming of the Lord so I believe the fall feasts will align with and be fulfilled by major prophetic events involving the 70th Week and Second Coming of the Lord. Therefore to help us establish a chronology of the 70th week we need take a more in depth look at the feasts of the Lord and their prophetic significance and implications. We will first examine the meaning of the word feast, which alludes to their significance.

> The Hebrew word translated 'feasts' means *appointed times*. The idea is that the sequence and timing of each of these feasts have been carefully orchestrated by God himself. Each is part of a comprehensive whole. Collectively, they tell a story. These feasts

are also called 'holy convocations'; that is they are intended to be times of meeting between God and man for 'holy purposes.'[123]

God instituted seven yearly feasts for the Israelites to observe. There were four spring feasts and three fall feasts. The feasts, in calendar order with their associated Hebrew dates, are:

1. The Feast of Passover—14 Nisan
2. The Feast of Unleavened Bread. 15 – 21—Nisan
3. The Feast of First Fruits—16 Nisan
4. The Feast of Weeks—50 days after first fruits.
5. The Feast of Trumpets—1 Tishri
6. The Day of Atonement—10 Tishri
7. The Feast of Tabernacles—15 – 21 Tishri

Not only are these feasts significant from a relationship standpoint between God and man, but they also have prophetic implications:

> These seven feasts typify the sequence, timing, and significance of the major events of the Lord's redemptive career. They commence at Calvary where Jesus voluntarily gave Himself for the sins of the world (Passover), and climax at the establishment of the messianic Kingdom at the Messiah's Second Coming...[124]

Paul alluded to this in Colossians 2:16,17 when he said.

16 Let no man therefore judge you in meat, or in drink, or in respect of an holyday, or of the new moon, or of the sabbath days: 17 Which are a shadow of things to come; but the body is of Christ.

Let's expound upon this thought and see exactly how each feast points to a prophetic event. Without going into too much detail, we will summarize the prophetic implication of each feast. For a more thorough understanding of the feasts of the Lord, I would recommend

---

[123] Howard, K and Rosenthal, M. *The Feasts of the Lord.* Nashville, TN: Thomas Nelson Inc. 1997.
[124] Ibid. p.14.

Kevin Howard and Marvin Rosenthal's excellent book *The Feasts of the Lord*.

> 1. The Feast of Passover points to Christ as the Lamb of God who takes away the sin of the world, and was fulfilled when Christ died on the cross for our sins on Passover on Nisan 14, 33 A.D.
>
> 2. The Feast of Unleavened Bread shows that Christ's sinless body would not undergo decay, and was fulfilled when Christ's body did not decay while in the grave.
>
> 3. The Feast of First Fruits shows that Christ had power over death and was the first fruit of the resurrection and was fulfilled when Christ rose from the dead on the day of the feast of first fruits on Nisan 16, 33 A.D.
>
> 4. The Feast of Weeks alludes to the pouring out of the Holy Spirit upon the initiation of the historical church period and was fulfilled on Pentecost on Sivan 6, 33 A.D.

It is clearly evident that the first four feasts were fulfilled at the time of Christ's First Coming and thus we can reason that the last 3 feast will be fulfilled in events surrounding Christ's Second Coming. Let's examine the tree remaining feasts and see how they may be fulfilled. The fifth feast, the Feast of Trumpets, or Rosh Hashanah, is practiced as a two-day feast.

> **Rosh Hashanah** (Hebrew: ראש השנה, literally "head [of] the year") is the Jewish New Year. The Biblical name for this holiday is called **Yom Teruah** (Hebrew: יום תרועה, literally "day [of] shouting/raising a noise") or the **Feast of Trumpets...** It is the first of the High Holy Days or *Yamim Nora'im* ("Days of Awe")...Rosh Hashanah is a two-day celebration, which begins on the first day of Tishrei.[125]

I believe that since it is a two-day feast that it may have two separate and different fulfillments. One of the events I believe this feast may align with, though I am not dogmatic about this, is the

---

[125] http://en.wikipedia.org/wiki/Rosh_Hashanah

rapture. The trump that is referred to at Christ's coming to the clouds at the rapture may be a reference to the trumpet blown at this feast.

> And then shall appear the sign of the Son of man in heaven: and then shall all the tribes of the earth mourn, and they shall see the Son of man coming in the clouds of heaven with power and great glory. And he shall send his angels with a great sound of a trumpet, and they shall gather together his elect from the four winds, from one end of heaven to the other. (Matt. 24:30–31)

The shofar blown on Rosh Hashanah is known as the last trump, which the apostle Paul mentioned in I Thes 4:16-17 and I Cor 15:52 in connection with the rapture.

> For the Lord himself shall descend from heaven with a shout, with the voice of the archangel, and with the trump of God: and the dead in Christ shall rise first: Then we which are alive and remain shall be caught up together with them in the clouds, to meet the Lord in the air: and so shall we ever be with the Lord.

> In a moment, in the twinkling of an eye, at the last trump: for the trumpet shall sound, and the dead shall be raised incorruptible, and we shall be changed.

This last trump of God will signal the beginning of the Day of the Lord in which the righteous will be delivered and the wicked will be judged. In fact, ancient Jewish tradition held that the resurrection of the righteous dead would occur on Rosh Hashanah with the blowing of the shofar (trumpet), which is why a shofar was engraved on Jewish gravestones. These two major occurrences signaled by the blowing of the trumpet are consistent with the historical use of the trumpet in Israel as explained by Marvin Rosenthal:

> The blowing of the trumpet in ancient Israel had two primary functions. The first was to call a solemn assembly; that is, when the children of Israel were to be summoned to God's presence, the trumpet was blown (Ex 19:13,17,19; Num 10:2). And second, when Israel, under divine direction, was to go to war, the trumpet was to be blown (Num 10:9; Jud 7; Jer. 4:19-21).[126]

Kevin Howard has this to say about the judgment aspect of the Feast of Trumpets

> Rosh Hashanah was often referred to as *Yom Ha-Din* ("Judgment Day") by rabbis since it began the Days of Awe, the traditional time of God's judgment.[127]

The prophet Zechariah tells of the judgment that will transpire when the trumpet is blown: "And the Lord shall be seen over them, and his arrow shall go forth as the lightning: and the Lord God shall blow the trumpet, and shall go with whirlwinds of the south" (Zech 9:14). The benediction given for the last 2,000 years during synagogue services on Rosh Hashanah also speaks of the trumpet being blown at Rosh Hashanah at the Lord's return, as explained by Kevin Howard:

> The benediction also speaks of the end of days when God will again reveal Himself through fire and the sounding of the shofar as He sends the Messiah: 'The Lord shall appear over them; his arrow shall go forth like lightning. The Lord shall sound the shofar and march amid the storms of the south. (cf Zech 9:14)[128]

Another interesting fact about the Feast of Trumpets that correlates it to the rapture is that, in the ancient observance of the feast, no one knew the exact start of the feast. It always started on the first day of the Jewish year, which is the first day of the month of Tishri, but no one knew the exact day when a Hebrew month started. The Hebrew months start by the sighting of the new moon, and it was the job of the Sanhedrin to announce the beginning of the month when the new moon was observed. Of course, one could calculate an approximate time by counting 29.5 days since the last new moon, but it did not officially start until the Sanhedrin observed the crescent moon, and then declared it so. This correlates beautifully with the truth that no one knows the exact time of Christ's return. Some even feel that Christ's own words, "No one knows the day or hour" is a direct reference to this feast for this reason. In Jewish tradition Rosh Hashanah is also known as Kiddushin/Nesu'in or the wedding

---

[126] Howard, Rosenthal. p.26
[127] Ibid. p.110
[128] Ibid. p. 111

ceremony of the Messiah.[129] The practices involving the ancient Jewish wedding ceremony closely parallel the Messiah's redemptive work. Pointing to the fact that the bridegroom/Christ will come for his bride—the church—at the rapture.[130] Thus these facts are a strong indication that this feast may be fulfilled at the rapture and possibly at another event that we will examine in the next chapter.

The Feast of Trumpets also starts the time period known as the Days of Awe. The Days of Awe are a 10-day period between Rosh Hashanah and the Day of Atonement in which observant Jews are to engage in a solemn time of self-examination. Tradition holds that these days are the last chance to repent before God's judgment is finalized.[131] Prophetically, I believe these days may be fulfilled when after the last trumpet of the Feast of Trumpets, which calls for a solemn assembly; Israel will assemble for seven days and will receive Christ as their savior on the eighth day, which will be the Day of Atonement.

> Yom Kippur or the Day of Atonement is the most solemn and important holy day of the Jewish calendar. In the Old Testament, the Day of Atonement was the day the High Priest made an atoning sacrifice for the sins of the people. This act of atonement brought reconciliation between the people and God.[132]

I believe this feast will align with the time after Israel repents and officially recognizes Christ as Messiah and will be saved. And when will this occur? Most likely after Israel flees into the wilderness after the abomination of desolation.

The final feast is the Feast of Tabernacles and is associated with Israel's time in the wilderness.

> Sukkot, Succot or Sukkos, Feast of Booths, Feast of Tabernacles is a biblical Jewish holiday celebrated on the 15th day of the month of Tishrei... The sukkah is intended as a reminiscence of the type of fragile dwellings in which the Israelites dwelt during their 40 years of travel in the desert after the Exodus from slavery in Egypt.[133]

---

[129] http://www.linkjesus.com/rosh.htm
[130] http://lloydpulley.com/2008/12/14/the-ancient-jewish-wedding--a-picture-of-christ--his-bride-the-church.aspx
[131] Ibid. p. 108
[132] http://christianity.about.com/od/biblefeastsandholidays/p/dayofatonement.htm
[133] http://en.wikipedia.org/wiki/Sukkot

I believe this feast will align with the time when Israel will once again find themselves in the wilderness after fleeing the antichrist. And once again God will watch over and provide for them for 3.5 years.

Putting It All Together
I view the prophetic implications of the fall feasts as follows:

1. The Feast of Trumpets is practiced as a two-day feast that alludes to the return of Christ during the event known as "The Day of the Lord" in which the righteous will be raptured and the wicked will be judged. This feast will start to be fulfilled at the beginning of the Day of the Lord when Christ comes to the clouds for His bride and will be totally fulfilled after God's enemies will be vanquished at the battle of Armageddon and Jesus takes His throne in Jerusalem. This feast may also align with the time when Israel is called into the wilderness to flee the antichrist.

2. The Day of Atonement speaks of the shed blood of Christ and the substitutionary work it accomplishes in covering our sins and restoring us to fellowship with God. This feast will be fulfilled after Israel repents and recognizes Christ as Messiah and are saved on the Day of Atonement.

3. The Feast of Tabernacles is a seven-day celebration in which the Israelites dwell in "booths" or shacks reminiscent of their journeying in the wilderness. This feast will be fulfilled when Israel will once again find themselves in the wilderness after they flee the antichrist after the abomination of desolation where God will protect and provide for them for 3.5 years.

Estimating the Timeline
Our examination of the last three feasts of the Lord and their prophetic implications has allowed us to succinctly align several end times events that will aid us in coming up with and end times chronology. In constructing an end times chronology we must not only consider the alignment of the feasts but we must also take into account several number parameters. Besides the 2520 days (7 years of 360

days), Daniel gives us three date parameters associated with the end times: 1260, 1290, and 1335 days.

> And one said to the man clothed in linen, which was upon the waters of the river, How long shall it be to the end of these wonders? And I heard the man clothed in linen, which was upon the waters of the river, when he held up his right hand and his left hand unto heaven, and sware by him that liveth for ever that it shall be for a time, times, and an half; and when he shall have accomplished to scatter the power of the holy people, all these things shall be finished. (Dan 12:6,7)

> And from the time that the daily sacrifice shall be taken away, and the abomination that maketh desolate set up, there shall be a thousand two hundred and ninety days. Blessed is he that waiteth, and cometh to the thousand three hundred and five and thirty days. (Dan 12:11,12)

These verses tell us that to the time when the power of the holy people will be destroyed there will be "time, times and a half" or 3½ years or 1260 days. They also tell us that from the abomination of desolation there will be 1290 and 1335 days. Thus we can assign the abomination of desolation as occurring on day 1230 (2520 − 1290 = 1230). Thus after the occurrence of the abomination of desolation on day 1230 there will be 1290 days to the end of the 70th Week. What will happen on this day? The Second Coming and the battle of Armageddon will occur. The 1260 days in Daniel 12 regards he who scatters the holy people. This is in reference to the reign of the antichrist and his persecution of Jews and Christians. This fact is again confirmed in Revelation.

> But the court which is without the temple leave out, and measure it not; for it is given unto the Gentiles: and the holy city shall they tread under foot forty and two months. (Rev 11:2)

> And the woman fled into the wilderness, where she hath a place prepared of God, that they should feed her there a thousand two hundred and threescore days. (Rev 12:6)

> And to the woman were given two wings of a great eagle, that she might fly into the wilderness, into her place, where she is

nourished for a time, and times, and half a time, from the face of the serpent. (Rev 12:14)

Realizing that the antichrist is given 1260 days to reign and persecute, and knowing that his reign will end at Armageddon we can subtract 1260 days from 2520 days and end up with day 1260 as the start of the rule of the antichrist.

Another date parameter regards to two witnesses who have an important role to play in the end times and the span of their ministry provides us with another end times chronological parameter. Their ministry is described in Rev 11:3-15.

> And I will give power unto my two witnesses, and they shall prophesy a thousand two hundred and threescore days, clothed in sackcloth. These are the two olive trees, and the two candlesticks standing before the God of the earth. And if any man will hurt them, fire proceedeth out of their mouth, and devoureth their enemies: and if any man will hurt them, he must in this manner be killed. These have power to shut heaven, that it rain not in the days of their prophecy: and have power over waters to turn them to blood, and to smite the earth with all plagues, as often as they will. And when they shall have finished their testimony, the beast that ascendeth out of the bottomless pit shall make war against them, and shall overcome them, and kill them. And their dead bodies shall lie in the street of the great city, which spiritually is called Sodom and Egypt, where also our Lord was crucified. And they of the people and kindreds and tongues and nations shall see their dead bodies three days and an half, and shall not suffer their dead bodies to be put in graves. And they that dwell upon the earth shall rejoice over them, and make merry, and shall send gifts one to another; because these two prophets tormented them that dwelt on the earth. And after three days and an half the Spirit of life from God entered into them, and they stood upon their feet; and great fear fell upon them which saw them. And they heard a great voice from heaven saying unto them, Come up hither. And they ascended up to heaven in a cloud; and their enemies beheld them. And the same hour was there a great earthquake, and the tenth part of the city fell, and in the earthquake were slain of men seven thousand: and the remnant were affrighted, and gave glory to the God of heaven. The second woe is past; and, behold, the third woe cometh quickly. And the seventh angel sounded; and there were

great voices in heaven, saying, The kingdoms of this world are become the kingdoms of our Lord, and of his Christ; and he shall reign for ever and ever.

Many over the years have debated their identity—these two witnesses, whoever they are, will prophesy and proclaim God's message of salvation and repentance to the world from Jerusalem. They will also have power, like Moses before Pharaoh, to inflict the world with many judgments.

The timing of their ministry has also been debated. However if you look to the end of Revelation 11, you will notice that right after the witnesses die and are resurrected, the second woe is past. The three woes are the last three trumpet judgments. Thus, their work on earth ends between the 6th and 7th trumpet judgment near the end of the 70th Week. If their ministry started just before or at the same time as the abomination of desolation on day 1230, then their ministry would end just before or on day 2490, thus establishing a beginning date for the bowl judgments.

Here is a chart summarizing this information.

Event	# Days After Beginning of 70th Week
Abomination of Desolation	1230
Beginning of the rule of antichrist	1260
Beginning of the bowl judgments	2490
Armageddon	2520
Beginning of the Millennium	2565

We have established general date parameters for several events in the 70th Week and we have also discussed the importance of the fulfillment of the fall feasts in end times chronology. We will now attempt to integrate the data into a more exact end times scenario.

Chapter 12
When?

That is the question everyone wants the answer to; when will the will these things take place? Are you ready for the answer? I do not know. But is there anything that we can look for that will enable us to come up with possible end times scenarios and maybe even a most probable end time scenario? Yes, I believe there is.

2014/2015 Lunar and Solar Eclipses
In 2014 and 2015 there will be 4 blood moon total lunar eclipses all falling on feast days.

1. Passover, April 15, 2014
2. Tabernacles October 8, 2014
3. Passover, April 4, 2015
4. Tabernacles, September 28, 2015

What is significant about this? A tetrad of lunar eclipses on feast days has only occurred two times in the last 500 years; 1949/50, and 1967/68. During each of those tetrads of total eclipses Israel was at war.

> Though Israel was declared an independent state sixty years ago in 1948, the war with its neighbors began after its first day and lasted for a year. Therefore, the first lunar eclipse of 1949 occurred during this war for the establishment of Israel. The next tetrad began on Passover 1967, which was just six weeks before the Six-Day-War. Therefore, these two significant wars of Israel were covered by each tetrad period.[134]

The time before those tetrads of eclipses on feast days was in 1493/4. In 1492 the Jews were kicked out of Spain. Another interesting fact is that all of these tetrads occurred in Hebrew "pregnant years" or years with 13 months. These facts lead us to

---
[134] http://www.fivedoves.com/letters/may2008/danielm517.htm

wonder if the upcoming tetrad is a sign from God that something significant will occur in 2014/15 in regards to Israel? Will they be involved in another major war at that time, possibly a war with her Arab neighbors where she regains the Temple Mount setting the stage for major events of the end times? This is something to ponder and watch for, and in my opinion gives us a definite indication that the end times are upon us.

The Great Pyramid

It is believed by many that the Great Pyramid complex at Giza in its design contains time markers or date ciphers pointing to the First and Second coming of the Lord. There are two scriptures that are the basis for this conjecture.

> In that day shall there be an altar to the LORD in the midst of the land of Egypt, and a pillar at the border thereof to the LORD. And it shall be for a sign and for a witness unto the LORD of hosts in the land of Egypt: for they shall cry unto the LORD because of the oppressors, and he shall send them a saviour, and a great one, and he shall deliver them. Isaiah 19: 19,20

> Which hast set signs and wonders in the land of Egypt, even unto this day... Jeremiah 32:20a

Prophecy researcher Daniel Matson has made some startling discoveries regarding the date ciphers of the Great Pyramid complex at Giza. In Chapter 16 of his book, *Signs of the End* he states;

> What is important is that there is valuable information that must be passed along that is a striking discovery concerning the Great Pyramid complex at Giza and its marking both advents of Christ. It is a discovery that is in line with the Bible, history, and the magnificence of the pyramids. It highlights the time in precise astronomical alignments. It is a discovery that fits the themes woven into the Bible concerning the coming King and it further supports the scenario developed in this book.

Thus his research has led him to believe that the Great Pyramid complex at Giza astronomically aligned with the First coming of the Lord, and he believes it will also at His Second Coming, and the alignment points to Rosh Hashanah 2017. What leads the author to this conclusion?

The basic idea is that the pyramid complex is a map of the heavens of a point in time when Christ the King returns with his armies. The pyramids show what is to be at meridian (Al Nitak in Orion), and also the causeways heading east from the pyramids show the importance of the rising sun or other items rising in the east. That the Sphinx also looks to the east is a factor as well. The point though was to see when there was a candidate for an alignment of Rosh Hashanah and the meridian alignment of Orion at dawn...Therefore, at dawn the morning before the Feast of Trumpets 2017, Al Nitak is precisely at meridian...

Let us not forget the all-important Christ angle to see where it might come into significance. At the moment Al Nitak is at meridian, Leo is in the east, but more importantly its star known as Regulus (the King) is precisely at the inclination of the Christ angle. Therefore, the Christ angle not only bisected Bethlehem at Christ's birth, but it also bisects Regulus at this possible time of his Second Coming. The year 2017 is the first year from present that Rosh Hashanah comes immediately after September 20th—the time Al Nitak hits meridian precisely at dawn, and also when Regulus hits the Christ angle...

In analyzing the positioning of the stars, moon, and sun at the time of September 20, 2017, there was also another alignment. Venus will be in conjunction with Regulus at this time. So at this moment Venus the "Morning Star" will be aligned with the "King Star", precisely at the Christ angle...

The ascending and descending passageways of the Great Pyramid share the common Christ angle, but one is actually the prime of the other. Looking at the computer model of the sky when Regulus and Venus are at the Christ angle just prior to dawn, there is again something suspicious. Below the horizon is Jupiter--referred to as the planet of the Messiah by the Jews...At the dawn of Rosh Hashanah 2017, Jupiter is at the precise Christ angle in the opposite scenario as the day before. Jupiter is below the horizon at 26.3 degrees...

So as there are opposite Christ angles, it would appear that the pyramid is a map of this event. Jupiter is the suffering Messiah at the descending angle, whereas the "morning star" and glorious king are on the ascending angle. Therefore, the Great Pyramid would be a map of this time when Rosh Hashanah coincides with the dawn meridian of Al Nitak and the positioning of Christ's representative planets at the Christ angle. What are the odds? It would probably be safe to say that this is practically the only time these alignments could occur in our era... (Used by permission of author. I would highly recommend reading the entire chapter, which is available at this link http://2010rapture.org/signsoftheend/giza.html)

As already mentioned these many significant alignments lead him to believe that the First Coming was marked by the celestial alignment of the Great Pyramid, and that events surrounding the Second Coming will be marked by the celestial alignments on Rosh Hashanah in 2017. I contend that the alignment at Rosh Hashanah in 2017 is a significant occurrence and will align with important end times events. Is this why the pyramids were built, and have withstood throughout time? Are they a "sign and witness" of events surrounding the First and Second Coming of the Lord? If they are, then they have profound prophetic significance for the year 2017, especially in light of the Revelation 12 sign of the woman clothed with the sun.

The Woman Clothed with the Sun

In Revelation 12 I believe that we are given a very important sign regarding the coming of the Lord

> 12:1 And there appeared a great wonder in heaven; a woman clothed with the sun, and the moon under her feet, and upon her head a crown of twelve stars: 2 And she being with child cried, travailing in birth, and pained to be delivered.

Here I believe we see a symbolic picture of the nation of Israel—the woman—and the coming of the Christ child. I believe this symbolism appeared as a sign in the skies over Jerusalem in the alignment of the stars on Rosh Hashanah 9/11/3 BC. (Note: Click on the following link to see the images of the celestial alignments I will be referring to in this section; Look Up for Your Redemption Draweth Nigh.) On that day the constellation Virgo was "clothed with the sun," and the moon was under her feet. Above her head 3 planets—Mercury, Venus, and Jupiter—were in alignment with the star Regulus in Leo, Regulus was also in conjunction with Jupiter. This Regulus/Jupiter conjunction is what David Larson, mentioned above, believes is the famed Star of Bethlehem. The 9 stars of Leo and the 3 planets aligning with Regulus make the crown of 12 stars.

Now let's examine the skies around the time that the Great Pyramid complex points to, Rosh Hashanah in 2017. On 9/20-21/17 Rosh Hashanah; Virgo is clothed with the Sun, the Moon is not under her feet but is in close conjunction with the sun, and there is an alignment of Jupiter, the Moon, Mercury, Mars, Venus, and Regulus, with Venus in conjunction with Regulus.

Three days after this alignment on 9/23/17, Virgo is "clothed with the sun," the moon is now under her feet, and above her head are 3 planets—Mercury, Mars, and Venus, which are in alignment with the star Regulus in Leo. The 9 stars of Leo and the 3 aligning planets make the crown of 12 stars. Thus this alignment meets the criteria of the Rev. 12 sign and is similar to the 3 BC alignment. Interestingly enough this alignment occurs the day after the second day of Rosh Hashanah on the day of Shabbat Shuvah—the Sabbath of Return.[135] We will discuss implications regarding this below.

So there we have it, the sign of Revelation 12 in the sky above Jerusalem on special days, of which in their alignments and their meanings point to major prophetic events surrounding the First and Second Coming of Christ. Thus I believe these celestial alignments in 2017 have major prophetic implications of which we will discuss more in detail after the next piece of data.

Rabbi Judah Ben Samuel Prophecy

The following is the write up of a prophecy made by Rabbi Judah Ben Samuel that I believe is significant in regards to answering the question when, and may point to a possible year of the Second Coming. The original article appeared in Israel Today, March 2008[136]

> In 1217 the Jewish Rabbi Judah Ben Samuel prophesied that the Ottoman Turks would rule over the holy city of Jerusalem for

---

[135] Shabbat Shuvah or Shabbat T'shuvah ("Sabbath [of] Return" שובה שבת or "Sabbath [of] Repentance" תשובה שבת) refers to the Shabbat that occurs during the Ten Days of Repentance, but is between (i.e. not including): the two consecutive Days of Rosh Hashanah; and the Day of Yom Kippur. The name Shabbat Shuvah comes from the first word of the Haftarah that is read on that day, Hosea 14:2-10, and literally means "Return!" It is alternately known as Shabbat T'shuvah owing to its being one of the Aseret Y'may T'shuvah (Ten Day of Repentance). http://en.wikipedia.org/wiki/Special_Shabbat#Shabbat_Shuvah
[136] http://issuu.com/ryaninzion/docs/israel_today_march_2008

eight Jubilees. A Jubilee is a period of 50 years according to Leviticus 25:8-13. Eight Jubilees would then be 400 years. Sure enough, 300 years later in 1517 the Ottoman Turks seized control of the city of Jerusalem and ruled over it for the next 400 years. They were finally driven out of the city and the holy land in 1917 by the Allied forces under the command of General George Allenby. The Rabbi's prophecy about the 400 years was fulfilled exactly to the year.

The Rabbi had also prophesied that during the ninth Jubilee Jerusalem would be a "no-man's land." This is exactly what happened from 1917 to 1967, due to the fact that the holy land was placed under British Mandate in 1917 by the League of Nations and literally "belonged" to no nation. Even after Israel's war of independence in 1948-49 Jerusalem was still divided by a strip of land running right through the heart of the city, with Jordan controlling the eastern part of the city and Israel controlling the western part of the city. That strip of land was considered and even called "no-man's land" by both the Israelis and the Jordanians. Anyone even stepping into that strip would be shot down. I lived during that period of time and well remember the reports in the newspapers and shown on TV about the division of Jerusalem. It was not until the Six Day War in 1967 when the entire west bank of the holy land was conquered by the Israeli army that the whole city of Jerusalem passed back into the possession of Israel. So once again the prophecy made by the Rabbi 750 years previously was fulfilled to the letter.

But that is still not the end of the matter. The Rabbi also prophesied that during the 10th Jubilee Jerusalem would be under the control of the Jews and the Messianic "end times" would begin. The 10th Jubilee began in 1967 and will be concluded in 2017.[137]

Let's consider the data;

Jubilees 1-8 (1517 to 1917): Turks will rule.

Jubilee 9 (1917 to 1967): Jerusalem a "no man's land."

---

[137] http://www.injesus.com/index.php?module=message&task=view&MID=ZB007HAL&GroupID=2A004N9G&print=1

Jubilee 10 (1967 to 2017): Jerusalem under Jewish control, Messianic end times will begin.

Jubilee 11: Begins at Yom Kippur 9/30/17.

Jubilees 1-8 and 9 were fulfilled as his prophecy stated. His prophecy also states "during the 10th Jubilee Jerusalem would be under the control of the Jews and the Messianic "end times" would begin." Therefore if the prophecy is to be trusted, then the Messianic "end times" would have to start within the time of the 10th jubilee, before the 11th Jubilee starts at Yom Kippur on 9/30/17. Thus if the Messianic "end times" refers to the beginning of the 70th Week, then the prophecy implies the Second Coming will be no later than 2024. If the Messianic "end times" refers to Jacob's trouble—the second half of the 70th Week—then the prophecy implies the Second Coming will be no later than 2021.

The Most Probable Scenario

Let's see if we can integrate all of the data discussed in this book into a "most probable scenario." Here is a synopsis of some of the data and their associated dates.

2014-2015: Tetrad of lunar eclipses on feast days—associated with Israel at war and or under persecution.

9/21/17: Pyramid alignments—associated with events surrounding the First and Second Coming of Jesus.

9/20-23/17: Rev. 12 Sign of the Woman clothed with the sun—associated with First and Second Comings of Jesus.

9/30/17: Rabbi Judah Ben Samuel prophecy—beginning of Messianic end times before Day of Atonement in 2017.

With this data in mind, and noting its important prophetic implications for Rosh Hashanah in 2017, I can foresee three possible scenarios based on that date;

1. The **Rapture will occur on 9/23/17**, with the Second Coming 2018-2020 necessitating a 2011-2013 start of the 70th week.

2. The **abomination of desolation will occur around 9/23/17**, with the Millennium beginning in 2021 necessitating a 2014 start of the 70th week.

3. The **70th Week will begin on 9/23/17** with the Second Coming in 2024.

Let's consider each scenario from a scriptural point of view; in regards to scenario #1, it would suggest knowing the day of the rapture, which I believe would violate the principle of scripture of no one knowing the day and hour. In regards to Scenario #3—that the 70th week would begin on that day or around that time—is certainly a possibility that we will have to watch for, but the dates do not synchronize with fall feast days. That leaves us with scenario #2; let's analyze this scenario to see if it is viable.

Here is the way I see the scenario; I believe the 2017 sign of the woman clothed with the sun, which aligns with the Sabbath of Return on 9/23/17, points to Israel "returning" to the Lord. As alluded to by Hosea 14:2 which is read on this special Sabbath day.

> Take with you words, and turn to the Lord: say unto him, Take away all iniquity, and receive us graciously: so will we render the calves of our lips.

Scripture tells us that this returning to the Lord by Israel is precipitated by the performing of the abomination of desolation by the antichrist after which Israel flees into the wilderness for 3.5 years.

> 14 But when ye shall see the abomination of desolation, spoken of by Daniel the prophet, standing where it ought not, (let him that readeth understand,) then let them that be in Judaea **flee** to the mountains:…18 And pray ye that your **flight** be not in the winter. Mark 13

1 And there appeared a great wonder in heaven; a woman clothed with the sun, and the moon under her feet, and upon her head a crown of twelve stars:...

6 And the woman fled into the wilderness, where she hath a place prepared of God, that they should feed her there a thousand two hundred and threescore days...

14 And to the woman were given two wings of a great eagle, that she might fly into the wilderness, into her place, where she is nourished for a time, and times, and half a time, from the face of the serpent. Rev 12.

This returning to the Lord, if it occurs on 9/23/17, would follow the sign of the Great Giza Pyramid alignment at Rosh Hashanah on 9/21/2017, and may align with a significant event regarding the antichrist, such as when the devil enters into him—hmm...maybe that is why the pyramid is on the back of the dollar bill.

During this flight into the wilderness, after recognizing the Lord Jesus Christ as the true Messiah, fulfilling the Sabbath of Return, they then call out to Jesus for salvation and thus their sins are atoned for, fulfilling the feast of the Day of Atonement that occurs on 9/30/17. And in the wilderness God provides for them and protects them, fulfilling the feast of Tabernacles that occurs on 10/5/17.

If this indeed will be the way it happens when will the beginning and end of the 70th Week be? If the 9/23/17 event is the abomination of desolation, which we have calculated to occur on day 1230, then calculating 1230 days before 9/23/17 brings us to 5/13/14—a possible beginning date of the 70th Week.[138]

Based on this possible starting point of 5/13/14 here is a chart showing the other date calculations.[139]

---

[138] It is possible to shift the date parameters up to 30 days past 5/13/14 to 6/12/14. Also remember Hebrew timing and inclusive and exclusive accounting would make all dates +- 2 days.

[139] The 45 days comes from 1335 days minus the 1290 days given to us in Daniel 12. 11 And from the time that the daily sacrifice shall be taken away, and the abomination that maketh desolate set up, there shall be a thousand two hundred and ninety days. 12 Blessed is he that waiteth, and cometh to the thousand three hundred and five and thirty days.

Event	Day	Date
Beginning of 70th Week	1	May 13, 2014
Abomination of Desolation	1230	Sep 23, 2017
Beginning of the rule of antichrist	1260	Oct 23, 2017
Beginning of the bowl judgments	2490	Mar 6, 2021
Armageddon	2520	Apr 5, 2021
Beginning of the Millennium	2565	May 20, 2021

This scenario takes into account the pyramid alignment, the importance of the alignment and fulfillment of the fall feasts, and other prophetic data. But the question remains; is it viable and or is there any confirmation of this scenario? Maybe; I just recently became aware of 2 more very important signs in the heavens that occur in 2021 that may offer a confirmation. I believe celestial signs are the most important signs that we can look for as indicated in Gen 1:14 "And God said, Let there be lights in the firmament of the heaven to divide the day from the night; and let them be for signs, and for seasons, and for days, and years."

The Sign of the Cross
The sign occurs in the heavens on 2/11/21 and was discovered by a prophecy researcher who believes the odds of this sign are as great as the odds of the 2017 sign—about 3 million to one.[140] (This sign can be viewed at the link in the footnote or at the link provided at the beginning of this chapter.) Therefore I agree with him that this is a significant sign and must be incorporated into any end times scenario. (Note: a cross sign also appeared at Christ's First Coming, again discovered by the same researcher.)

In the chart above the end of the 70th Week, which would be 1290 days after day 1230, is calculated as 4/5/21, and the beginning of the Millennium which would be 1335 days later is on 5/20/21. And as you can see these end dates do not align with the important Cross sign of 2/11/21, giving the initial indication that this new scenario or the sign is not viable. However consider what happens at Trumpet 4.

---

[140] http://www.youtube.com/watch?v=RyjzZYRnEIA

> And the fourth angel sounded, and the third part of the sun was smitten, and the third part of the moon, and the third part of the stars; so as the third part of them was darkened, and the day shone not for a third part of it, and the night likewise. Rev 8:12

Basically what this verse tells me is that after the sounding of the 4th Trumpet 1/3 of the day and night is gone. Since both the day and night appear to be shortened by 1/3, could this mean that the earth's daily rotation speeds up so that a day occurs in 1/3 less time—that a day would now only be 16 hours long instead of 24 hours long? This is something that I never considered before in my date calculations.

If the days were shortened by 1/3 and the earth's progression around the sun stayed the same, then what this would mean practically is that the days would still be counted as normal, but the earth would not be in its normal position relative to the sun for that date. For example on any particular day of the year the earth reaches a certain position relative to the sun, and one year later it should have gone around the sun and be in the same approximate position. However, If the days were shortened by 1/3, then one year later on the calendar, the earth would only be 2/3 the way around the sun. Thus causing the position of the earth in regards to the sun to not be in sync and the earth would fall behind the calendar date. Numerically, the 365 calendar days would be shortened to about 243 days in earth/sun position days.

If the days will be shortened because of the 4th Trumpet, and Trumpet 4 occurred on 7/30/20, then the 294 days from 7/30/20 until 5/20/21 would be shortened to 196 days in earth/sun position days. Thus the earth's position in regards to the sun at the calculated day of the beginning of the Millennium (5/20/21) would now align with its normal earth/sun position on 2/11/21, and if the moon appeared in the same place in the sky, then the sign of the cross would be in the skies that day.

The Sign of the Infernal Trio

On 1/12/21 another sign appears in the skies discovered by the same prophecy researcher mentioned above.[141] He believes this sign is a depiction of Jesus—the rider on the white horse defeating the false prophet, the antichrist, and the devil, and throwing them into the lake

---

[141] http://www.youtube.com/watch?v=mtQDbKTFh2w

of fire. He also believes the odds of this sign are about 3 million to one. In this celestial alignment we have Venus—the bright morning star/Jesus—in the constellation Sagitarius—the horse. We also have the three planets, Jupiter, Mercury, and Saturn—the antichrist, false prophet, and satan—in Capricorn—the goat. This occurrence is described in Revelation 19.

> And I saw heaven opened, and behold a white horse; and he that sat upon him was called Faithful and True, and in righteousness he doth judge and make war. 12 His eyes were as a flame of fire, and on his head were many crowns; and he had a name written, that no man knew, but he himself. 13 And he was clothed with a vesture dipped in blood: and his name is called The Word of God. 14 And the armies which were in heaven followed him upon white horses, clothed in fine linen, white and clean. 15 And out of his mouth goeth a sharp sword, that with it he should smite the nations: and he shall rule them with a rod of iron: and he treadeth the winepress of the fierceness and wrath of Almighty God. 16 And he hath on his vesture and on his thigh a name written, King Of Kings, And Lord Of Lords. 17 And I saw an angel standing in the sun; and he cried with a loud voice, saying to all the fowls that fly in the midst of heaven, Come and gather yourselves together unto the supper of the great God; 18 That ye may eat the flesh of kings, and the flesh of captains, and the flesh of mighty men, and the flesh of horses, and of them that sit on them, and the flesh of all men, both free and bond, both small and great. 19 And I saw the beast, and the kings of the earth, and their armies, gathered together to make war against him that sat on the horse, and against his army. 20 And the beast was taken, and with him the false prophet that wrought miracles before him, with which he deceived them that had received the mark of the beast, and them that worshipped his image. These both were cast alive into a lake of fire burning with brimstone.

How does the sign occurring on 1/12/21 confirm the scenario that I presented above? On the chart above I have the Second Coming—when Jesus returns to the earth at Armageddon, which we know is when the infernal trio gets thrown into the pit—as occurring on 4/5/21. In shortened days 4/5/21 in earth/sun position days aligns with 1/12/21—the day of the sign of the Infernal Trio!

Thus these 2 signs in the heavens may offer a confirmation of this scenario. Here is a chart indicating the shortened dates.

Event	Day	Date	Shortened Date
Beginning of 70th Week	1	May 13, 2014	---
Abomination of Desolation	1230	Sep 23, 2017	---
Beginning of the rule of antichrist	1260	Oct 23, 2017	---
Trumpet 4	2271	Jul 30, 2020	---
Beginning of the bowl judgments	2490	Mar 6, 2021	Dec 23, 2020
Armageddon	2520	Apr 5, 2021	Jan 12, 2021
Beginning of the Millennium	2565	May 20, 2021	Feb 21, 2021

To further confirm this scenario I decided to check some of the other dates. I checked the skies for three dates 10/23/17: When the antichrist is supposed to take over the world, 7/30/20: When Trumpet 4 is supposed to occur, and 3/6/21 (12/23/20): When the bowl judgments are supposed to occur. What I found in the skies on those days surprised me and may offer another confirmation of this scenario. You can see and read about these signs at The End Times Forecaster blog; What Prophecy Time is it? A Few More Confirmations!?.

I also decided to check some of the dates in the scenario with the Hebrew calendar. What I found also surprised me. 7/30/20—the possible day of Trumpet 4—falls on Tish'a B'Av, the day when the First and Second Temples were destroyed—a fitting day for retribution to be brought upon the world for their unrepentant sins. 3/6/21—the possible day for the bowl judgments to start—falls on the Sabbath Parah or Sabbath of the Red Heifer. This is when the Red Heifer would be sacrificed before the priest as recorded in Numbers 19. This Sabbath has many allusions to Jesus and His Second Coming. 4/5/21—the possible day for the Second Coming and Armageddon—falls on the last day of Passover/feast of unleavened bread. This feast commemorates Israel's deliverance from Egypt and also has many allusions to the coming Messiah who will deliver Israel from the persecution of the antichrist at His Second Coming. 5/20/21—the possible day for the beginning of the Millennium—falls on the day after the second day of Shavuot and depending on how you count and round things off could also be a hit. Shavuot is the day Israel was given the Torah and became a nation, it is also known as Pentecost—the birthday of the Church and has illusions to the time when the kingdom of God will be established on earth.

Thus we have 6 critical dates in our scenario that align with important Jewish days, we also have many signs in the skies on several dates in our scenario. Does all of this information confirm our scenario? That is certainly something to ponder. I have put all of this date information into a diagram entitled "The 70th Week of Daniel," viewable at the link.

Conclusion

Thus in light of all the prophecy data I have at this time, I can foresee three possible scenarios based on the important signs of 2017;

1. The **Rapture will occur on 9/23/17**, with the Second Coming 2018-2020 necessitating a 2011-2013 start of the 70th week.

2. The **abomination of desolation will occur on 9/23/17**, with the Millennium beginning in 2021 necessitating a 2014 start of the 70th week.

3. The **70th Week will begin on 9/23/17** with the Second Coming in 2024.

Further I believe that scenario #2—"the **abomination of desolation will occur on 9/23/17**, with the Millennium beginning in 2021, necessitating a 2014 start of the 70th week"—is the most likely scenario.

Is scenario #2 the way it will work out? As always time will tell, but realize that this scenario takes into account and synchronizes all the date parameters, Trumpet 4, the 2 major signs of 2017, the cross sign of 2021, the infernal trio sign of 2012, the fulfilling of the fall feasts, several important dates in the Jewish calendar, and several other signs in the heavens.

If this scenario is the one, then here are some things that we can watch for. First let me mention that if this scenario is valid we do not have to have seen anything of major prophetic importance happen around 5/13/14, for I believe it is highly possible for the 70th week to start silently. Also if this scenario is valid then we will see the first 4 Seals of Revelation occur between 5/13/14 and the calculated midpoint of 10/23/17. Further if this will be the case and the antichrist will arise and take over the world on 10/23/17, then we will see the 6th Seal rapture sometime between 10/23/17 and early 2020. Also if the rapture will align with Rosh Hashanah then, Rosh Hashanah in 2018 and 2019 would be the years to watch.

So let's get back to the original question; when? I do not know the exact year, but I do believe that we are getting close, as the prophetic data and the "most probable scenario" seems to imply. As the saying goes; time will tell, look for WWIII (Seal 2), which will most likely be the definitive sign that we are about to enter into the time period of the great tribulation in which the rapture will occur. "And when these things begin to come to pass, then **look up**, and lift up your heads; for your redemption draweth nigh." Luke 21:28.

Of course there is always the possibility that there is other pertinent prophecy data that I am not aware of, and thus another scenario may be the correct one. **However in light of the important signs around Rosh Hashanah 2017, I do not see the Second Coming (when Jesus returns to earth at Armageddon) occurring any later than 2024—meaning we are very close to seeing major prophetic events occurring**.

Here is something else to consider; if the 2017 hypothesis is correct and WWIII and the other seals will be opened in the near future, are you ready? Are you spiritually, mentally, and physically prepared for the end times? That is what we will discuss in the next chapter—being prepared.

Chapter 13
Be Prepared

Many years ago, I had the wonderful experience of being a Boy Scout. I learned many important skills and character traits through the Scouts. One of the first things I learned was the Boy Scout motto—"Be Prepared." There is nothing worse than being faced with an adverse situation and not being prepared. In the Scouts, we were taught to think ahead about situations that we might encounter while camping and prepare accordingly.

Many difficulties that we face in life, likewise, can be overcome if we think ahead and plan and prepare accordingly. In this chapter, we will think ahead to what difficulties we will face in the 70th Week and I will suggest ways that we can plan and prepare accordingly. By the time you read this book, even though I am writing it before the 70th Week starts, you may already be in it. Even if that is the case, it is still not too late to prepare.

In endeavoring to prepare for this time, you must first realize that many people will be deceived and will not recognize the signs of the prophetic times in which we live. For as the Apostle Paul said, Christ's return to the clouds and the rapture will catch many people off guard and will come upon them as a thief in the night:

> But of the times and the seasons, brethren, ye have no need that I write unto you. For yourselves know perfectly that the day of the Lord so cometh as a thief in the night. For when they shall say, Peace and safety; then sudden destruction cometh upon them, as travail upon a woman with child; and they shall not escape. (1 Thess. 5:1-3)

When the rapture happens, the people of the world will pretty much be going about their daily routines. Even though the 70th Week will have started and the first five seals will bring about much death and destruction, the majority of the people will be so deceived that they will not be able to recognize the prophetic times in which we live.

> But as the days of Noe were, so shall also the coming of the Son of man be. For as in the days that were before the flood

> they were eating and drinking, marrying and giving in marriage, until the day that Noe entered into the ark, And knew not until the flood came, and took them all away; so shall also the coming of the Son of man be. Then shall two be in the field; the one shall be taken, and the other left. Two women shall be grinding at the mill; the one shall be taken, and the other left. (Matt. 24:37-42)

So we see that, even though the first five seals will be opened, and tribulations and sorrows will be experienced by the world, the vast majority of people will not recognize that we are in this prophetic time period and will be caught off guard by the Day of the Lord because they will be deceived by the devil and his cohorts.

But that is not to be the case for the believer. The believer, as Jesus says, is to watch:

> Watch therefore: for ye know not what hour your Lord doth come. But know this, that if the goodman of the house had known in what watch the thief would come, he would have watched, and would not have suffered his house to be broken up. Therefore be ye also ready: for in such an hour as ye think not the Son of man cometh. (Matt. 24:42-44).

The Apostle Paul also echoes the same idea and further tells us that the Day will not overtake *us* as a thief:

> But of the times and the seasons, brethren, ye have no need that I write unto you. For yourselves know perfectly that the day of the Lord so cometh as a thief in the night. For when they shall say, Peace and safety; then sudden destruction cometh upon them, as travail upon a woman with child; and they shall not escape. But ye, brethren, are not in darkness, that that day should overtake you as a thief. Ye are all the children of light, and the children of the day: we are not of the night, nor of darkness. Therefore let us not sleep, as do others; but let us watch and be sober. (1 Thess. 5:1-6)

Note what it says in reference to the Day of the Lord, that it will not overtake the brethren as a thief. Why? Because any serious student of the Bible will recognize the signs of the times and, more specifically, will probably be able to know that the 70th Week has started and will be able to discern the occurrences of the seals. Thus, after seeing the signs, they will know that the Lord's return is imminent. Hopefully, you will be walking close enough to the Lord that you can recognize His pending return and prepare many years in advance for the difficulties that lie ahead.

The most important consideration in getting ready for the Lord's return is to make sure you are prepared spiritually. Jesus told a parable that teaches the importance of being spiritually ready for His return:

> Then shall the kingdom of heaven be likened unto ten virgins, which took their lamps, and went forth to meet the bridegroom. And five of them were wise, and five were foolish. They that were foolish took their lamps, and took no oil with them: But the wise took oil in their vessels with their lamps. While the bridegroom tarried, they all slumbered and slept. And at midnight there was a cry made, Behold, the bridegroom cometh; go ye out to meet him. Then all those virgins arose, and trimmed their lamps. And the foolish said unto the wise, Give us of your oil; for our lamps are gone out. But the wise answered, saying, Not so; lest there be not enough for us and you: but go ye rather to them that sell, and buy for yourselves. And while they went to buy, the bridegroom came; and they that were ready went in with him to the marriage: and the door was shut. Afterward came also the other virgins, saying, Lord, Lord, open to us. But he answered and said, Verily I say unto you, I know you not. Watch therefore, for ye know neither the day nor the hour wherein the Son of man cometh. (Matt. 25:1-13)

Are you ready for the bridegroom?

Spiritual Preparation

The starting point for being spiritually prepared is to make sure that you are a Christian. "Examine yourselves, whether ye be in the faith; prove your own selves..." (2 Cor. 13:5a) Becoming a Christian is a very simple yet profound process. There are four things one must know in order to become a Christian:

> 1. **We are sinners**. As the Bible says; "For all have sinned, and come short of the glory of God" (Rom. 3:23). Sin is falling short of God's perfection. Everyone has sinned many times in life. We have all lied, or stolen, or cheated, or done something

wrong at some time in our lives. "As it is written, There is none righteous, no, not one" (Rom. 3:10).

2. We deserve Hell. Realize that there is a punishment for being a sinner, and that punishment is death. "For the wages of sin is death" (Rom. 6:23). The punishment for sin is not just physical death, but also spiritual death. The place of spiritual death is Hell. "But the fearful, and unbelieving, and abominable, and murderers, and whoremongers, and sorcerers, and idolaters, and all liars, shall have their part in the lake which burneth with fire and brimstone: which is the second death" (Rom. 21:8). We all have sinned and we all deserve the punishment of Hell for our sin.

3. Jesus died for our sins. "But God commendeth his love toward us, in that, while we were yet sinners, Christ died for us" (Rom. 5:8). Jesus willingly went to the cross, shed His blood, and died for our sins. On the cross Jesus paid the price for our sins, He suffered the punishment that we deserve, He suffered Hell for us. Hell is a place of total separation from God. When Jesus was on the cross, God the Father separated Himself from God the Son. That is why Jesus cried out "with a loud voice, saying, Eli, Eli, lama sabachthani? That is to say, My God, my God, why hast thou forsaken me?" While Jesus was on the cross He was experiencing separation from God the Father. In other words He was suffering Hell. He was suffering the Hell that we deserve. While on the cross Jesus paid for all the sins of mankind, past, present, and future.

4. We must receive Christ by faith. In order to receive the forgiveness of our sins and become a Christian it is not enough to know that we are sinners, that we deserve Hell, and that Christ died for our sins, but we must receive Christ by faith. "For by grace are ye saved through faith; and that not of yourselves: it is the gift of God: Not of works, lest any man should boast" (Eph 2:8,9).

Notice that that verse tells us that we cannot earn our way to heaven. We obtain salvation through faith, not by works. Faith basically boils down to placing your trust in something or someone. If you are sitting down while reading this book, you are placing your faith or trust in the chair that you are sitting upon. Faith requires more than just an intellectual belief; it involves an action of your will. For example, if there were a pond covered with ice, and there were people standing around saying that the ice could hold them up, but they were not willing to walk on the ice, then they would only be demonstrating an intellectual belief and not faith. If they stepped out onto the ice, they would be demonstrating faith.

One can place their faith in Christ by simply calling out to Him in prayer, for the Bible says, "For whosoever shall call upon the name of the Lord shall be saved."

I placed my faith in Christ by sincerely praying a prayer like this: **"Dear Jesus, I am a sinner. I deserve Hell. Thank you for dying for my sins. Save me. Come into my life. Make me the kind of person that you want me to be. I thank you that you have and that you will take me to heaven when I die. Amen."**

If you sincerely pray that prayer with all your heart, then the Lord Jesus will come into your life and forgive your sins, and save you from an eternity of Hell. If you were to die tomorrow, you would go to heaven. Not because you are good enough to get there, but because you have received the payment of your sins. It is that simple.

> Verily, verily, I say unto you, He that heareth my word, and believeth on him that sent me, hath everlasting life, and shall not come into condemnation; but is passed from death unto life. (Jn 5:24)

So the first thing that one needs to do in order to get ready spiritually for the Lord's return is to make sure that you are a Christian. I would encourage you, if you are not sure of your eternal destiny, to take a moment right now and bow your head and sincerely pray the prayer listed above and place your faith in the Lord Jesus Christ. Once you are saved, nothing can separate you from the love of God. For more on the security of your salvation, see the article "Eternal Security" at www.thecomingepiphany.com.

Righteous Living

The next step in being spiritually prepared for the Lord's return is to make sure that you are living a righteous life — that is, a life without offence toward God and man. There are serious consequences for the believer who is not living in obedience to our Lord's commands.

> For this cause many are weak and sickly among you, and many sleep. For if we would judge ourselves, we should not be judged. But when we are judged, we are chastened of the Lord, that we should not be condemned with the world. (1 Cor. 11:30-32)

These verses suggest that the disobedient Christian will be subject to problems, sickness, and even death for their disobedience. You certainly do not want to be in a disobedient state when the Lord returns.

How do you live a righteous life? Righteous living is summed up in just two commandments:

> Jesus said unto him, Thou shalt love the Lord thy God with all thy heart, and with all thy soul, and with all thy mind. This is the first and great commandment. And the second is like unto it, Thou shalt love thy neighbour as thyself. On these two commandments hang all the law and the prophets. (Matt. 22:37-40)

Thus, the two most important things for a Christian to do is to love God with all his heart and love his neighbor as himself.

How does a Christian love God? Jesus answered that question succinctly:

> If ye love me, keep my commandments." (Jn 14:15)

> He that hath my commandments, and keepeth them, he it is that loveth me: and he that loveth me shall be loved of my Father, and I will love him, and will manifest myself to him. (Jn 14:21)

Jesus told us the way that we love God is to keep the commandments.

There are some Christians who say to make a list of items that you should obey is legalism. No, to *not* have a list of things a Christian should obey is licentiousness. Legalism is when you say that one must obey a list of "dos and don'ts" for salvation. To have a list of dos and don'ts from the Bible to show love to God is godly living. Those who say the Christian is free or at liberty to do as they wish are not free. Rather, they are enslaving themselves to sin at the dictates of their misguided imaginations and fleshly desires. If someone is legalistic in saying, in order to love God you must keep the commandments, then Jesus was legalistic when He commanded us to keep them. We know that this was not the case. Therefore it is not legalism to obey God.

Here are some of the many things that the Lord, either directly or by application of principle, commands Christians to do:

- Pray and read the Bible daily
- Be baptized
- Attend church
- Give tithes and offerings
- Love our neighbor as our self
- Share the gospel
- Obey authorities
- Forgive others
- Dress modestly

Here are some of the many things that the Lord, either directly or by application of principle, commands Christians to *not* do.

- Lie
- Steal
- Cheat
- Cuss
- Covet
- Murder and commit acts of violence
- Hate
- Harbor unforgiveness
- Fornicate
- Commit adultery
- Listen to rock and rap music
- Looking at unwholesome things

Unfortunately, many Christians have swallowed—hook, line and sinker— the lie of the devil that a Christian is free to live as they please. This philosophy is contrary to the teaching of scripture. I have worked with Christian young people for 20 years, and I have seen a steady progression of worldliness and unrighteousness in the lives of the children and their parents. And sadly enough, many of these young people have fallen into grievous sins and brought great destruction to their lives. For more information on how to live righteously, see the article entitled "Living Righteous" at www.thecomingepiphany.com.

Remember we obey God, not for the purpose of earning salvation, but because God has saved us from a terrible hell and we out of love for the Lord want to glorify Him by abstaining from sin and living a Godly life. Let us not use our liberty in Christ as a license to sin. The Apostle Paul gives us a strong admonition if we continue in sin:

> Be ye therefore followers of God, as dear children; And walk in love, as Christ also hath loved us, and hath given himself for us an offering and a sacrifice to God for a sweetsmelling savour. But fornication, and all uncleanness, or covetousness, let it not be once named among you, as becometh saints; Neither filthiness, nor foolish talking, nor jesting, which are not convenient: but rather giving of thanks. For this ye know, that no whoremonger, nor unclean person, nor covetous man, who is an idolater, hath any inheritance in the kingdom of Christ and of God. Let no man deceive you with vain words: for because of these things cometh the wrath of God upon the children of disobedience. Be not ye therefore partakers with them. (Eph. 5:1-7)

Dear Christian, as we see the Day of the Lord approaching, let us sincerely examine ourselves before the Lord with a humble and contrite heart to make sure that we are in the faith and that we are living a life that is pleasing to Him. Let us all strive to hear the words "Well done, thou good and faithful servant enter into the joy of thy master" (Matt. 25:21). Do not try to claim that you love the Lord if you do not obey Him. Jesus said; "He that loveth me not keepeth not my sayings: and the word which ye hear is not mine, but the Father's which sent me." (John 14:24)

This may seem difficult, but you don't have to do it alone. The power and ability to live the Christian life comes through the controlling and empowering of the Holy Spirit. In scripture, this is referred to as walking in the Spirit or being filled with the Spirit.

> Wherefore be ye not unwise, but understanding what the will of the Lord is. And be not drunk with wine, wherein is excess; but be filled with the Spirit. (Eph. 5:17,18)

> This I say then, Walk in the Spirit, and ye shall not fulfil the lust of the flesh. (Gal. 5:16)

How can a Christian be filled with the Spirit? Colossians 2:6 answers that question: "As ye have therefore received Christ Jesus the Lord, so walk ye in him." This verse is basically saying that in the same way that we received Christ, we should also walk in Him. How does a Christian receive Christ? Through faith, thus, we are to walk in Him by faith or be filled with the Spirit through faith. So in order to be filled with the Spirit, we must first desire to be filled. Then we must make sure that we have all sins confessed — for God will not fill a dirty vessel — we must also present ourselves to God as a living sacrifice to be used any way that He may wish, and ask to be filled and believe by faith that we are filled.

Here is a suggested prayer to be filled with the Spirit: **"Dear God I present myself to you to be used any way that you desire. Fill me with your Spirit, direct me, control me and empower me. Live your life through me. I thank you that you will. Amen."**

Mental Preparation

In order to be ready for the return of the Lord, we must not only be spiritually prepared, but we must also be mentally prepared. To do this, we need to have a good working knowledge of prophetic truths. The Lord admonishes believers to not be asleep in regards to prophetic matters:

> But of that day and that hour knoweth no man, no, not the angels which are in heaven, neither the Son, but the Father. Take ye heed, watch and pray: for ye know not when the time is...Lest coming suddenly he find you sleeping. And what I say unto you I say unto all, Watch. (Luke 13:32-37)

Here, Jesus warns believers of being asleep at His return. I believe He is specifically referring to being mentally and spiritually asleep, or unaware of the prophetic times that we live in, and the pending sorrows and tribulations that Christians are going to have to endure during the 70th Week. This description would probably classify the vast majority of sincere Christians that, due to a lack of fervency in seeking after the truth in relation to end times prophecy, have blindly adhered to what their well-respected, but erring pre-trib teachers have taught them.

So I say, wake up, Christian, know that we are very close to entering the 70th Week of Daniel, and by the time you read this we may already be in it. Do not remain asleep to the pending trials that are going to come upon the world with the opening of the seals. Christians who remain asleep and do not prepare spiritually, mentally and physically for those trials will be subject to extreme difficulties and hardships. After the Abomination of Desolation, the antichrist will require all to take the mark in order to buy or sell.

> And he causeth all, both small and great, rich and poor, free and bond, to receive a mark in their right hand, or in their foreheads: And that no man might buy or sell, save he that had the mark, or the name of the beast, or the number of his name. (Rev. 13:16,17)

What are Christians who have not prepared for those times going to do when they are faced with the choice of not being able to buy or sell unless they take the mark? And yes, it will be a choice, and will not be forced upon anyone as was depicted in the popular, but scripturally inaccurate, *Left Behind* series. Many misinterpret Rev. 13:16, which says, "And he causeth all, both small and great, rich and poor, free and bond, to receive a mark in their right hand, or in their foreheads," to read "And he forces" instead of "And he causeth." The Greek word in question here is *poieo*. Strong's Greek and Hebrew dictionary defines it as "to produce, construct, form, fashion, to be the authors of, to make ready, to prepare." The word in no way means, "to force."

It will be a choice that all alive at the time will have to make, and I fear some nominal Christians will choose the mark, undoubtedly reasoning it away somehow, especially when they are faced with not being able to buy or sell. Some may even be faced with a choice of taking the mark or being put to death. Unfortunately, the threat of death will, along with the many deceptions and persecutions, will be part of the reason there will be a great falling away from the faith.

Scripture even indicates that many nominal Christians *will* fall away to the point where they will even betray family members.

> Now the brother shall betray the brother to death, and the father the son; and children shall rise up against their parents, and shall cause them to be put to death. And ye shall be hated of all men for my name's sake: but he that shall endure unto the end, the same shall be saved. (Mark 13:12,13)

If somebody takes the mark are they really doomed to hell? The answer is found in Rev. 14:9-12:

> And the third angel followed them, saying with a loud voice, If any man worship the beast and his image, and receive his mark in his forehead, or in his hand, The same shall drink of the wine of the wrath of God, which is poured out without mixture into the cup of his indignation; and he shall be tormented with fire and brimstone in the presence of the holy angels, and in the presence of the Lamb: And the smoke of their torment ascendeth up for ever and ever: and they have no rest day nor night, who worship the beast and his image, and whosoever receiveth the mark of his name.

So yes, those who take the mark are doomed to hell. Do not let any fantasy series convince you otherwise. The *Left Behind* series portrayed an individual who was forced to take the mark and who later was saved. This is in contradiction to the scripture above. Taking the mark will be an eternal choice with clear ramifications.

Physical Preparations

Along with making spiritual and mental preparations for the return of the Lord, one must also make physical preparations. Preparing for the future is a basic life principle. "Go to the ant, thou sluggard; consider her ways, and be wise: Which having no guide, overseer, or ruler, provideth her meat in the summer, and gathereth her food in the harvest." (Prov 6:6-8) "A prudent man foreseeth the evil, and hideth himself: but the simple pass on, and are punished." (Prov 22:3) These verses make it clear that a Christian is to prepare for the future. So how can a Christian prepare physically for the 70th Week? We must first consider what we are likely to be faced with. As already discussed, Christians will be faced with living through the first five seals.

Let us re-examine again what the first five seals entail:

First seal (white horse): Establishment of the world religion and or government through deception.

Second seal (red horse): War and or anarchy on the earth.

Third seal (black horse): Famine due to crop failures and or a worldwide economic collapse.

Fourth seal (pale horse): Death of one-quarter of world's population by various means, possibly culminating from the first four seals.

Fifth seal: Persecution and martyrdom of Jews and Christians.

The first five seals will span a length of time from at least 3.5 years to a maximum of six years in total duration. See the charts entitled "The Afflictions of the 70th Week" and "The Three Sevens '777'" at the end of this book for a pictorial representation of this data. Things will become more severe upon the opening of the fifth seal, which starts after the 3½ year point. That time period is called the great tribulation and is when Christian and Jews will be persecuted and no one will be able to buy or sell without having the mark of the beast. Even though the first four seals present many difficulties, the fifth seal will be the most difficult to withstand. This is the time that Christians will need to concentrate on preparing for.

Realizing the great tribulation, as already discussed, will most likely last from ½ to 2½ years, thus Christians will probably be faced with up to a maximum of 2½ years of time where they will not be able to buy or sell and will have to prepare for. In considering how to prepare for those times realize that saving money for that time will most likely be of no help, for with the initiation of the mark the world will be under a cashless monetary system and money will be obsolete and become worthless. Thus to prepare one should concentrate on making preparations which will allow you to make it through those times without money.

The first and most important necessity for life is water. Unless you have vast economic resources, and large amounts of storage space, you will not have the ability to store several years' worth of water. In my opinion the best way to provide for your water needs would be to obtain a good water filter that will remove all harmful materials. With a good filter, you could use rainwater, pond water, and or stream water and, after filtering it, you could use it for whatever you wanted. I prefer gravity filters, which use silver impregnated ceramic "candles" to filter out the impurities and pathogens. Missionaries have used these for years. You can take muddy pond water and pour it in the top and you will get out clean water. The replaceable filter elements are good for a couple thousand gallons. These units cost about $200 to $300. They are well worth the investment.

The next most important preparation is food. If Christians will not be able to buy or sell for up to 2.5 years then ideally you should try to have that much food stored. Since we do not know when the 70th Week will begin you want to buy foods that will keep for extended periods of time. Thus, we are talking about dried or canned foods. There are many companies that sell freeze-dried foods and also offer package deals on case lots. Or you could gather the foods yourself from local businesses and package them for long time storage.[142] At present many foods suitable for long time storage can be obtained quite inexpensively. Rice, pasta, flour, dried beans, oatmeal, dried soups, canned vegetables, nuts, chocolate, raisins, sugar, dried potatoes, dried milk, etc. There are numerous grocery stores and wholesale centers that offer bulk quantities of food at reasonable prices. You want to make sure that you cover all the basic food groups, the greater the variety the better. To fulfill your protein needs, freeze-dried meats are available, but they can be a little costly. Vegetable proteins, such as beans, are also an excellent cost effective source of protein. Also having a supply of seeds and knowing how to grow vegetables would be another good idea. One could grow large amounts of fresh vegetables or obtain them from a farm and can them. There are whole books devoted to emergency preparedness, and it would be a good idea to consult them to become more knowledgeable in this area.

It would also be helpful if one learned how to hunt and fish. Being able to harvest fresh meat would be a good addition to any diet. To be able to hunt or fish would necessitate purchasing hunting and

---

[142] http://www.youtube.com/watch?v=vW7_cTn6YpE

fishing equipment. Rods, reels, lures, line, guns, ammunition, bow and arrows, hunting clothes, and skinning knives are all needed to help gather fresh meat. And do not naively think that just owning those items makes you a hunter or fisherman. It takes practice.

The next concern we should consider is shelter, which includes housing and clothes. Most of us probably have enough clothes to make it through a couple of years. But if you have smaller children that will be growing, you may want to make sure that you have some bigger size clothing pre-bought for them. As for housing, it is unclear exactly what will transpire. From what we have previously discussed about the seals, we know that there will be a severe economic collapse. Whether people will be able to keep their houses without paying their mortgages is unknown. Most likely, they will not. Also those who pay rent will not be able to do so either after the mark comes about. We will consider some possibilities of what one can do about this later in this chapter, but in case all else failed it wouldn't hurt to have a tent.

Another consideration is electricity. Most likely, at some point we will be without it. This may be a result of natural disasters, wars, and or not being able to buy or sell. As a matter of fact, Iran has claimed that it has the ability to destroy our power grid and take out all items with computer chips, including modern automobiles, using electromagnetic pulses.[143] Lt. Col Thomas E. Bearden (retd.), who has done extensive research in scalar weaponry, asserts that hostile forces will conduct an asymmetrical war against the U.S. in the future and will eventually take out the power grid and collapse the economy.

> Selected portable weapons of such types are to be inserted — probably some have already been inserted — into the U.S. and used internally by the Yakuza in its coming destruction of our centralized electrical power system... the loss of our national electrical power system is intended to evoke the catastrophic collapse of the entire U.S. economy, followed by the fall of other Western nations' economies like toppling dominoes.[144]

---

[143] Farah, Joseph. *Iran Military Journal Eyes Nuclear EMP Attack on U.S.* April 29, 2005. WorldNetDaily.com

[144] Bearden, Lt. Col Thomas. Scalar Electromagnetic Weapons and their Terrorist Use: Immediate Strategic Aspects of the Asymmetric War on the U.S. Oct 13, 2004

Whether God allows this to occur is yet to be seen but the possibility of being without electricity in the near future is real. Being without electricity presents a problem for most of us because we rely on it for heat, refrigeration, cooking, and much more.[145] So with the possibility of losing electric, we have to make a choice of whether to generate it ourselves or live without it. If you choose to generate it yourself, solar and or wind power is probably the way to go. Generating power with a fossil-fuel-driven engine would necessitate storing huge amounts of fuel and would be impractical. The downside of solar or wind power is the cost, these setups can be quite expensive. If you have unlimited resources, solar and or wind would probably be the best way to provide electricity during the 70th Week. And if you could not afford a solar set up to power your whole house you could maybe just get a big enough one to power essential appliances like your refrigerator and or freezer. The other choice is to prepare to live without electricity. With no electricity, to meet your heating and cooking needs, all you would need to get is a wood stove. If you have a large house, you may have to get a second one. Wood is a readily available source of fuel that one would be able to collect themselves. Solar ovens are also a good way to cook food.

The next consideration would be for necessities such as but not limited to: Bibles, soaps, toothpaste, toilet paper, medicines (including herbal remedies), diapers, candles, solar charger, disposable lighters, camping equipment, flashlights, batteries, crank-up radio, first aid kit, baking soda, salt, hydrogen peroxide, sun screen, vitamins, tea tree oil, personal hygiene items, and tools.

I believe that it would be wise to purchase and learn how to use a gun for defense purposes and or hunting. The best type of gun for home defense is a shotgun. They are relatively easy to use and easy to accurately fire. In an attack, you would probably not have to even use the gun. Just showing it will send most criminals running. Some Christians feel that it is wrong to protect themselves and that guns are evil or bad. This is far from the truth. The use of weapons for protection against criminals, and or in war is promoted in scripture. The most famous example was when David slew Goliath. He used a slingshot, a weapon, to defend Israel and fight the Philistine giant, and then he cut off Goliath's head with his own sword. Thus, weapons for

---

[145] Here is an article that describes what life without electricity would be like. http://rense.com/general80/pwrff.htm

self-defense, guns included, are not bad, only the improper use of them is wrong.

When food and money become scarce, the "have-nots" are going to seek out the "haves," and some will stop at nothing to get what they want. Thus, Christians should be ready to fight off criminals if necessary to protect their families. Of course deadly force should only be used as a last resort in the face of imminent danger. Another consideration is that you should not let anyone know about any of your preparations, even your relatives. Be very discrete about all that you do. Keep all stores in a safe and secure place, if you can hide them, all the better.

During the 70th Week there will be places in the world that will be more dangerous to live than others, and these places should be avoided. The troubles of the 70th Week, as we know, will include various distresses at various places. The Bible indicates that several places will be hotbeds for destruction, including but not limited to Jerusalem, Damascus, and end-times Babylon. Other areas that will probably be most prone to troubles will be the big cities. Not only are they targets for mass destruction, but also when things get tough, riots could break out, making them very dangerous. Thus rural areas would more likely be less dangerous. Also, the farther a rural area is from a big city, the better. For instance, if a nuclear bomb exploded in a city, or a plague hit, you would want to be far enough away so that you were not directly affected. Also in case of widespread nuclear fallout you should have some potassium iodide on hand.[146]

So if one wanted to move to a less dangerous location during the 70th Week, where should they go? God has a perfect will for all of us. Go to Him and ask Him what it is, and when the time comes, If it is His will for you to move He will show you what you need to do. Something to keep in mind and pray about is that after the opening of the fifth seal, and the persecution of the antichrist begins, God commands Israel to flee into the wilderness and He may want you to do the same.

During the beginning of the 70th Week, plagues and diseases will be unleashed upon the land. As already discussed many Bible scholars feel that the fourth seal contains plagues:

---

[146] http://www.nitro-pak.com/product_info.php?cPath=37&products_id=1127

And when he had opened the fourth seal, I heard the voice of the fourth beast say, Come and see. And I looked, and behold a pale horse: and his name that sat on him was Death, and Hell followed with him. And power was given unto them over the fourth part of the earth, to kill with sword, and with hunger, and with death, and with the beasts of the earth. (Rev. 6:7-8)

What can one do to protect themselves against plagues? Many think that a daily intake of colloidal silver will prevent one from getting certain diseases. Jerry Golden has written an article entitled "Learning to Survive an Attack! Colloidal Silver!"[147] which discusses this possibility. In light of this information a colloidal silver generator would also be another item one would want to purchase. A substance that has been proven to be effective in fighting viruses is Sambucol, which is made from elderberries.[148] Another great defense against viruses is taking large doses of vitamin C. Bird flu has been in the news in recent years and could be one the viruses that could afflict the population in the future. Vitamin C is very effective against this virus.[149] Let me also mention that many feel that vaccinations will offer little or no protection against future pandemic viruses because the viruses spread and change so rapidly.[150] Some also think that during this time evil forces may use some vaccinations to spread disease.[151]

Financial Preparations

One must also make wise financial investments. As already discussed, the third seal will probably entail an economic collapse.[152] Believe it or not, there are groups out there who would love to see such a collapse happen, including a secret occult group called The Illuminati, which has had plans in the works for years. [153]

---

[147] http://www.thegoldenreport.com/specialinterest.asp
[148] http://www.israel21c.org/bin/en.jsp?enDispWho=Articles^l1209&enPage=BlankPage&enDisplay=view&enDispWhat=object&enVersion=0&enZone=Health
[149] http://www.healthfreedomusa.org/resources/newsletters/pandemicflu.shtml
[150] http://www.whale.to/v/rapp.html
http://foundingfather1776.wordpress.com/2009/03/06/flu-vaccine-accidentally-contaminated-with-live-avian-flu-virus/
[151] http://educate-yourself.org/nwo/nwopopcontrol.shtml
[152] http://foundingfather1776.wordpress.com/2009/03/07/this-is-what-a-collapse-looks-like/
[153] http://rense.com/general80/protc.htm, Eric Rainbowlt, 1001 Facts Surrounding 9-11-01, Austin, Texas, available for download at Three World Wars.

I am not a financial advisor, and the suggestions herein are not to be deemed as financial advice, but if the economy does collapse, I believe it's important to be debt-free. The banks will come collecting their loans. If you are not able to pay, they will foreclose. So make it your goal to get out of debt. If you have a home mortgage and cannot pay it off before the coming collapse and the mark of the beast is instituted here is an idea that could possibly work; try to anticipate the timing those events, and if possible, pre-pay — by whatever righteous means you can — a couple years worth of mortgage payments, taxes, insurance, and utilities. If you rent seek to do the same. To do this, you need to concentrate on saving as much money as possible now. Also realize that a financial collapse would also involve a collapse of the stock market far worse than what happened in 1929. At such a time most stocks would lose their value. Again I am not a financial expert but if such a collapse of the stock market were to occur during the third seal then it would be wise to move investments to "safer" investments before the collapse occurred. Safer investments could possibly include sector funds, and commodities like grains, oil, and precious metals.[154] Though no investment is guaranteed to be safe these are probably less risky and those sectors are likely to rise in value. One sure investment is wheat, after the third seal a measure of wheat will cost a days wages! (Rev 6:5,6)

But also realize that *all* money will become worthless after the antichrist takes control and establishes the mark. Thus, any money you have just prior to the 3.5-year point should be used to purchase

---

[154] During the economic collapse of the third seal, and possibly before, it is probable that the dollar will suffer a tremendous hit and lose most of its value and with the onset of the mark will eventually be declared obsolete. In such a scenario it may be wise to invest in items that have barter value such as gold, silver, food stores, ammunition, etc. These type items would be a great medium of exchange and would most likely increase in value. Be careful about investing in gold because it may be confiscated as it was in 1933. http://www.the-privateer.com/1933-gold-confiscation.html Note: Some claim that numismatic gold (pre 1933 gold coins) would not be confiscated but a recent treasury document has defined numismatic gold as coins that are at least worth two times the bullion value. Therefore, according to the treasury, most pre 1933 gold coins are merely bullion and may be subject to confiscation. (http://www.fincen.gov/antimoneylaundering060905.pdf http://www.conspiracypenpal.com/columns/whirly.htm) Thus silver may prove to be a better investment than gold. Here are some books that I found helpful concerning investment strategies before and during a financial collapse: Rubino/Turk, *The Collapse of the Dollar and How to Profit from it.* Leeb/Strathy, *The Coming Economic Collapse*, Schiff/Downes, *Crash Proof.*

necessities to make it through the great tribulation. Any other medium of exchange may have some value after the mark comes about, but it would be limited to being used to barter with private individuals.

In regards to when you should make physical preparations; Realize that it is possible that the 70th Week may start this year, it is also possible that it may not start for another 30 years or more, though things are looking like it will be sooner than later. You should make this a matter of prayer, but to be on the safe side preparations that may take a longer time to complete such as saving money, learning to hunt and fish, etc can be started now. Food storage can also be started now as long as you buy foods that can be stored for a long time without perishing.

It is unclear when things will first start to "get bad." All kinds of things could happen before and at the beginning of the 70th week. Some locales may experience troubles before others. For instance what if God allows the American Hiroshima—the threatened nuking of 10 or more American cities—to occur[155], which would be catastrophic for the United States. If it occurs it may occur before the 70th week or could be part of one of the seals. Also there could be severe economic downturns in various places leading up to and at the beginning of the 70th week. More than one financial expert has predicted that the United States will suffer a severe economic downturn before the end of 2008.[156] If any of these scenarios develop life could become very difficult for many. So to be on the safe side it would be better to make preparations sooner than later.

In God's Hands

Of course, these are just examples. I have presented a general outline of how I am attempting to prepare and some ideas for how others might prepare, as well. However, these things should be used as a guideline. Your situation may be different and require different preparations. Some will never be able to prepare. What about the senior citizen living from check to check? What about children living in a home where their parents are not saved? Or what about someone who does not get saved until they actually see the mark of the beast come about? People in these situations will not be able to prepare at

---

[155] Some are saying that the American Hiroshima will occur before the end of 2008 and or shortly after the U.S. attacks Iran.
http://www.wnd.com/news/article.asp?ARTICLE_ID=49950
[156] http://www.europe2020.org/spip.php?article527&lang=en

all. What can people who cannot prepare properly do (or, for that matter, what can any of us do, for none of us can prepare totally for what lies ahead)? The answer is to do the best you can and trust God for the rest. Believers should attempt to prepare as best they can with the resources that God has given them. Due to financial constraints, I have not even been able to prepare to the full extent that I have recommended, but as the Lord provides, I will seek to do those things. Also, do not let me give the false impression that if you prepare you will be guaranteed to have "smooth sailing." Even if you prepare to the fullest you may still face great difficulties during the tribulations of the 70th Week.

At the same time, let me encourage those with means to prepare for and take care of their brothers and sisters in the Lord who do not have the means to take care of themselves:

> Charge them that are rich in this world, that they be not highminded, nor trust in uncertain riches, but in the living God, who giveth us richly all things to enjoy; That they do good, that they be rich in good works, ready to distribute, willing to communicate; Laying up in store for themselves a good foundation against the time to come, that they may lay hold on eternal life. (1 Tim. 6:17-19)

Our first responsibility in life is our relationship with God. Then our responsibilities are to others, which starts with providing for our family. "But if any provide not for his own, he hath denied the faith, and is worse than an infidel" (I Tim 5:8). After we provide for our family, then we are to minister to others and try and meet their needs. You may be the one that God wants to use to meet the needs of that senior citizen in your church living from check to check. We will need to all pull together and help each other make it through that time. It would also probably be advisable to form groups of true believers that can work together to provide for the needs of the group. During the trying times ahead wise pastors would do well to organize their church into such groups.

Prayer will be our most important asset during this time, and Christians should gather together as often as possible to pray about that time and to pray against the plans of the NWO and the antichrist. We can pray even now that the damage, destruction, control, etc of the antichrist and his NWO forces would be kept to a minimum and that their plans would be frustrated. We should also pray for the salvation of the many that will be deceived during these times. We can also pray now that we would be spared from persecution and that we would be left alone to live a life glorifying the Lord till we are raptured.

Let me also remind you that Christians are to never trust in their preparations or weapons to protect them and or deliver them from the tribulations that lie ahead:

> There is no king saved by the multitude of an host: a mighty man is not delivered by much strength. An horse is a vain thing for safety: neither shall he deliver any by his great strength. Behold, the eye of the Lord is upon them that fear him, upon them that hope in his mercy; To deliver their soul from death, and to keep them alive in famine. Our soul waiteth for the Lord: he is our help and our shield. For our heart shall rejoice in him, because we have trusted in his holy name. Let thy mercy, O Lord, be upon us, according as we hope in thee. (Ps 33: 16-22)

At the same time, however, trusting in the Lord does not negate proper preparation. If you knew a hurricane was coming your way, would you be "lacking in faith" by preparing for it, and even evacuating if necessary? Or would you stay in harm's way and be washed out to sea and claim that you were trusting Jesus? We are all supposed to trust Jesus. However, I do not feel one can say, I am not going to prepare because I am trusting in God. We must do all that we can and trust God for the rest.

Was it wrong for David to get five stones out of the brook to prepare to fight Goliath? Or should he have gone out there with no stones and said I am just going to trust God? No, he would have been just dead by his own fault because he did not prepare. Joseph interpreted Pharaoh's dream and told Pharaoh that a seven-year famine was looming in the future. Joseph instructed Pharaoh to prepare, and you know the rest of the story. He did, and many people were saved from the famine. In one of his sermons, Dr. Bob Jones Sr. said, "God will not do for you what He has given you strength to do for yourself." Do all you can trusting in God's power and guidance to prepare for the 70th Week.

What if you are in no financial position to prepare at this time? Pray to God and ask Him to provide for you. Remember the Word of the Lord; "And this is the confidence that we have in him, that, if we ask any thing according to his will, he heareth us: And if we know that he hear us, whatsoever we ask, we know that we have the petitions that we desired of him" (1 John 5:14,15). We know that it is God's will for us to have food and shelter. Remember the wonderful promises of God. "The Lord is our shepherd and we shall not want." Do all you can to get ready, but trust in Him to see you through the difficult times that lie ahead.

Prepare yourself spiritually by making sure of your salvation and removing evil practices from your life. Draw close to the Lord through prayer, Bible reading, and fasting. Prepare yourself mentally by studying prophetic truths so you know what to expect and can make educated decisions based on fact and not panic. And, finally, prepare physically by making sure, as much as is possible, that you have enough necessities to make it through the trials and tribulations ahead. And in all, remember to trust in the Lord. My prayer for you is this: "And the Lord make you to increase and abound in love one toward another, and toward all men, even as we do toward you: To the end he may stablish your hearts unblameable in holiness before God, even our Father, at the coming of our Lord Jesus Christ with all his saints (1 Thess. 3:12,13). Be a good scout; be prepared!

Chapter 14
Jehovah Jireh

Jehovah Jireh my provider His grace is sufficient for me, for me, for me! Jehovah Jireh my provider His grace is sufficient for me. My God shall supply all my needs according to His riches in Glory. He shall give His angels charge over me Jehovah Jireh cares for me, for me, for me! Jehovah Jireh cares for me. Have you ever sung the song "Jehovah Jireh"? If you have, then you know the meaning of those words: "Jehovah Jireh—my provider..." Jehovah Jireh is a name of God that focuses on His ability and promise to provide for His children and take care of their needs. During the 70th Week, it will be no different; God will provide for us and take care of us. After reading this book, some Christians—realizing that they will not be raptured until after the sixth seal is opened—may become frightened. It was not the intention of this book to scare you, although that may be a natural reaction to the things that you have read. The intention of this book was to share the truth of what is about to take place on the earth so that you may properly prepare yourself and your loved ones—spiritually, mentally, and physically. Being properly prepared can help bring you comfort and peace. Not being prepared will bring about the most fear. Panic, many times, is the result of being caught off guard when traumatic situations arise. This book is not about scaring you. It is about giving you information so you may properly prepare for the days leading up to the glorious appearing of the Son of God and have peace through the Lord when times become difficult.

> But ye, brethren, are not in darkness, that that day should overtake you as a thief. Ye are all the children of light, and the children of the day: we are not of the night, nor of darkness. Therefore let us not sleep, as do others; but let us watch and be sober." (1 Thess. 5:4-6)

What does God tell us about fear? God has commanded us hundreds of times to *fear not*! Remember, God will take care of you. Here are just a few of the many scriptures that remind us of those facts.

> Be strong and of a good courage, fear not, nor be afraid of them: for the Lord thy God, he it is that doth go with thee; he will not fail thee, nor forsake thee. (Deut 31:6)

> Be strong and of good courage, and do it: fear not, nor be dismayed: for the Lord God, even my God, will be with thee; he will not fail thee, nor forsake thee, until thou hast finished all the work for the service of the house of the Lord. (1 Chron 28:20)

> And fear not them which kill the body, but are not able to kill the soul: but rather fear him which is able to destroy both soul and body in hell. Are not two sparrows sold for a farthing? and one of them shall not fall on the ground without your Father. But the very hairs of your head are all numbered. Fear ye not therefore, ye are of more value than many sparrows. (Matt. 10:28-31)

If you are a Christian, then God is your Father. Just as a loving earthly father will watch out for and protect his children, so God in a greater way will protect His children. A sparrow cannot fall from the sky unless God allows it. If God cares for the sparrows, how much more does He care for you? God sees your needs; He will help you through whatever may come your way. Go to Him with your needs in prayer and He will answer.

> And I say unto you, Ask, and it shall be given you; seek, and ye shall find; knock, and it shall be opened unto you. For every one that asketh receiveth; and he that seeketh findeth; and to him that knocketh it shall be opened. If a son shall ask bread of any of you that is a father, will he give him a stone? Or if he ask a fish, will he for a fish give him a serpent? Or if he shall ask an egg, will he offer him a scorpion? If ye then, being evil, know how to give good gifts unto your children: how much more shall your heavenly Father give the Holy Spirit to them that ask him? (Luke 11:9-13)

One of the most beautiful and familiar passages in the Bible is Psalm 23. It eloquently speaks of the care, comfort, and protection that God will give to all His sheep.

> The Lord is my shepherd; I shall not want. He maketh me to lie down in green pastures: he leadeth me beside the still waters. He restoreth my soul: he leadeth me in the paths of righteousness for his name's sake. Yea, though I walk through the valley of the shadow of death, I will fear no evil: for thou art with me; thy rod and thy staff they comfort me. Thou preparest a table before me in the presence of mine enemies: thou anointest my head with oil; my cup Runneth over. Surely goodness and mercy shall follow me all the days of my life: and I will dwell in the house of the Lord for ever.

Let me briefly elaborate on the truths contained in this passage. It says that we "shall not want." That means that God will meet our needs, which include physical, mental, and spiritual needs. "To lie down in green pastures," tells us that God will not only meet our needs, but also do it lavishly. "Leadeth me beside the still waters" says that He will give us peace. "He restoreth my soul" speaks of how He will revive our spirits after we have fallen or been dismayed. "Leadeth me in the paths of righteousness" witnesses to the fact that He will lead us into truth and righteous living.

And here is the most important verse in light of the information presented in this book: "Yea, though I walk through the valley of the shadow of death, I will fear no evil: for thou art with me." The first six seals of the 70th Week of Daniel are at times going to be like walking through the valley of the shadow of death. But what are we to do? *Fear no evil!* And why are we to fear no evil? Because *He is with us!* Trust in Him, rely on Him. He will not fail you, and He will show Himself mighty through you to do His work if you let Him. Not only are we not to be afraid, but we can trust that God will meet our physical needs, too. He will give us food and clothing; we can trust Him for that. "I have been young, and now am old; yet have I not seen the righteous forsaken, nor his seed begging bread." There is a verse that we can put our confidence in. Read this Psalm carefully and be assured God will take care of His own:

> Fret not thyself because of evildoers, neither be thou envious against the workers of iniquity. For they shall soon be cut down like the grass, and wither as the green herb. Trust in the Lord, and do good; so shalt thou dwell in the land, and verily thou shalt be fed. Delight thyself also in the Lord: and he shall give thee the desires of thine heart. Commit thy way

unto the Lord; trust also in him; and he shall bring it to pass. And he shall bring forth thy righteousness as the light, and thy judgment as the noonday. Rest in the Lord, and wait patiently for him: fret not thyself because of him who prospereth in his way, because of the man who bringeth wicked devices to pass. Cease from anger, and forsake wrath: fret not thyself in any wise to do evil. For evildoers shall be cut off: but those that wait upon the Lord, they shall inherit the earth. For yet a little while, and the wicked shall not be: yea, thou shalt diligently consider his place, and it shall not be....For the arms of the wicked shall be broken: but the Lord upholdeth the righteous. The Lord knoweth the days of the upright: and their inheritance shall be for ever. *They shall not be ashamed in the evil time: and in the days of famine they shall be satisfied.* But the wicked shall perish, and the enemies of the Lord shall be as the fat of lambs: they shall consume; into smoke shall they consume away....The steps of a good man are ordered by the Lord: and he delighteth in his way. Though he fall, he shall not be utterly cast down: for the Lord upholdeth him with his hand. *I have been young, and now am old; yet have I not seen the righteous forsaken, nor his seed begging bread*....But the salvation of the righteous is of the Lord: he is their strength in the time of trouble. And the Lord shall help them, and deliver them: he shall deliver them from the wicked, and save them, because they trust in him." (Psalm 37)

So do not be afraid. As long as you are living a life pleasing to God, He will protect you, provide for you, and pour out His Spirit upon you in a mighty way. In a lot of ways, it will be a time to look forward to. It will be a time when the Lord will work mightily on the earth. Yes, there will be problems and trials and tribulations, but God will take care of you. Consider this comforting quote from *The Days of Praise*.

> Let your conversation be without covetousness; and be content with such things as ye have: for he hath said, I will never leave thee, nor forsake thee. (Heb 13:5)... Actually, the promise is even more emphatic in the original Greek. The word "leave," which means to uphold or sustain, is preceded by a twice-repeated negative. It literally means, "I will not, I will not cease to uphold you!" The word "forsake" implies forsaking one in a position of hopelessness, and is preceded

by a thrice-repeated negative: "I'll never, never, never abandon you in a hopeless state!" JDM.[157]

The fact that God will take care of you, however, does not negate the fact that we also need to prepare as best that we can. Of course one should never trust in his preparations, and it is possible that our preparations might be taken from us. In that regards, we should start praying now against that happening. We should also give everything—possessions, family, health, everything—to God and trust Him to take care of it. God can protect his possessions better than we can, so give everything to Him and trust Him with it. An excellent story that illustrates this spiritual concept is "The Pineapple Story," which can be obtained from The Institute In Basic Life Principles. At the same time, we realize that a non-Christian and or disobedient Christian has no claim to the protection of God, but can expect to receive chastisement

Will We Suffer?
Some Christians will be called to suffer during the 70th Week. Yes there will be difficulties, problems, trials, and sorrows. But God will be there with us and He will help us if we go to Him. Some Christians will be martyred during the 70th Week. Should Christians be afraid of being killed? No, absolutely not! Would you be afraid if your boss came to you and said, "I hate you because you are a Christian and I am going to send you on a lifetime all expense paid vacation to Hawaii?" No, you would be rejoicing. Heaven is a million times better than any "paradise" on earth, and if somebody kills you, you will immediately enter into paradise and be able to live with God forever. As many have said, "You cannot threaten me with Heaven." Besides, martyrdom is an honor. Being killed for the cause of Christ brings many eternal rewards. I am not saying that you should seek to be martyred, but if that is God's will for you, do not worry or fret, but rejoice for great is your reward in Heaven. Our attitude should be "Nevertheless not my will, but thine, be done." (Lk 22:42) Reflect upon the words of our Lord in these regards:

> But beware of men: for they will deliver you up to the councils, and they will scourge you in their synagogues; And ye shall be brought before governors and kings for my sake,

---

[157] Morris, John D., The Institute for Creation Research, Days of Praise, Friday June 26 entry, June – August 2009.

for a testimony against them and the Gentiles. But when they deliver you up, take no thought how or what ye shall speak: for it shall be given you in that same hour what ye shall speak. For it is not ye that speak, but the Spirit of your Father which speaketh in you. And the brother shall deliver up the brother to death, and the father the child: and the children shall rise up against their parents, and cause them to be put to death. And ye shall be hated of all men for my name's sake: but he that endureth to the end shall be saved. But when they persecute you in this city, flee ye into another: for verily I say unto you, Ye shall not have gone over the cities of Israel, till the Son of man be come...And fear not them which kill the body, but are not able to kill the soul: but rather fear him which is able to destroy both soul and body in hell. Are not two sparrows sold for a farthing? and one of them shall not fall on the ground without your Father. But the very hairs of your head are all numbered. Fear ye not therefore, ye are of more value than many sparrows. (Matt. 10:17-31)

So as one proceeds through the 70th Week of Daniel, draw nigh to God and He will draw nigh to you. Go to Him as a child goes to his or her daddy. Pour out your heart before Him. He will be with you all the way. God loves you more than you realize. Do not be afraid. When we are afraid, we are telling God that we do not trust Him. This saddens Him as it would any mother or father if their child was afraid that they would not take care of them. "Commit thy way unto the Lord; trust also in him; and he shall bring it to pass" (Psalm 37:5). Remember the words of our Lord:

Let not your heart be troubled: ye believe in God, believe also in me. In my Father's house are many mansions: if it were not so, I would have told you. I go to prepare a place for you. And if I go and prepare a place for you, I will come again, and receive you unto myself; that where I am, there ye may be also. And whither I go ye know, and the way ye know." (John 14:1-4)

Should I Be Angry?

Another reaction to reading this book may be one of anger. You may feel anger toward God for not planning it so that the Christians will be raptured before the 70th Week begins, or you may be angry that you have been taught a wrong rapture view by many well respected Bible teachers.

First, it is impossible for God to do anything wrong. "In Him is no sin" (1 John 3:5). He is perfect and holy and righteous. Anything that God does is right and perfect. We also know that anything that God allows to happen to believers is for our good. "And we know that all things work together for good to them that love God, to them who are the called according to his purpose" (Rom. 8:28). Thus, we have no right to be angry with God.

Some may be angry with those who have taught them a wrong rapture view. That is not right either, because we are responsible for our relationship with God and it is our responsibility before the Lord to make sure that we believe in correct doctrines. We cannot place the blame for believing in incorrect doctrine at the feet of someone else. In most cases, our respected Bible teachers have given many years of service, sacrifice, and study in trying to accurately preach and teach the word of God. I know none who intentionally try to teach error. I believe modern Christianity fell into the trap of believing in a wrong rapture view because it was easy and pleasant to believe that Christians would not have to endure any "sorrows" at the end of the world. So if we are going to be angry, then we have no one to blame but ourselves. But there is a better reaction. "Brethren, I count not myself to have apprehended: but this one thing I do, forgetting those things which are behind, and reaching forth unto those things which are before. I press toward the mark for the prize of the high calling of God in Christ Jesus" (Phil. 3:13-14).

Do not be afraid of the trials and tribulations that are coming upon us. Do not be angry that you have to go through it. God will take care of you. Draw nigh to Him and He will draw nigh to you. Seek the Lord and He shall be found. Remember Jehovah Jireh cares for you, for you, for you!

Conclusion

It is my desire and prayer that, in the past or as a result of reading this book, you have had an "epiphany" regarding prophetic events, and that you now realize that the rapture will occur after the sixth seal is opened, at the beginning of the Day of the Lord. An epiphany concerning the return of Christ will come to all; it is just a matter of when. For some, the epiphany will come when the peace treaty is signed and the rapture does not happen as many are expecting. Or it may be when the sorrows of the seals are experienced. For unbelievers, it will be after they see Christ in the clouds at the rapture, but by that time, it will be too late. I pray that you will have your epiphany before it is too late.

I hope you also realize that since the rapture will not occur until after the sixth seal is opened, Christians will be subject to the sorrows of the first five seals. Considering the rapid changes in world events, especially the Middle East these times may be upon us shortly. I hope you also realize that at some point of time in the future, probably after the opening of the first seal, the world will be taken over by the New World Order and for the last 3.5 years, the antichrist. After the antichrist comes on the scene, times will get rough, with believers being persecuted and the mark being instituted where no one will be able to buy or sell without it. It is your responsibility to prepare for what lies ahead. You would be wise to make every effort to fulfill these responsibilities, trusting in the Lord for strength and guidance. If you are a Jew living in America and or Israel, and you do not recognize Christ as Messiah, then you need to be ready and prepared to flee to the wilderness of Israel, which will be a place of refuge for you, as God has commanded. But it would be far better to recognize Christ as Messiah now and be raptured. Christians should also be prepared to flee, if necessary, after the fifth seal is opened and the persecution begins.

If you have had your "epiphany" concerning these things, then I encourage you to spread the word, especially about when the rapture will occur. I am afraid that many of our brothers and sisters in the Lord will be caught off guard unless they are awakened. We should do all we can to try and awaken them.

Again the word of the Lord came unto me, saying, Son of man, speak to the children of thy people, and say unto them, When I bring the sword upon a land, if the people of the land take a man of their coasts, and set him for their watchman: If when he seeth the sword come upon the land, he blow the trumpet, and warn the people. Then whosoever heareth the sound of the trumpet, and taketh not warning; if the sword come, and take him away, his blood shall be upon his own head. He heard the sound of the trumpet, and took not warning; his blood shall be upon him. But he that taketh warning shall deliver his soul. But if the watchman see the sword come, and blow not the trumpet, and the people be not warned; if the sword come, and take any person from among them, he is taken away in his iniquity; but his blood will I require at the watchman's hand. So thou, O son of man, I have set thee a watchman unto the house of Israel; therefore thou shalt hear the word at my mouth, and warn them from me." (Eze. 33:1-7)

Let me also remind you that it is your responsibility to warn people of "the sword coming upon the land." How do you think your fellow church members, relatives, and friends will feel when the bad times hit and they see you are prepared and you did not tell them? Worse yet, what if they take the mark because they have not prepared? Awaken as many as you can.

Standing on the sure foundation of the Word of God I call on pastors to preach the truth about the end-times boldly. Fulfill your duty and awaken your congregation and preach the truth to them about what is shortly going to come to pass on the earth. I have been a Christian for over 25 years and I have never heard one message on the New World Order and their plan to take over the world. Why not? The plan has been exposed for a long time. It is time for the message to go forth because people need to know the truth about the end times.

Woe to the pastor who misleads his congregation and does not prepare them for what lies ahead. Let this not be true of the shepherds of God's flock. The flock has gone astray in its end-times beliefs because of lackadaisical attitudes and the errors that have been preached from the pulpit. As a result, they are in danger of suffering a devastating attack. "My people hath been lost sheep: their shepherds have caused them to go astray, they have turned them away on the mountains: they have gone from mountain to hill, they have forgotten their resting place" (Jer. 50:6). The men of God need to fall to their knees and ask God for forgiveness and go out and preach the truth like they have never done before!

In the troublous times ahead, Christians need to unify and quit all of their squabbling over minute doctrinal issues. We are going to need each other. If we are disjointed, we will be more susceptible to satan's attacks. It will become more apparent as the days continue who the true Christians really are. Beware of the false ones. Not all who claim the name of Christ are in the Body of Christ. The nation of Israel will also undergo some very serious times during the 70th Week. True Christians must be ready and willing to support them and their right to the land.

The "things which must shortly come to pass" are going to be very trying to say the least. The road ahead will be rough, but the Lord will be there for us. You can trust Him and we should look forward to His coming.

> And, behold, I come quickly; and my reward is with me, to give every man according as his work shall be. I am Alpha and Omega, the beginning and the end, the first and the last. Blessed are they that do his commandments, that they may have right to the tree of life, and may enter in through the gates into the city... I am the root and the offspring of David, and the bright and morning star. And the Spirit and the bride say, Come. And let him that heareth say, Come. And let him that is athirst come. And whosoever will, let him take the water of life freely...He which testifieth these things saith, Surely I come quickly. Amen. Even so, come, Lord Jesus. The grace of our Lord Jesus Christ be with you all. Amen. (Rev. 22:12-21)

Reference

(The charts in this section can be viewed in a better format at http://thecomingepiphany.com/Special.html)

The 70 Weeks of Daniel and the "2 Days"

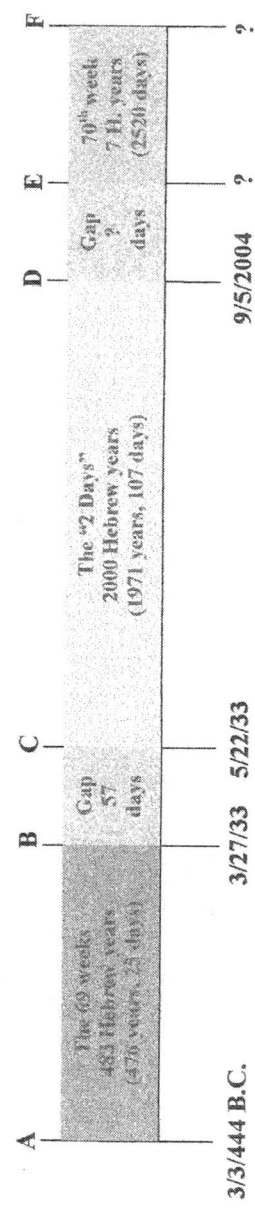

A. Decree to Rebuild Jerusalem, Start of 69 Weeks.
B. Triumphal Entry, End of 69 Weeks.
C. Pentecost, Beginning of Historical Church Period.
D. End of Historical Church Period.
E. Beginning of 70th Week, Peace Treaty.
F. End of 70th Week, anointing of Christ as king of the world.

(ALL DATES ARE GREGORIAN)

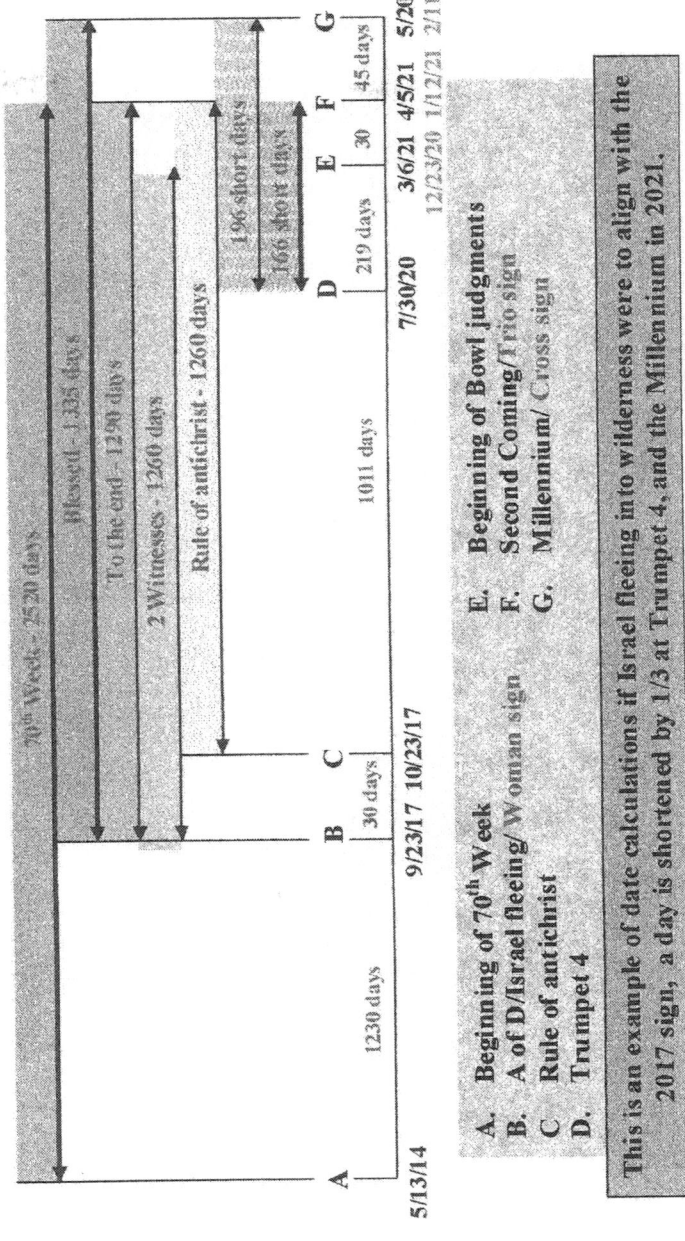

An Explanation of the Computation of the Dates in the 70th Week of Daniel

Assuming the abomination of desolation will align with the sign of the woman clothed with the sun on 9/23/17, then we would subtract 1230 days from 9/23/17 and arrive at a date for the beginning of the 70th Week on 5/13/14.

At this same time as the abomination of desolation or just a few days prior, the two witnesses will begin their ministry that will end 1260 days later just before the bowl judgments begin on 3/6/21.

30 days after the abomination of desolation the antichrist will take over the world and his 3.5 year/1260 day reign will begin on 10/23/17.

The reign of the antichrist will end 1260 days later or 1290 days after the abomination of desolation at Armageddon on 4/5/21.

The Millennium will begin 1335 days after the abomination of desolation on 5/20/21.

If the days are shortened by 1/3 at Trumpet 4 on 7/30/20, then on 4/5/21 the earth will be in its normal position for 1/12/21, and on 5/20/21 the earth will be in its normal position for 2/11/21.

The Three Sevens "777"

The 7 Seals

1. Conquering world power
2. War and anarchy (WWIII)
3. Famine, plagues & economic collapse
4. Death of ¼ of the world population
5. Persecution of Christians and Jews
6. Moon to blood, sun darkened, Earthquake, Rapture!!!

7. **The 7 Trumpet Judgments**

    1. Hail and fire
    2. Meteorite/Volcano
    3. Comet
    4. 1/3 Light removed
    5. Demon locusts
    6. Demon army

7. **The 7 Vial Judgments**

    1. Boils
    2. Sea turned to blood
    3. Freshwater to blood
    4. Great heat
    5. Darkness
    6. Euphrates dried up

Tribulation/Sorrows

Great Tribulation

Day of the Lord

A Chronological Synopsis of the End of the World According to God's Holy Word; The Bible.

1. Last 7 years begins. (Dan 9:27)
2. Seal 1: Explosion, conquering political and or religious force begins to take over the world. (Rev 6:1,2)
3. Seal 2: World War III. (Rev 6: 3,4)
4. Seal 3: World wide economic collapse, famine. (Rev 6:5,6)
5. Seal 4: Plagues, death, ¼ of world's population dies. (Rev 6:7,8)
6. Antichrist performs abomination of desolation. (2 Thes 2:1-4)
7. Ministry of 2 witnesses begins. (Rev 11:1-15)
8. Antichrist takes over the world. (Rev 13:5-9)
9. Seal 5: Worldwide persecution of Jews and Christians. (Rev 6: 9-11)
10. Seal 6: Signs of the sun, moon, and stars, worldwide earthquake, appearance of Christ in the sky, Christians raptured, wrath of God begins. (Rev 6:12-17)
11. America (end times Babylon) destroyed in a nuclear holocaust. (Rev 17:16-18:24)
12. Sealing of the 144,000 (Rev 7)
13. Seal 7: 7 Trumpet judgments. (Rev 8:1-6)
14. Trumpet 1: Horrific hail and fire, 1/3 of plants burned up. (Rev 8:7)
15. Trumpet 2: Meteorite/Volcano explodes in the ocean, 1/3 ships and sea life destroyed. (Rev 8:8,9)
16. Trumpet 3: Comet explodes on the earth, 1/3 of fresh water poisoned, many men die. (Rev 8:10,11)
17. Trumpet 4: 1/3 of sunlight removed. (Rev 8:12)
18. Trumpet 5: First woe—Demon locusts, men tortured. (Rev 8:13-9:12)
19. Trumpet 6: Second woe—Demon army, 1/3 of men die. (Rev 9:13-21)
20. Ministry of 2 witnesses ended. (Rev 11:1-13)
21. Trumpet 7: Third woe—7 Vial Judgments. (Rev 11:14-19)
22. Vial 1: Boils on men. (Rev 16:1,2)
23. Vial 2: Sea turned to blood. (Rev 16:3)
24. Vial 3: Freshwater turned to blood. (Rev 16:4-7)
25. Vial 4: Great heat. (Rev 16:8,9)

26. Vial 5: Darkness. (Rev 16:10,11)
27. Vial 6: Euphrates dries up. (Rev 16:12-16)
28. Vial 7: The Lord Jesus Christ and His saints return to the earth and defeat the antichrist and his armies at Armageddon with 100-pound hailstones. Great earthquake, every island and mountain destroyed, America the Babylon sinks under the ocean. (Rev 16:17-21, Rev 18:21, Jer 51:42)
29. Jesus is anointed as King of the World and the Millennium begins! (Rev 19)

A Comparison of the Rapture Theories

Prophetic truth/principle	Pre-trib	Mid-trib	Post-trib	Pre-wrath
A Christian will not be subject to God's wrath	√	√	×	√
No one knows the day of Christ's return	√	×	×	√
The rapture occurs after the moon is turned to blood after the sixth seal is opened	×	×	√	√
The rapture occurs after the antichrist is revealed	×	√	√	√
The rapture is not imminent until all the prerequisites are fulfilled	×	√	√	√
Christians will be subject to sorrows and tribulations.	×	√	√	√
Jews and Christians are persecuted by the antichrist	×	×	√	√
Christians are removed out of the midst of the great tribulation	×	×	×	√
Jesus will return to the clouds at the rapture	√	√	×	√

The only theory that agrees with all of the end-times scriptural principles is the Prewrath theory.

"If you eliminate the impossible, whatever remains, no matter how *improbable*, must be the truth..." Sherlock Holmes.

About the Author

William Frederick has been teaching and preaching God's Word for over 20 years as a Christian Education Minister. He is also the Sunday School Superintendent in the local Independent Fundamental Baptist church he attends.

William has written another book entitled *Christian Rock Music; Wolf or Sheep? A Theological Analysis.* William's book lays before the reader, in an easy to understand format, essential spiritual truths which succinctly answers the question of whether Christian rock music is good or bad. In this well documented book the reader will be able to know for sure if Christian rock music is good to listen to. For more information about this book go to William Frederick's storefront at Lulu.com

Miscellaneous

If you would like to partner with us in helping others know the truth about the end times then please tell others about *The Coming Epiphany*, which can be obtained in print at leading book retailers and through our website. The e-book version is available at our website as a FREE download which we encourage you to email, or copy on disc, and give to as many people as possible. We also accept donations at our website. Please also pray with us that God would use this book to reach many with the truth of His Word.

William Frederick has started Blog entitled The End Times Forecaster. It is a good place to keep up to date with current prophecy events, ask questions, and discuss the end times. The End Times Forecaster Blog is located at **http://endtimesforecaster.blogspot.com/**

Most reference articles pertaining to this book can be found at The Coming Epiphany Website located at **http://thecomingepiphany.com**. New articles will be added as prophecy developments unfold.

The prophecy charts in this book are available full size and in color at this link **http://thecomingepiphany.com/Special.html**

Questions and comments may be directed to:
email@thecomingepiphany.com

The information provided in this book is without warranty of any kind and, in particular, no representation or warranty, expressed or implied, is made nor to be inferred as to the accuracy, timeliness, or completeness, of any such information. Under no circumstances shall William Frederick have any liability to any person or entity for a loss or damage in whole or in part caused by, resulting from, or relating to any error (neglect or otherwise) or other circumstances involved in procuring, collecting, compiling, interpreting, analyzing, editing, transcribing, transmitting, communicating, or delivering such information, or any direct, indirect, special, consequential, or incidental damages whatsoever, even if William Frederick is advised in advance of the possibility of such damages, resulting from the use of or inability to use, such information

Made in the USA
San Bernardino, CA
13 March 2017